Praise for Bruce Northam's In Search of Adventure: A Wild Travel Anthology

"...Pops the top off objective travel writing . . . Lives up to the adage that travel writers fear boredom more than death."

— Time International

"...100 pithy travel stories ... tales that are smart, funny and even risqué."

— National Geographic Traveler

"This collection of travel tales doesn't just push the envelope, it shreds it."

— San Francisco Examiner

"...A collection of extraordinary memories, memories that conjure our own most moving journeys and make us hunger for more."

— Salon

"Body and soul are individually served."

— Publishers Weekly

"...an engrossing read. And, for anyone who has ever dreamed of escape or imagined a wilder existence, this refreshing and sometimes over-the-top compilation will not disappoint."

— Newsweek.com

"...the wanderlust-addicted writers of these exciting travel essays undergo physical challenges and life-changing insights as they explore seldom-visited places . . . zany, enthusiastic adventurers and hippie journalists push travel writing far beyond Sunday supplement fare."

— Boston Herald

"Anything can happen when you travel. And in the new anthology . . . just about everything does . . . dozens of writers share 100 amazing tales and take you to places you might never go. The book celebrates the wild side of travel."

— New York Post

"Roughing It: The rough-and-ready contributors would probably eat their luggage before they'd pack a velvet tea gown or shooting tweeds. If they have luggage at all — this is the crowd that travels with a toothbrush, a pair of jeans, and a passport. They're an eclectic crew of adventurers..."

— Washington Post

"...be entertained, enlightened, and sometimes shocked by these honest slices of life on the road."

— Travel Weekly

"Lovers of storytelling and anyone looking for summer vacation inspiration shouldn't miss this."

— San Francisco Bay Guardian

"The anthology is a fresh, irreverent look at international travel, and delves into areas often glossed over, including experiences with crime, sex, and religious fraud."

— San Francisco Chronicle

Praise for Bruce Northam's Globetrotter Dogma

Cited by National Geographic as one of "Ten better choices: insightful travelogues that will inspire rather than dictate." (Geographic's list included The Travels of Marco Polo, by Marco Polo.)

Praise for Bruce Northam's The Frugal Globetrotter

"...there's no shortage of travel books on the shelves, but most aren't worth your time. We found (one) worth recommending: The Frugal Globetrotter."
— Men's Health

"For more cheap travel ideas, read The Frugal Globetrotter."
— Mademoiselle

"...an offbeat look at saving while seeing ... delving into subjects such as endangered paradises and women traveling alone ... lots of practical advice."
— Boston Globe

Praise for Bruce Northam's Keynote Presentation

"Bruce is a great storyteller. His unique style grabs the audience, gets them laughing, and inspires everyone to follow their dreams wherever they might lead."
— Scott Flaherty, I LOVE NEW YORK Media Coordinator, on Bruce's New York State Governor's Conference on Tourism keynote

"Insightful . . . Excellent program . . . adventures that are available to everyone with an open mind . . . highly recommend [his] program to other campus organizations."
— North Carolina State University

"Bruce Northam rocks! ... This guy is exciting, fun, and full of enough information to get anyone interested in truly enjoying life . . . shows us that we're only confined to the extent that we limit our dreams . . . This guy needs to hit every college campus in the nation."
— University of Tulsa

"Ingenious methods to grasp hold of an enormous range of traveling opportunities . . . well-organized, entertaining and vibrantly clear, offering information that immediately elicited a positive response . . . an intriguing and valuable guest speaker at any institution."
— University of Virginia

"It was obvious that his presentation was enjoyed ... informative and funny and very knowledgeable."
— Oklahoma State University

"Lecture was both fun and informative . . . everyone who went thoroughly enjoyed it. You inspired a lot of people to go out and explore the world as you have done."
— University of the Pacific

"Wonderful presentation... people around here are still talking about it."
— Rutgers University

"Envious of your energy and enthusiasm. The students appreciated your vitality, but particularly responded to your varied interests evidenced by your travel experiences and your practical advice. In your presentations there is wit, humor, and a sly commentary on life."

— Lynchburg College

Praise for Bruce Northam's The Directions to Happiness
"A literary compass: 135 Countries, Infinite Lessons, One Book."

— Travelgirl Magazine

"By the end of the book, you like the author, you believe him, and you've had a fun ride--because this is no namby-pamby travelogue."

— Travel+Leisure

THE DIRECTIONS TO HAPPINESS

A 135-Country Quest for Life Lessons

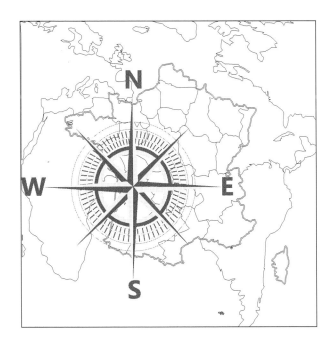

Bruce Northam

Also by the Author

American Detour

Globetrotter Dogma

In Search of Adventure: A Wild Travel Anthology

The Frugal Globetrotter

Table of Contents

PROLOGUE

I have felt the lungs of the world expand, and this is my exhale. Our planet is trying to tell us something. There is a global disconnect of understanding, as we are often led to believe that the world is an unwelcoming place. I'm not a preacher, a guru, or a therapist but a working-guy explorer on a cross-continental mission, a messenger sharing the local bliss that's always out there, if you know where to dig. By asking the right questions—or the wrong ones—I've discovered what keeps people striving for their dreams.

Pursuing and compiling these teachings reminded me that diversity is a great teacher. There are volumes of inspiring life lessons that have yet to be published, televised, or digitized. Gems of understanding have been passed down through generations to the people you'll soon meet on these pages. Capturing simple moments that inform without leaning on arcane dogmas, I'm inviting you on a world-ranging holiday to far-flung places away from the gadgets that threaten to disengage us from our deeper senses and sensibilities.

This isn't about my quest for happiness, though the hunt for how others find their joy inspires mine. Wisdom from a stranger fires the imagination—individuals in strange lands often have the power to realign our beliefs.

Patriotism should be redefined as improving every country, not just our own. That's why I strive to be a frontline worker in the battle against bad news and boredom. I've explored our world tailing timeless news—some people call it "travel writing." Mobile street anthropology reveals what happens when curiosity conquers the fear of the unknown.

It's easier to behold what people really think once you cut to the chase. Thanks to a merry vagabond I met while hitching across Australia, I'll never forget that the real measure of wealth is how much you'd be worth if you lost all your money. Likewise, a musical encounter in the Philippines taught me that the enlightened never ask who is teacher and who is student. And, I won't soon forget when a self-proclaimed Honduran expert in pirate chic declared, "If you have to ask what's hip—you're not!" These life lessons from seven continents double as contemporary wisdom updates. Socrates and the ancient gang studied contentment intensely, but we need a recharge. Happiness, purely defined, is the love of living. Seize moments, set your gypsy blood afire, and discover insights you can't find online.

Cultural anthropology studies why people do what they do—and asks how society manages itself. A number of academics spend more time studying indoors than out on the world's streets, which encourages the redefinition of some PhDs as merely Piling it Higher and Deeper. Formal education may be an essential preparation for life, but it's no substitute for it. Humanity lives "out there," under the bridges, on remote mountaintops, or sitting beside you. Don't spend your vital years warming a chair.

We're here to find and teach love, and I don't just mean the nude version. The emergence of our individual wisdom tends to loom a few years or decades ahead of us. So I pursued my own, country by country, state by state, person to person, moment by moment. Check out this world before the next.

Bruce Northam
AmericanDetour.com

Live Loving
Die Dreaming
—Epitaph in an Ecuadorian cemetery

WHERE IT ALL BEGAN

The detour is the journey.

W e all start somewhere—love it or leave it. If I could blitz the U.S. with air-dropped leaflets, they would urge: *Pack a small bag, march outside, wander into a different neighborhood, ask strangers fun questions.* Faithfully beholding this tactic—anywhere and everywhere—turned most of my life into a working vacation. First, I had to wrestle the establishment to learn a few lessons about freedom.

My first income involved petty theft. As an eight-year-old living across the street from the Hempstead, Long Island golf course driving range, I was motivated by the pro shops' return policy, which netted a nickel per ball. The pilfering ring began with me coaxing balls through the fence using a long stick. The scheme matured into fence-hopping sprints onto the driving range to load as many balls as possible into the belly of my shirt and then bounding back over the rusted eight-foot chainlink fence using the free arm not securing the loot. Older brother initiations aside, this midday one-armed banditry delivered my earliest adrenaline rushes.

Ball burglary was only a symptom of the recreational terrorism my two older brothers and I routinely enjoyed inside those

4

suburban-liberating golf course fences. We'd camp overnight, buried deep in the courses' leaf piles, sled year-round on any slope, and spend hours clinging to soaring treetops. In an early stride toward independence, I constructed and maintained my own treehouse in a lumbering white pine to spy on a sport I'd never fancy, except as a caddy.

When the dreaded greenskeeper, Tony Matueza, finally captured me red-handed snatching balls on the driving range, he drove me in his supply-laden golf cart onto the street and into my driveway. As we walked up to my front door, his chunky claw still clutching my arm, he threatened, "You're in a world of trouble." After citing abundant crimes to my mother, he remanded me to her custody and left me to ponder a troubled planet.

Skip to now, as the news media continue fanning that world-of-trouble myth (my mom let me off the hook and didn't tell dad), my worldwide search for guidance reconfirmed that we actually reside on a very friendly planet. Tony was *wrong*.

Don't let blanket travel warnings, the bruising 24-hour news cycle, and other implanted delusions limit your scope of the world. Heed the common sense revealed by unlikely sages in faraway places and just down the road from you. Detour away from ill-advised gloom and the scorn of crotchety pessimists. It's never too late to have a happy childhood.

DIRECTION

DON'T PREDICT THE FUTURE, INVENT IT (China)

Why peer through the keyhole when your hand rests on the doorknob?

I was backpacking in the newly "opened" China in 1987 when Chen, a multilingual restaurateur and the unofficial mayor of Yangzhou, entered my life. He had a kindly way with backpackers, and one afternoon he invited me to join him on a 70-mile journey in a rickety delivery truck across southeast China's surreal limestone-peak landscape.

En route, we passed a seemingly ancient man and his goat. They were walking on the roadside in the opposite direction. Barefoot, the man plodded along the rough, hot road, two immense bags of rice suspended on a long, flexible pole across his back.

We passed him without a word, but upon returning to Yangzhou several hours later, we found him again—still plodding along. I suggested to Chen that we offer him a lift. After we pulled over, the old man and Chen had a brief exchange. Then Chen got back behind the wheel, and we drove off, leaving the man in the road. Puzzled, I asked Chen to translate their conversation.

He explained that the man wasn't due to arrive in Yangzhou until the following day. If he were to show up in advance, he wouldn't know what to do with the extra time.

"You see, my friend," said Chen, "Not all of us are in a hurry."

I asked him to turn back, as I wanted to ask the old man a few things. Chen parked, and I hopped out. The old man stopped, balancing on his walking stick, and grinned. We pondered each other, beings from opposite sides of the planet—different planets really, worlds and ways apart.

Chen translated my questions.

"What's the most important thing in your life?" I asked.

The old man looked to his left and made a peculiar honking call for his straying goat. Was the goat the most important thing? When the animal arrived at his side, the man looked at Chen and spoke slowly.

Chen interpreted, "He said that if you can't help people, don't harm them."

"Why are people hurtful?" I asked.

I didn't look at Chen as he spoke but rather stared into the old man's eyes. He was human art, more serene than a drowsy cat.

"If you decline to accept someone's abuse, then it still belongs to them," he replied.

"Why do we quarrel?" I asked.

"The rise of a man's mind from his scrotum to his skull can be a long haul." We all burst into laughter. The goat bleated. "Ready?" Chen asked.

The old man and I shook hands and waved goodbye. The truck

rolled away.

Today, I often recall the man's deeply wrinkled face, and I know that the infuriating fixtures of modern life—traffic jams, rude people, the arrogance of ego—are only options. His words remain a permanent, benevolent echo.

I departed Yangzhou a month later. Chen walked with me to the bus stop. After mutual pats on the back, I told him how much his companionship meant to me, and that the old man's words were unforgettable. I thanked him for those too.

"Use those words to end a book," Chen said.

"Come on, Chen," I replied. "Do you know how old I'll be by the time I get published?"

"The same age you'll be if you don't," he winked.

∞ ∞ ∞ ∞ ∞

…Well, two decades and several books later, I received a letter from Chen that delivered a shock. He confessed—in that letter—that he hadn't actually translated the old man's words. Everything I'd learned that day had actually been Chen's sage advice.

But, I got the best of Chen, and started this book with him…

DIRECTION

NEVER GIVE UP (India)

Make choices and stick with them.

Crossing humid southwest India, a sluggish train chugged slowly enough to stay inside a cloud of its own dust. It eventually stopped in a nameless station featuring a canine envoy. One of the dogs, gaunt and glum, sat before the train's open window near a seat where he knew a couple was eating. Sitting lopsided on his haunches, the gaunt dog was missing patches of fur, giving him the charm of a plucked chicken. He had, however, a clever, longing face with eyes that illuminated his thoughts: hunger, optimism, patience, and a weary intuition of what seemed to be pending disappointment.

The rotund couple next to the window chewed blindly—stuffing themselves—sensing no obligation to the dog who continued eyeing them. Farther up the platform, another dog was treated to a tidbit thrown by an elderly man. The yet-to-be fed dog glanced sideways for an instant, wondering whether to abandon his current bid for food. The couple might relent at any moment, as they had ample rations. Desire spread across his face, and his nostrils flared with the scent of meat. He chose to stay put, his eyes infused with such yearning that it seemed impossible the couple could ignore him. Surely they would return his gaze and pitch him at least a crust, but they didn't look away from their meal.

Abruptly, the whistle sounded, and the train bucked forward. The dog cantered along with it half-heartedly, eventually striding into a loping gallop. When the train was nearly out of sight, the hungry dog trotted back to reclaim his spot on the station platform and wait for another train. After all, hope is not only a commentary on the past but also a promise for the future.

DIRECTION

DON'T BE AFRAID TO ROAM OUT
OF BOUNDS (Laos)

*Savor the pleasure in gambling when you don't care
if you win or lose.*

T he State Department's warning about Americans traveling to Laos is vaguely based on a sniper who shot at a bus carrying tourists, killing two Swedish passengers in 2000. As the unpopular Iraq war unfolded, Americans traveling abroad were sometimes met by a previously unsurpassed level of wariness, mostly by Europeans and other English-speaking travelers. Meanwhile, most Laotians seemed to have already forgiven the U.S. for the carnage committed there during the Vietnam War. While The State Department didn't consider Laos to be a worthy gamble, I bet otherwise.

I visited Laos armed with the knowledge that expert trackers—people who make a living finding people lost or hiding in the wilderness—can usually predict that a person missing in the woods, desert, or elsewhere will eventually re-cross their own path. I learned this while attending survivalist Tom Brown's Tracker School. Lost humans have a knack for gradually traveling in circles because one of our legs is typically stronger than the other. That dominant leg is the one we favor when using one leg to jump, and that same leg always works harder when we stride. Therefore, when walking, our non-dominant leg rides the breeze and takes longer steps. While on our daily strolls, instead of gradually turning because of this uneven stepping pattern, we adjust and walk in a straight line.

But, if you lead a challenger in betting mode to the end zone of a large field (rugby, football, schoolyard, or otherwise), blindfold them, and bet he or she can't walk from one end to the other without first straying out of bounds, you'll probably win the bet. Without eyesight to self-correct, the individual will drift in the direction led by his or her weaker leg.

Years later, with this in mind, I wagered for a chicken by posing the blindfold challenge to a Laotian acquaintance. In mountainous Northern Laos, I walked with Sert, a 40-year-old carpenter, to a makeshift field on the outskirts of his village that was only accessible by river. Here, the vertical limestone cliff formations created a cathedral panorama, and a dramatic setting for a gamble. The chicken followed us.

We first aligned fallen jungle debris to define the sidelines and the end zones. It wasn't long before 50 villagers showed up to witness the event. Hearty laughter was already erupting as I secured Sert's blindfold, a red bandana that I had been using to secure my backpack for months. Sure enough, not only did Sert swerve out of bounds before making it halfway to the end zone, but the crowd's hilarity also made him buckle over with laughter. His snickering stumbles turned him around so that he roamed straight back to where he'd started.

Kids everywhere began taking off their shirts, tying them around their heads to cover their eyes, and walking randomly into each other. Our little wager had started a blind human bumper-car riot whose joy seemed worthy of national holiday status. We were all happy, carefree children at heart. After an hour, Sert handed me the chicken and we walked back to the village for a barbeque. Later, I insisted that he accept the chicken as my gift, along with the red bandana.

The next morning, my last in these gnarly mountains, I came across Sert as he pedaled down the main drag, a car-free, rutted dirt road. While he rolled to a stop, a Hall of Fame smile spread across his face as something rustled in the basket perched on the bicycle's handlebars. You bet it was the chicken, decked out in a red bandana which was tied around its neck.

The rebirth of a country's soul is a splendid thing—no matter the stakes.

DIRECTION

MEASURE YOUR WEALTH BY HOW MUCH YOU'D BE WORTH IF YOU LOST ALL YOUR MONEY (Australia)

Put the currency blues on the run.

B efore email and cell phones, letter writing was still vital, as many long-term backpackers could rarely afford to call home. Such isolation made Australian hospitality even more welcome, especially after a year in Asia without a turkey hero.

In the late 1980s, after a year-long Southeast Asian tour, a college friend and I hitchhiked 1,000 miles up Australia's east coast to attend an AC/DC rock concert. Somewhere near Bundaberg, rides were in short supply. Our money evaporated, and we forgot that the buck is an endangered species that can't be eaten. We stood by the road, yearning to overcome poverty's limitations.

Across the baked intersection, a quintessential Outback man twice our age was hitching in the other direction and smoking a homemade cigarette that would get him tossed out of most U.S. establishments.

"How's it goin', mates?" he quizzed from across the pocked

pavement, his voice rising above a soundtrack merging crickets with distant chainsaws.

"We ran out of money," groaned my friend Pete.

The grinning Aussie rambler, a talent-at-large, notched up his tattered wide-brim hat and, unknowingly narrating timeless mythology, replied, "No worries guys, I started out with nothing and still have most of it left."

A mirage no doubt belonging in the gallery of sainted survivors, he had a primitive affluence that reminded us that you can rise from the pits to the Ritz, in your head.

After scaring away our *purse-onalities*, he added, "Don't spend time; enjoy it."

There are a million options in the enterprise of starting from scratch.

∞ ∞ ∞ ∞ ∞

"They'd raise the rent, and I couldn't raise the money." — Mozambique musician

"Beware of *loan* wolves." —Emirati businesswoman observing an unfinished, rusting skyscraper skeleton in her neighborhood.

"The funny thing about money is that if everyone threw in their *two cents* about it, there'd be 15 billion cents." —overheard in Israel's Negev Desert

DIRECTION

CALL IT A DRAW (Japan)

"Without wood a fire goes out; without gossip a quarrel dies down." —Manhattan horse-drawn carriage driver quoting *Proverbs 26:20*

A decade before the internet eliminated the getting-away-from-it-all element from traveling, I hitchhiked from Osaka to Tokyo, Japan, with a pal keen on winning an argument. Some Japanese road signs include English pronunciations, others don't. A sign on Osaka's outskirts reading Neyagawa-shi landed our dissimilar pronunciation styles on the chopping block. I enunciated the village as one swift syllable, whereas she methodically broke it into three. Driving past another Neyagawa-shi sign, we clung to our interpretations, confidently voicing our articulations and amusing the truck driver who'd picked us up and bought us lunch.

Me: Nayagawashi (nearly phonetically, in one breath, as I imagined a local would).

Her: Knee–agah–washeee (an outmoded laundromat command?).

So, instead of becoming angry with each other's elocution, we motioned to our gracious driver to pull over, so we could ask a local to verbalize the verdict. We entered a roadside restaurant and approached a young woman stationed behind a cash register.

"Excuse us, can you please slowly say where we are?"

"Burrr–Gurrr–King," she replied.

DIRECTION

RESPECT YOUR FOOD'S JOURNEY
(Ifugao Province)

There is no burnt rice to a hungry person.
—Philippine proverb

O ur first urge to travel was motivated by finding food. This transient lifestyle requires a mobile crash pad. Tracking migratory herds, primeval wanderers fashioned portable shelters out of stones, branches, and animal hides. Today, our movable shelters—tents and the like—have roots in archetypal havens like Native American tepees, Inuit tupiks, and Mongolian gers. Even well-fed never-get-their-knees-muddy city kids want to build forts inside of their apartments.

While many are now concerned with our food's farm-to-table odyssey, we rarely have to worry about defending it while it grows. Grown in water, rice is the staple food of three billion people. In traditional rice paddies, a hidden few take shelter and wait to defend their crops. While trekking in the mountainous northern Philippine highlands, I came across a recurring curiosity, farmhands who seemed to be watching the rice grow. I discovered that the rice business requires 24-hour surveillance where live scarecrows protect mountainside rice terraces from persistent rice-loving birds. These farmers spend their days in temporary thatch-and-bamboo huts called *ab-hungs*, makeshift sheds built for two. They are built into manmade mountainside terraces and provide relief from the sun and rain for the people whose job it is to spy and scare off the thieving birds.

These human scarecrows rely on tactics that evolve with the growing seasons. Early on, pounding on a barrel or a basin would suffice in frightening the birds away. When the birds tired of that ploy and returned to the crime scene, the farmers created noise by pulling on strings attached to rows of jingling cans. When that jig was up—the birds don't fall for the same tricks for long—ab-hung security ultimately had to shoo the birds away by running after them.

Fortunately, this mode of occupational scaremongering does pay off. Highland rice is tastier, more aromatic, and more nutritious than the lowland's industrial version. Then again, more work goes into it, as it takes six to seven months to grow, three times longer than chemically fertilized rice. Locals perform planting and harvesting rituals to invoke ancestral spirits who watch over the crops—and it seems to work. The International Rice Research Institute wasn't so lucky. When it tried introducing new strains here, they didn't yield. Farmers then resurrected their ancient methods after rejecting a non-governmental organization's pesticide invasion, which killed tiny fish and snails—additional food sources—that also grow in the rice-paddy ponds.

Savoring moments in an ab-hung, I'm reminded of the ancient nomad musings today's weekend warriors enjoy inside their camping tents. Entering one makes the hut smaller but the world bigger. While avoiding some midday rain in this bird-spy shack, I chatted with a local elder about rice watchmen until the sun came out. Inside the primitive lean-to, I offered the farsighted, squinting man a pen, and he doled out a pinch of tobacco for me to chew, redefining the notion of insider trading. He then trotted out a thought that was loosely rendered by an eager kid who had been tailing me. I later employed the eager one as my guide, and the old man's quote as fact...

"A peace on birds would probably work better than this war on birds." —Rice wisdom, and an ageless take on disputes

DIRECTION

BE NICE TO STRANGERS (New Jersey)

*The people you meet on your way up in life might be the same
ones you'll encounter on your way down.*

R ushing to make an early morning flight in Newark,
New Jersey, I was due in San Francisco for a speaking
engagement. Unfortunately, the previous night's rock concert
meant token sleep and an unkind hangover. Because I had packed
travel gear and a box full of *Globetrotter Dogma* (my then current
book), my torso was sandwiched between two backpacks while
a free hand balanced the books like a waiter's tray. Resembling
an inept pack-mule, I stumbled up Seventh Avenue. I also had a
container of plain yogurt—supplied by my girlfriend with whom
I was quarrelling about my behavior at the concert—zipped into
my around-the-waist fanny pack. She offered to escort me to
the train station but actually walked backwards in front of me,
repetitiously reminding me why I'd overslept and how out of
sync I was with virtue.

Lumbering into Manhattan's Penn station, airport rail ticket in
hand, a conductor verified that I'd been misinformed on train
departures. A woman wearing a blue suit appeared beside me
and frowned when she learned we had the same dilemma. I

21

asked her if she wanted to share a cab to the airport. She glanced at me optimistically, then at my agitated girlfriend, and politely declined.

I hailed a costly taxi, one that jerked and stalled in Lincoln Tunnel traffic for an hour. Exiting the taxi at the terminal required me to perch forward, which audibly exploded the yogurt container in the pack around my waist, saturating my plane ticket, presentation notes, and wallet.

Because I was using frequent flier miles from one airline to fly another, I confused the two and found myself waiting in line at the wrong terminal. A ticket agent swore I wouldn't make the flight at the correct terminal anyway. Eyeing him suspiciously, I darted onto the monorail to switch terminals, a charging pack mule with slimy milk product oozing from my midsection and drooling kneeward.

The line at the correct check-in counter was a half-mile long. My flight departure in 20 minutes demanded I become that snake who cuts the line. Of course, by that time the cutoff for issuing boarding passes had come and gone. I pleaded with an insistent clerk. After emptying the contents of my waist-sack on the counter and waving my flight confirmation, which was marinated in slime, a boarding pass appeared and I was warned that my only shot was at the boarding gate. I sprinted to the security post where an X-ray lawman denied my advance unless I took off my shoes—until his eyes scrolled south from my tortured face down to my leg where the creamy lava had invaded a shoe.

Bolting toward hope on the moving walkway, I combated nausea, 60 pounds of tackle rabbiting around my body, and a frothy meringue dribbling from my private area. Just as the gate came into view, the airport PA system barked, "Passenger Bruce Northam, report immediately to the check-in counter to claim your wallet." Alarmed and intent on dropping my baggage to quicken my dash back for the wallet, I pleaded with the lineup of passengers—who were boarding the plane—to part so I could slip through and drop my gear on a chair.

Needling between two people, I turned right prematurely, causing my rear backpack to knock over a middle-aged woman. When I spun the other way to lend aid to the fallen one, my frontal backpack banged into another customer who staggered backward, yelping for help. The entire congregation focused on me, a profusely sweating packman in a state of panic. I dropped my bags, then immediately fled at the speed of light from whence I came.

Slowing this leg of the marathon to a canter, I met four policemen and two canines standing at the check-in counter, all staring at my gooey wallet lying atop the counter. "Why is this coated in a powdery white substance?" a baritone voice probed. It had dried a bit and, apparently, resembled an igniting agent. Instead of waiting for my mind to present a new scheme, I weighed every syllable and swore, "Yogurt." Demonstrating even-handed scholarship and maintaining eye contact with the cop chaperoned by the hulkier German shepherd, I slowly dunked my hand into my on-board milk culture pouch, inserted those five fingers into my mouth, and swallowed.

I then zipped my wallet back into the fanny pack (why not) and fled. Closing in once again on the now sealed gate, dizzied between memory and dream, the airport PA system thunderclapped, "Passenger Northam, your luggage has been confiscated and will be destroyed. Return immediately to gate 113." In this newly terrorist-paranoid country, it's amazing I hadn't already been tackled and tied by fatigue-wearing brutes.

There was a flurry of activity near my gate. The ruckus was fronted by a manager who faced me with arms folded, head cocked, and broadcasting an eerie expression that said war. I panted before her, nearly fainted, and was locked in open-mouthed astonishment. First, I noticed the uniformed herd racing up behind me, then the army of security guards behind her rummaging through my luggage like rabid hyenas ripping apart a rhino carcass. My belongings were spread over the entire boarding area. One guard was even rifling through copies of my book. Hyperventilating and with blurred vision, I anticipated a voice, "God will see you now."

Coming to terms with missing my flight and being a no-show for my keynote-speaking gig, I decided it was time for a remark verifying the crucible of my legitimacy. "I am not a criminal or a terrorist. I've never been arrested. I love airline people. Missing this flight will destroy my career and my ability to provide for my family (sort of a fib, that one). Today, I've missed trains, been held hostage by tunnel traffic, boomeranged between two terminals and three airline desks carrying 60 pounds. My yogurt broke (show and tell: sack, leg, and foot) and ruined my flight confirmation ... (pause) My girlfriend hates me."

The army continued burrowing into my ready-for-yard-sale belongings. Adjusting her stance, the manager unfolded her arms and made a decision.

"And I'm a frequent flier," I assured her.

She peeped at the officer radiating with the most medals, then nodded approvingly to the person blocking the gate. "Let him go," she sighed. As I made a prayer sign with my hands and rushed away, the manager suddenly reminded me of someone I'd met before.

My curtain call was a march down the aisle of the crowded plane, to a rear seat by the toilet; a hundred irate eyes burning into my saturated forehead. I sat next to a passenger who'd obviously witnessed my pirouetting backpacks trick take out those two folks waiting on line for the flight. Summarizing my beer fragrance, puss-ridden pant leg, and sweat-soaked shirt and hair, he bristled. When he saw the squad of security guards carrying my rashly repacked belongings onto the plane and helping the flight attendants cram them into random overhead compartments, he evacuated his elbow from the armrest and shifted his body the other way.

I pressed the flight attendant call button to request eyeshades, which were salvaged from business class. In the dark, it dawned on me. The manager who let me board the plane was the same blue-suited woman I'd met earlier that morning at the train station, the one I had offered to share a taxi with to the airport.

Surely, an essential item we pack for any journey is ourselves— but the crap you lug can injure the portability, and back, of that self. "I'm not a devil," was the first thing I told the passenger beside me. "I'm a man with a devil on his back."

DIRECTION

ASK FOR DIRECTIONS (Cuba)

*It's tough enough for one lost man to ask for directions—
tougher when four guys sail into the unknown.*

U nexpected rewards for loyalty are divine. In the summer of
2005, I visited the off-limits island of Cuba. At the time,
Fidel Castro was aged but still healthy and in power. I was the
monthly travel columnist for *The Improper Hamptonian*, an
amusing print magazine for Long Islanders. When the editor
fled to start her own venture, she invited me to write a similar
column in her new magazine, which paid more. That is, only if I
ceased writing for the other magazine.

I pleaded to write original columns for both publications, but
the offer only stood if I cut my ties to the magazine in which
I'd been a regular contributor for years. For maintaining my
loyalty—I was the only columnist who did—the publisher off
The Improper Hamptonian offered me a trip to Cuba by boat
from the Florida Keys.

6:43p.m. Just off Cuba's coast, as we're scouring the shoreline
for an inlet leading to a port, two huge boats race towards us.

6:44p.m. "Give us your keys," they shout to our boat.

"Why?" I scream back. I'd never been mugged by pirates, so I dash below deck to stash valuables on my body. Back on deck, I can't argue with the impatient, AK47-wielding crews on the steely larger boats flanking ours. Only one of the 20 guys on either boat wears anything resembling a uniform. Both boats have big cannons, and nobody is smiling. After a useless protest against surrendering the keys, I throw them the keys and the line they use to tow us into port. They then start "the investigation."

7:28p.m. Waiting on the dock is a 50-person convoy of drug-sniffing dog handlers, scribbling policemen, brooding military personnel, doctors, interrogators, and interpreters. Welcome to Cuba!

Americans having to fly through Mexico, Canada, or elsewhere to visit the largest island in the Caribbean has always struck me as tedious. I wanted to conquer Cuba by boat, and *The Improper Hamptonian* publisher, Lenny, made it happen. For years, he had pondered venturing there with his father, Lenny, Sr., a retired steamfitter of merit who had previously traveled there by boat. Lenny, Jr., and I flew to Fort Lauderdale, boarded his dad's 30-foot fishing boat, the Steamfitter, motored south and soon reaffirmed: The adventure begins when the plan fails.

Although our captain planned on docking near Havana, headwinds burned more gas than expected, so the straight line from Marathon Key, FL, led to the marina in Varadero, 80 miles east of Havana. As Cuban soil rose into view, we made several unsuccessful attempts to radio the marina. Roaming 100-yards offshore, hunting for the inlet, the only other boat we'd seen in Cuban waters was a dilapidated 120-foot rusty vessel that kept its distance but mimicked our movements. When we turned and approached them to ask directions, another rusting steel beast raced onto the scene, and our vacation went into shock, just as the sun began to sink into the ocean.

9 p.m.—until the moon finishes its slow arc across sky. They search and pick apart the boat, as I occasionally nap on the comfy wooden dock, using a pylon base as a pillow.

A team of quarantine doctors follow the drug-sniffing dogs.

"Anybody want a soda?" asks Lenny, Jr.

10:50p.m. A young female physician gives us full physicals. Using the pilot's bench as an exam table, she probes our abdomens and wears an expression of deep concern. She suggests the captain keep his legs elevated, and returns later to retake his blood pressure.

1:33a.m. A technology expert steps on to the boat, gives us nods of confidence, and then completely dismantles each of our cell phones, taking ferocious notes about each part and their serial numbers. Spy stuff.

3:54a.m. I become keenly aware that several stone-faced men are photographing and filming the entire show because when the cameraman films part four of my nap, his camera light wakes me.

Tensions were spiking again between Cuba and America. The previous year, Bush and company sanctioned Swiss banks for the "laundering" of Cuban currency. Cuba's retaliation, starting in 2004, outlawed the previously common U.S. dollar for all goods and services, switched to the Euro, and imposed a 20-percent fee for mandatory dollar conversions. And, Yanks arriving unannounced by boat also became a tad more problematic. Technically, while it's not illegal for Americans to visit Cuba, U.S. law declares it illegal for them to spend U.S. dollars there.

6:16a.m. Detainment by Cuban Coast Guard and friends continues through sunrise.

6:17a.m. Emerging from a dream about missing a meal while

in solitary confinement because my Spanish is rusty, I wonder aloud if we should call a lawyer. Lenny, nursing an imported Coke, winks, "Spending that quarter could multiply our legal problems."

6:18a.m. "Ham sandwich, please," says our captain. The Captain's cryptic request dawns on me later. We have no food, only cases of beer and soda.

10a.m. Officials, in a variety of outfits ranging from medaled general to sly undercover detective, test-drive our boat for the second time.

11:11a.m. Undercover dude seats us outside the grilling office near the dock and formally permits us access to our bucket of beer and soda.

11:12a.m.—until the sun sets again. They interrogate us individually in a small windowless office. Using a Spanish-speaking quizzer with an interpreter, high-volume questions range from "Do you have any Cuban friends in the United States?" to "Have you ever been in trouble with the CIA?" Four other serious *padre* types look on without blinking. Thoughtfully, the interrogator skipped any real toughies, like, "Who is cooler, you, or your older brother?"

2p.m. Mildly panicked paranoia sets in. Cuban detention takes me back to the many hours I'd restlessly endured in my junior high school principal's office. "We're calling your parents," I think I hear someone mumble in Spanish. Images of a $10,000 Uncle Sam fine and a year in prison swirl in my head.

3p.m. Every two hours, I peek back into the interrogation chamber—two olden computer printers busily chugging propaganda—to ask when we'll be free to go enjoy their country's famous tranquilizing rhythms. They maintain poker faces and predict a few more hours. "We're checking with your government," says the interpreter. Is he joking? If I'm here trading with the enemy, why the hell are you calling Washington? Am I going to become an international media example, exposing the flipside of the Cuban refugee boating issue?

4p.m. Revelation: It's amazing that Cuba is only 90 miles from Florida, because the cultural differences fly in the face of proximity. I've visited hundreds of diverse cultures and seldom experienced such lifestyle variation in such a short distance. Typically, when I'm in travel-writer mode, I intentionally wander into bad neighborhoods to get the street beat in towns all over the world. On the other side of those tracks, I'm used to paranoid locals first screening me as possible DEA, FBI, CIA, or Immigration. It seems ironic to raise that intelligence antenna in Cuba when I'm actually attempting a vacation. Then again, remnants of the Cold War endure.

4:01p.m. I want my mom.

4:02p.m. "Gimme another ham sandwich." —Captain's code words for "Someone please deliver me another Miller Lite."

7:05p.m. We're still slumped in chairs outside the administrative cell as another sun sets. A Canadian boat dweller muses by and attempts to illustrate the bright side of Cuba's militarized bureaucracy: "Thick bureaucracy, thin crime."

7:15p.m. Our 24-hour detention concludes with an apology.

Lack of radio communication aside, we had no idea that our beachfront search for the inlet had raised red flags. Occasionally, speed boat mercenaries do storm beaches and ferry locals to Florida. And, some cell phones have GPS chips that could help navigate a rafting refugee seeking diplomatic immunity. Considering our phone dismantlings, you'd think they were hunting lasers. Who knows what else prompted their paranoia. Obviously, most Cubans can't afford boats, but you also don't see anybody in any sort of recreational floating devices near the beaches. The Cuban government discourages Cubans from floating on anything. It's even illegal for foreign boat visitors to use the kayaks they've brought along; any craft could become a local's ticket to a Dolphin's game.

For sure, very few Americans storm their shores by sea, and their lawmen didn't seem to have much going on otherwise. If it was an embargo formality, at least they now have a training video for ambushing and shaking down weekend warriors.

7:37p.m. Group discussion in a Havana-bound taxi cab. Perhaps the adage about men refusing to ask for directions when lost has merit—the rare moment when the four of us asked at once, the banana hit the fan.

11:25a.m. (one week later). On the boat ride back to Florida, we see only one other boat from afar as we cross from Cuban into international waters.

"Oh sh*t, is that the U.S. Coast guard?"…"Dump the cigars!"

DIRECTION

SHARE THE LIGHT (Nepal)

Enjoy the light of a distant star that no longer exists.

While trekking high in Nepal's Himalayas, a 10-day walk from electricity and political sex scandals, I happened upon a medicine-chest-sized mirror hanging on a teahouse wall. In an action reminiscent of my juvenile era, I removed the mirror from the wall, walked outside, and used it to transmit the immensely powerful sun's reflection around the village. An amped up team of Nepalese villagers, led by a curious elderly woman, soon gathered to witness the miracle of this invention that had started to beam the almighty solar laser several miles to villages across the valley.

For the remainder of the day, as I gradually hiked up and away from the village, the elderly woman sun-beamed me every 20 minutes. Though they'd always had the means to flash, things may never be the same there.

Weeks later, back in Kathmandu, miscellaneous trekkers provided consistent reports about a small arcane mountain village that emitted a mysterious twinkling that seemed to be directed at recreational hikers.

DIRECTION

DO MORE WITH LESS (Utah)

Your mind is the strongest muscle in your body.

As I was jetting to Salt Lake City, throwing back pretzels, musing at the endless desert below, I was blissfully unaware that 9/11 would re-prioritize the need for survival skills in a new world of terrorist awareness. Hours later, I'm one of eight apprehensive fellows—in search of something not found anywhere near concrete—seated in a semicircle at the bottom of a southern Utah canyon. We're taking in a sunset lecture by a female outdoor survival guide on how to wipe our backsides using a handful of fine red sand or sagebrush. Pine needles and sticks wound, she warns. This is a prelude to a three-day fast that begins with an overnight speed hike through sandstone-cactus backcountry. We are relentlessly mobile, eating nothing, and drinking only the fish-tankish water we find, frequently from puddles.

The 14-day field course is a canyon-country wilderness four-stage marathon covering more than 200 walking miles. It's an odyssey with missions—primitive wilderness living skills and a total detox from fast-paced advertising and internet addiction. Out here, we elect to be forced into many situations as diverse as

33

deep thought and starvation, which I learn go hand in hand. Like most people, I took survival for granted.

On departure, hard learning follows hard lessons, many of which are magnified in the wake of three days of extreme trekking without food. We set off at dusk, wearing only waist packs minus water bottles. Our belts dangle with tied-off garments and one blue enamel cup. We pause to suckle water from potholes that are also home to darting tadpoles. The Olympic walking passes through myriad terrain changes in Escalante National Park, the elevation rising and falling from 10,000 to 5,000 feet. We're being pushed to simulate a survival situation. Jet-lagged and visiting from sea-level cement, I'm punchy with hungry exhaustion, reminding myself I can quit, but there's no refund. I could die, but there's that death waiver I signed.

En route seminars involve identifying animal tracks (rear bear tracks look amazingly human), eating river birch leaves (tasting like…leaves), and explaining why it's necessary to pack two pairs of underwear (a backup for when you shit yourself from either nerves or lapping up buggy puddles). There is no angst resolution seminar.

Two routines emerge: We duct tape blistering toes and ergonomically strip and tie off clothing onto our belts as the sun demands. The breakout sessions on using knives and making fire without matches are the big leaps for humankind. We combust fire from carved sticks—imagine a mad pyro-fiddler contraption—then appreciate matches for life.

Still no food. The mood swings from chatty to solemn. Guides are intentionally elusive about even the near future. They only act as safety nets in the event of an emergency. Five-minute breaks collapse into instant group naps.

As I am climbing out of canyon number 90 on day three, my supposedly high-tech sneaker boots herniate by flapping shoe-sole rubber like an 18-wheeler losing a retread. Branded into various zones on the sole are logos indicating the miraculous ability of each engineered area—intricate parts of footwear able to turn me into a wilderness machine. Soleless, I plod on, now wearing the equivalent of hospital slippers.

My contemplation on wearing slippers for the next 11 days is interrupted when the business school graduate and his associate become the Gatorade brothers by kneeling simultaneously to vomit lime-green antifreeze. Yakking up bile is normal under extreme exertion circumstances without food. The body expects scheduled snacks and when denied secretes superfluous bile, causing nausea.

The sneaker-boot blowout, however, is abnormal, so I duct tape my soles back on. In the midst of slicing tape sections to mummify my footwear, I glance away at the heaving-again Gatoradors and plant my knife a half-inch inside my thumb. Mommy flashes into my mind. Fortunately, nobody else notices her.

Marching into another night—everyone sporting duct-tape somewhere—we wonder how much more we can take. By day four, I down a half-cup of oatmealish veggie mush and feel bloated. Workshops continue on stone toolmaking, munching dandelion greens (the yellow part too), tying knots, and setting animal traps. All this while aiming to expend fewer calories finding food than the caloric value of the food found, a necessity to endure in the outdoor supermarket.

We're now handy at stone-grinding oats and barley into flour. The guide surmises that, "Consumers, never knowing where their food comes from, are out of touch with the circle of life." Think about your next burger. The next day, we humanely killed, dissected, and ate a sheep—the entire thing. This was predominantly a vegetarian outing, and there was no mention of meat in the course literature. Ironically, on the course application, which required an okay from your doctor regarding your physical ability to handle this challenge, they also ask you to list allergies. There, I wrote only "Detest liver." Enter: Diced-organ stew. Still in starvation mode, most of the group don't second-guess ingesting organs. After all, what are hot dogs and sausages? The smell of liver repeatedly triggers my dry-heave response and I go another day without eating. The sheep's hide becomes a cloak, the bones become tools, fishhooks, and jewelry. Not attempting to be funny, the craftsman fashions the scrotum sack into a purse.

One of our staples becomes sheep jerky, made by dangling strips of raw sheep meat on a rack baking in the sun. On a 1,500-calorie-per-day diet, it all tastes good, even the spongy texturized vegetable protein (TVP). But the no-trail power walking isn't over. Our mobile homes are hand-tied backpacks made from military-issue ponchos wrapped around wool blankets. We ration supplies for the next five days: carrots, cornmeal, garlic, lentils, millet, potatoes, powdered milk, onion, salt, pepper and vegetable bouillon—plus a cloth bag with enough peanuts and raisins to gorge a kitten.

Thinking our hard days are behind us, we begin to notice the little things. The aromas shift from juniper to armpit to sage to digestive gas from people battling the TVP. Living like a hunter-gatherer tribe shaved down to our humanity, we think the only apparent hazards are inhaling campfire smoke, relaxing to the point of collapse, or getting a whiff of someone's breath (only baking soda is permitted to clean teeth).

At sunrise, it's no bother that my canteen of mossy agua is nearly frozen solid. I'm alone in a red canyon with two dilemmas:

While doing laundry naked by the river, I sunburnt my butt cheeks, and must therefore sleep on my stomach. Consequently, I find myself face down in an ant ranch.

Once the stomach unbloats, an amazingly small amount of food suffices, and I must find other things to consider, such as the chasm between modern and ancient living. I consider an observation made by the Crow Indians: They build small fires and stand close; white men build large fires and stand far away.

Eating uncooked food has blessed me with gas and diarrhea rivaling an experience I sampled in Nepal. So I'm mellow, slow moving like a patient 80-year-old yoga devotee. Time is irrelevant, an opportunity to rethink the period from sun up till down. And, as surely as cottonwood trees and animal tracks usually lead to water, my love handles vanish and are replaced by skin stretched over my lower ribs.

My fiddling-for-fire machine won't behave. The ointment cap I use atop the fiddle burned through and cut into the palm of my hand. Now I have no fire or cap for the ointment. I've got matted hair, a crusting scalp, and am in the midst of an involuntary cleanse. My savage reawakened, I brave the hours either reapplying a body mud-sheen to repel bugs or reckoning that's it high time for a bug snack.

A vision quest usually gives the quester a direction, a plan, a dictum, or a new purpose for their life from that point on. The scope of this experience remains unclear, because I'm consumed by a few rudimentary issues, like suffering from ant-fly madness complicated by widespread itchiness. Food fantasies wane behind a daydream of a hot shower that will soothe skull-dermis decay and cactus attacks.

Knocked out, I amuse myself by watching an ant war and wonder how the ages revolve, rockwise. Night birds conduct low flybys as a lizard bursts away on lightning-speed legs. But I'm too tired even to create the indents in the sand that will prevent my hip and shoulder from falling asleep. Through a process of elimination (eating only sheep jerky), I link sheep jerky to diarrhea.

The group rejoins and is split in two, and we're on our own traveling 30 miles in two days without a guide. I'm heading into the river canyon with three other guys, and one of them begins stretching to prepare for exertion. I wonder: Do wild animals stretch before going for a run?

Not surprisingly, the common realization concluding survival schools—and getting in touch with any desert—is that you can do more with less. You also gain a renewed appreciation for modern convenience.

Dyed red-orange after two weeks in Mother Earth's sandbox, I lull myself to sleep on the final night with thoughts of lizards and ants and anticipate bliss in the morning gas can of powdered lime-ade.

"Do tadpoles contain protein?" —Survival school cohort, after suckling water from a pothole

Upon reentry, a van ride back to Salt Lake City flirts with the present, though we still smell like cavemen. I wake at 4:00a.m. in a friend's den in Salt Lake City, where it takes me a minute to recognize that I am not in a really nice shelter. In the first mirror I see, I think, "Hey, you can survive in the wilderness." I am cutting a better self-image and still snacking like a fashion model—until I fly the next day, on assignment, to Scotland's Glenlivet Estate to sample a different sort of barley, the single-malt-scotch version. In flight, I look out the plane window into a desert canyon and take a bit more with me. And wonder if ants like sheep jerky.

DIRECTION

PICK YOUR OWN WINNERS (Brazil)

"Your hometown makes you think of silly things, New York City makes you talk of them ...and Rio makes you do them." —an unofficial Rio street-crossing guard/hustler.

R io de Janeiro, a buzzing urban landmark infused with lush tropical foliage, is home to 14 million. The gorgeous metropolis is encircled by soaring granite mountain pinnacles and enjoys 46 miles of oceanfront, but most visitors see only the famous four-mile crescent strip—a sunbathing beachfront tripling as a volleyball training center and a thong runway.

As opposed to being a tourist, I propose traveling as a poorist— gravitating to each country's impoverished regions, because they need the cash and that's often where the real fun hides. This sort of roaming is a lateral breed of responsible tourism, one that leaves money in the neediest pockets, not the greediest. Spending time and cash in poor neighborhoods helps sustain them better than some of the bloated aid organizations trickling a minimal percentage back to the needy.

Nearly one-quarter of Brazil's population lives rent-free in *favelas*, ramshackle cubicle communities that are custom-built on unclaimed land. The squatters in Rio's favelas don't perceive their neighborhoods as slums, because many of them border or tower over high-rent zones with prized views of the undulating cityscape. Like waterfalls defying gravity, these mountain-hugging, beehive-ish colonies crawl up narrow valleys behind posh neighborhoods—the equivalent of shantytowns overshadowing Malibu.

Traditionally detached from the government, these self-policing neighborhoods eventually became independent states. Although still odes to free enterprise, they are integrating with the rest of society. Well, sort of. Favelas are typically named after streets that pass through them. Residents randomly construct amateur, code-free, brick and concrete compartments atop existing compartments. Rooftop decks endure until other apartments are built upon them. Often arranged in expanding concentric circles, some clusters rise 12 stories. The explanation for why these cubicle stacks don't tumble down the hilly slopes bears a resemblance to why it's impossible to keel over in a crowded subway. Typically, construction on these homes is never completed, so the government can't demand property taxes. Many of the elaborate fort builders I met also seemed to have a bit of electrician in them. The haphazard webs of overhead electrical wiring celebrate a free-market energy piracy I'd only witnessed in India.

One favela maze I explored overflowed with wires, humanity, and talk of the *recorde*, a word whose meaning was lost on me. Entering this self-sufficient community meant navigating narrow, curving alleyways and improvised cinder-block steps. Every other corridor had dorm room-sized businesses, including grocery stores, tire repair shops, and beauty salons. As I wove through the maze—looming above Rio's twilight buzz—several locals either nodded or pointed me in the same direction while soberly announcing, "recorde."

Winding through my last turn, a young girl took me by the hand and presented me to an elderly bald man who was sitting on a short stool and wearing oversized black eyeglass frames without lenses. His faint smile seemed permanent. In the thin man's lap sat a mutt fusing dachshund, beagle, and apparently a bit of platypus. Both the man and the dog tilted their heads to the same side and gazed at me.

"Hello, I am Fabio…" There was a silent pause as the elderly gentleman used his fingertips to uniformly elevate both of the dog's droopy ears so they were level with the horizon, and posed them there.

"…and dis is de most loved dog in de world." The man and the great one cocked their heads to the other side.

"Really… how do you know?" I asked.

"Looook at him!" Fabio gushed. He released the dog's ears and began petting his head, each backstroke temporarily widening both sets of their eyes. The dog didn't seem to be thrown by his fame, but Fabio certainly was. Simultaneous with appreciating that recorde is Portuguese for record, I also petted the tail-wagging idol while surveying Fabio. A treasure near the end of a chapter in his existence, Fabio was glowing with the surety that his amazing partner went unrivaled for adoration on the planet. No doubt a sainted hero among these hillside dwellers, he adjusted his lens-free eyeglasses, flashed a calendar-resistant smirk, and hummed, "World record."

I wasn't the first wanderer led to this reputable duo. But, like a perfect song, they intrigue and charm every time. After an hour of celebrity worship, and just before spinning on my heel to stride downhill through the mesh of cables, uneven steps, and passages leading back onto flat streets, a final question for Fabio, "What is your dog's name?"

"Recorde," he exhaled, and then re-elevated Recorde's ears in tribute to his accomplishment. Two diamonds in the Rio rough. It's within us all to set our own records. While we can't all be the most loved, we can certainly love beyond measure.

∞ ∞ ∞ ∞ ∞

Recorde tugged a heartstring connected to a beagle named Ben, my companion beginning in 1976 when he was presented as an abandoned puppy at my front door after being found near railroad tracks by a neighbor. I thank him, a long-legged beagle mutt, for some important life lessons. For instance: Your territory extends far beyond your yard.

You don't train beagles, they train you. Once a month, this wayward male fled on two-day no-look-back female dog hunts. For the first year of Ben's monthly disappearing act, my family panicked, roaming the neighborhood day and night, calling his name and interviewing people walking their dogs on leashes. As the years passed, a pattern emerged. He always came back, albeit exhausted, to collapse on the kitchen floor for a world record nap. Soon after, Ben would turn back into an enviable pet—nobody could pass him without stooping to bond.

When it was announced in 2008 that a beagle won the Westminster Dog Show for the first time since 1939, I sensed the universe sharing my enthusiasm.

Ben also helped me understand how standard education models can backfire. In fenced-in yard mode, he occasionally refused to come into the house upon request. Training him to come inside for a treat soon flopped because he figured out that rushing back outside again created another treat cycle. Improvisation has its rewards.

DIRECTION

TAKE WING (Martinique)

It is easiest to bounce ideas off of flexible surfaces.

I routinely visit elementary schools around the world. With permission from the proper say-so, it's blissful to sit in on a class, or if invited, teach part of one. During my schooling years, while limping along in some subjects, physics was one of my early loves. So when I call on young learners, I pose scientific conundrums. In the hilly, tropical heart of French Caribbean Martinique, I stood before a class of bilingual seven-year-olds and asked them why the ball I'd just dropped on the floor bounced.

An eager scholar shot his hand high in the air and exclaimed, "Because it wants to fly!"

Faith, of any variety, is the only true and rational answer. We can learn from the naïve. Optimism needs no flag.

∞ ∞ ∞ ∞ ∞

"Don't let the bastards bump you from your orbit." —Advice from a Singaporean department store (imported Northern Irish) Santa Claus

DIRECTION

HUG SOMEONE AND REMIND THEM OF WHO THEY ARE (Ireland)

There will be moments when you don't know if you can visit a certain place ... there will be a lifetime of knowing that you did.

I n 1922, my grandfather, James O'Sullivan, a captain in the fight for Ireland's independence, emigrated from Ireland to the U.S. via Canada one year after the partition of Ireland and simultaneously with the death of his friend and brother-in-arms Michael Collins. He traveled west, laying Canadian rails, ranching in Montana, and then hitchhiking to Manhattan's Upper West Side, where he opened and ran the popular O'Sullivan's Chophouse for 35 years. Shortly after establishing himself, his wife-to-be also emigrated from Ireland.

With that in mind, my mom and I visited Eire in tribute to her parents and to see if the Irish would reciprocate the hitchhiking hospitality my grandfather enjoyed in 1925 America.

In this land of fiercely independent people who value their poets as highly as their warriors, our strategy was to be road-warrior day-trippers and elegant country-inn evening guests—upscale vagabonds, so to speak. At first, mom waved at cars to request rides, but the drivers only waved back. We needed a hitching sign, so I crafted four cardboard appeals: Mom, Angel, Innocent, and Pub, which worked best at small town intersections.

"So Mom, where should we venture today?"

"Never ruin a hike with a reason," she replied.

At that moment, a car, piloted by an 85-year-old woman, pulled over. After climbing in, we traveled on narrow, stone-walled roads past thatched cottages, castles, fortresses, churches, and other noble dwellings. A primetime radio talk show host mused about gardens and the comings and goings of birds in the yard, followed by a lost pet alert and a stolen bicycle appeal. In response, mom reported, "Dad won't put out bird seed. He thinks it's welfare." As it began to rain, our driver said, "The rain is fond of Ireland."

As the landscape changed to sheer cliffs, wet meadows, rocky moonscapes, and roofless abbeys, we passed a lush lime-colored farm teeming with cattle. Pointing to cows, mom chimed in with "mootopia!" Our driver tooted her horn.

Despite using the "Angel" sign to attract the ride, we're dropped off at a pub. There, we eased into the social glue of pub life with a Guinness. Mom sat close to the band playing music by the fireplace. Foot tapping gave way to knee slapping. Soon she was dancing.

Then it dawned on me—the sign I forgot to make for her, representing what all moms stand for: Love.

∞ ∞ ∞ ∞ ∞

"Wherever they may in the distance roam, this country is never forgotten by its born." —Barman, looking over at my mother doing the Irish jig to live pub music.

"An Irishman will never use one word when 100 will do" —
Grandpa O'Sullivan

"I only have eyes for you." —my dad, singing to my mom lying
in a hospital bed just before having knee replacement surgery.

DIRECTION

DON'T JUDGE A COUNTRY BY ITS STATE DEPARTMENT WARNING (Philippines)

With a bit of luck, sometimes the mane event is not the main event.

On a trek through the Philippine "boondocks," a mountainous, rice-terraced cloud forest called the Cordillera, I discovered highlanders relaxing in a state of eleventh century harmony—still unscathed by roads, electricity, or other people's gods. Boondocks, or boonies, are terms derived from a native Filipino word meaning "out in the woods." (Filipinos speak tagalong). Their word for mountain is *bundok*. U.S. Marines imported the slang after WWII. Incidentally, I've come to challenge the U.S. State Department's warning against traveling here—where it's not uncommon to encounter a man with a mullet hairstyle brandishing a machete.

The Philippines is the lone Christian country in Southeast Asia. The majority of its 75 provinces swiftly caved into Jesus when Spain embarked on a short-lived Asian experiment in the 1650s. In spite of that, six of those provinces—within a secluded mountain-range jungle in the country's cooler north—fiercely

47

resisted Spain's take on God. The semi-tropical Cordillera is the country's most rugged and least populated region and is still a thorny place to plot a route and get a haircut. Native Ifugao, Igorot, and other pagan tribes remained warring headhunters until the 1950s.

From my jungle, New York City, it required three flights, two bump'n'weave bus marathons, a motorcycle-sidecar hitchhike, and a hoof over a 6,000-foot mountain saddle to behold the base camp of auto-free Batad, the starting point for my trek in this chiseled otherworld. This magnificent village is a triumph of ancient community planning because the rice-terrace irrigation technology created two thousand years ago still works today. An incredible labyrinth of mountainside water-dispersing canals flow from rivers and waterfalls into outlying crops. The effect is a valley-dwelling paradise encircled by an amphitheater of stone wall-rimmed rice-paddy terraces engraved like enormous steps into steep mountainsides.

In the misty distance, stooped rice planters, standing in two-feet of mud and wearing wide-brimmed grass sunhats, color the scene. Women weed the wall's earthen gaps while kids on other terraces bother pigs. Silence is interrupted only by roosters, cascading waterfalls, and the slush of workers tilling the mud, knee-deep in soupy, stilted earth. High on a terrace across the crystal-clear river, water buffalos pull two manned ox-and-yoke tilling plows—all-purpose 4x4s that venture anywhere. It's all rather timeless, apart from one of the buffalo-plower pilots, a teen wearing a hooded heavy-metal sweatshirt embossed with the words Sin Basher.

Roaming between valley villages in these boondocks means trudging up the ridges and then descending into the rainforest it chain-links together. Some inclines would be rated triple-diamond by extreme skiers, yet they've been conveniently sculpted for thousands of years to maximize rice harvesting on land that's anything but flat. Long ago, the stones used to reinforce retaining walls were carried up from river beds.

Although the never-hike-alone rule holds true, I longed for solitude. So after consulting locals about various trail routes, I rambled upstream to Cambulo, whose 1,300 residents still gaze in awe at a solar power panel that arrived a month before me. The footwork to get there required balance-beam style walking on wet, mossy wall crests that frequently meant being one slip away from a 100-foot tumble to paralysis or death. Surviving such a slip, and then being luckily discovered was only the beginning. Here, one mile "as the crow flies" translates into five zigzag miles. Locals would then have to carry you on a handmade stretcher for at least a full day to find a road leading to a rudimentary hospital and then a flight to Manila. As a result, I focused on each and every step rather than pay such a price.

As darkness fell, I found Cambulo and checked into a guesthouse, a.k.a. Lolita's house. Over dinner, Lolita explained that she gave birth to her nine children between the ages of 21 and 47. Her youngest is three-years-old. Lolita looks to be about 30. Her mother, looking on and grinning, spoke only Ifugao. During WWII, grandma's husband was a local message runner for U.S. troops fighting the Japanese, thus the family's yen to accommodate me was genuine.

I was awakened at dawn by an unrelenting pounding sound. Uncomfortable because I thought it was Lolita's husband, Alberto, going for kid number 10, I tiptoed down the stairs to go for a walk but discovered Alberto underneath his stilted house, thumping rice. This was the first of many encounters I had with people de-husking large stone bowls of rice stalks by pound-milling the grains using cone-tipped logs as smashers.

Here, six to 12 children per couple is the norm. So are basketball courts with cement backboards and dueling, wilting rims due to monkey business. Most of the five villages I visited had courts, and a 10-year-old trick-shooter always surfaced. We'd compare hook shots from every angle and distance. Meanwhile, several teens were often busy playing video games with ill-gotten chicken-thievery booty; modernity can spell trouble in the boondocks. A very recent drift into these far-flung communities are solar-powered DVD players—the first import to inspire a crime wave. For the first time in oral history, kids are caught stealing (chickens, mostly) to finance insidious video game addictions. A town meeting addressing this nefarious dilemma resulted in punishing the busted kid-robbers by making them care for the free-ranging chickens, night and day. And there they would be, sulking through the night, dreaming of their joysticks, their mullets silhouetted by a background that could pass for the Blue Ridge Mountains. In the end, these were the most notorious rapscallions in a rugged terrain thought to be worthy of a State Department warning.

Continuously gaining elevation, a few days later I met two barefoot betel-nut fans on the trail. Tooth-free and beaming, they adamantly advised against my side-trail detour. I was lost, and when they tired of trying to redirect me, they attached me to commuting school kids, who happily led the way. I soon learned that the best way to stay on the right trail was tailing school kids, moms carrying babies on their backs, or dads transporting tools or animals to an adjoining village.

In hillside-hugging Pula, another village without electricity, I was enlightened by Meliza, a teacher at a two-room schoolhouse. Meliza insisted that Cordillera hairstyles haven't suffered the whimsy of trend because the archetypal mullet haircut was invented here. A traditional Ifugao men's haircut, she explained, is executed by placing the customer's forehead on a block of wood and draping their frontal bangs over its side. Then a buddy-cum-barber uses one machete hack to trim his bangs to mid-forehead length, leaving the rest of the hairdo flowing like a Woodstock devotee.

From Pula, I hiked high up into another climatic zone, where conifers abruptly overtook rainforest. The trail eventually led into another valley village and another way of life. Standing on the breezy saddle that divided these worlds, as far away from traffic jams as one can get, I spotted a man and his dog ambling along the saddle towards me. I glimpsed something steely glimmering on his hip. My State Department cynicism took a breather. I considered hiding but waited for our paths to cross. His dog had already smelled me. When he was 100 feet in front of me, I distinguished the bulky machete dangling from a rope around his waist. Marching to a fallen log five feet in front of me, he stopped, looked at me, and then at his dog. I waved hello. Seemingly startled, he took off his handmade backpack and laid it on the ground. He walked the remaining feet towards me and presented an inquisitive nose-to-nose look into my eyes.

Tapping on my own chest and nodding yes, I murmured, "Me Bruce."

I pointed calmly toward his chest and inquired, "You name?"

Pause. Tree leaves rustled.

"Hygee," he asserted. He then playfully tapped on my chest to reconfirm my customized handle, "Boose."

Wedged between two thoughts, I think either I've made a new friend or it's time for a wild-Boose chase on his turf. Alas, he opened his backpack, pointed to the log we sat on, and we exchanged snacks—LAX airport granola for camp-fired flat bread. As we sat there snacking, he spoke no Tagalog or Spanish, only smiled and repeatedly pointed toward the massive, looming, fogged-in mountain—the Philippines highest point—and called out, "Amuyo."

I couldn't help noticing that he sported the typical mullet haircut. Snacks traded and devoured, we stood up to part ways. But my apprehension returned when he pointed to my forehead and then tapped on the machete swinging from his hip. Seeing my confusion, he reached out and used his fingers to flick the sweaty bangs that were hanging in my eyes. He nodded toward his knife again. I remained bewildered. He hunched his shoulders, smiled, and continued down the trail. It later occurred that he might have been offering me a shot at sporting my own Ifugao mullet.

The next morning, before the long return trek to Batad, I purchased a basketball from a ramshackle general store in Barlig—a different province with different looking people. The ball was deemed for Pula, the village strewn with deflated basketballs and a rumored spike in video game addiction. I hoped my gift could stem the tide of the chicken-pinching kid crime wave.

Back in the mist, I met Hygee again, now under the cover of jungle, both of us doubling back home. This time, he immediately began tugging at my backpack with a sense of urgency. Fear and curiosity raced through me in equal parts. One minute later, after indecipherable articulations in rapid-fire Ifugao, I realize that, unbeknownst to me, he was telling me my backpack zipper was open, and its contents were moments away from tumbling to the ground. Initially, I thought he meant, "Hand over the pack, pal." Relieved not to experience a remote Southeast Asian shakedown or revise my State Department opinion, I zipped up my pack and shook his hand. Hygee flashed me a smoky grin, but his concern didn't end there. Inside the soggy, slippery, leech-infested jungle, he noticed the bleeding leech bites covering my legs, and the medicine man in him shined. He treated my wounds with a topically applied salve of powdered lime, a mix of chewed betel nut and ground snail shells. It dried the bites and prevented jungle-rot infection.

Before parting ways with Hygee, I reconsidered his previous offer to cut my hair. In America, our hair obsession has been brainwashed into a toilsome slavery demanding a regimen of shaves, plucks, waxes, coloring, and $100-plus trims. Lacking locks or presenting back fur is taboo; hair has become way too complicated. I gave Hygee the nod and rested my head in prayer onto a fallen tree. He elevated his glistening machete blade of steel over me and a thundering whack shattered the dawn air. I slowly raised my head and looked about the highlands anew—no follicles obscuring my view, proudly sporting an Ifugao mullet. Hygee then pointed his thumb to the sky, smiled like he'd just received a huge raise, said "Boose" twice, and then strode off with a gait of unwavering altruism.

Continuing to retrace my steps, I learned that the schoolteacher in Pula was Lolita's daughter. Cloud forest news, walked-in gossip, preceded me. I presented the basketball to the entire town and gave a brief geography lesson using a similar sized globe. I think I spotted a couple of video game junkies loitering around a hut with wires protruding from it. Only they smirked at my haircut.

I returned to my trek's starting point, Batad, pounds lighter, speckled with leech wounds, unconcerned with electronic communiqués, and with a clearer outlook—literally. Perhaps I should advise the State Department to warn Americans to avoid traveling to this region with chickens, video games, or hair in their eyes. I stood tall above the rice terraces, unfettered after an officially unrecommended jaunt, clearly viewing my path from afar through the window of my mullet. Some ancient ways of life—and hairdos—never go out of style.

DIRECTION

THINK OUTSIDE THE FENCE (Botswana)

The problem with fences is, once built, you don't know if you're inside or outside. —Thoughts of a Kalahari Desert bushman, roughly translated.

In 2003, South Africa was a country in transition, and seemingly on track to begin reversing the atrocities forced upon its native people. After being whisked between South African wineries and safari lodges, I managed a border-crossing revelation.

The age-old ways of Africa's Kalahari Desert Bush people, innately bound to their ancient ancestry, is vanishing. Traditionally, San Bushmen were expected to provide meat for their women, and the women were expected to gather roots, fruits, and herbs. Boys could get married by age 10, if they could bring home the meat. Women were initiated after puberty, and then stayed inside for four months before emerging to select a husband. If Mrs. judged Mr. a slacker, she could trade him in for another man.

This traditional way of life went up in smoke when white colonists assigned Kalahari tribes particular precincts. The bushmen had difficulty embracing private property and animal ownership. They were perplexed when they were arrested for hunting and eating cattle that were grazing on land their people used to inhabit and roam freely. But the bush winds have shifted again. In the late 1990s, South Africa's president flew to a dusty squatter camp on the edge of the Kalahari and ceremoniously handed over to two bushmen leaders—likely having no idea they were in Botswana—the rights to their ancestral lands from which they had been evicted half a century before.

Bush people are shy and tend to keep their distance from non-familial groups. Surviving on hunted meat, edible insects, and wild fruits and vegetables is pretty much a thing of the past. Yet elements of their kinship structure remain, for instance, they don't comprehend community and employment outside of their immediate families. I was told of instances where bush descendants went through months of job training, then after three months, just as they were approaching proficiency, they'd disappear and "give" the job to an untrained relative.

San Bushmen average 5'5" in height, and every face tells a story. Their natural rows of peppercorn hair, almond-shaped eyes, yellowish skin, and high cheekbones meld an attractive likeness found nowhere else on earth. I meandered with my bushman guide, Teeho, cresting endless parallel sand dunes that make up the epic Kalahari Desert's wavy signature. In search of animal tracks and edible plants and bugs, we forged a path that eventually met a barrier, officially called the Veterinary Cordon Fence.

This 1,500-mile series of barriers, mostly five feet high, was built to separate wild animals from cattle ranches. Unfortunately, it impedes natural migration routes and prevents animals and bushmen from reaching water when routine water holes go dry.

Teeho set his hand on the fence, fell silent, and peered through it like a savant conducting valuable research despite scant resources. He whispered a native word that sounded to me like he way saying phish-stok. I stared through the fence, eyeing only desert sand and brush. He peeked my way and said it again, then began pacing alongside the fence. He sauntered back and forth several times, trading his glance between me and the "property" on the other side of the fence.

Later, back on my own in a lodge 50 miles away, I tried various spellings and pronunciations of the native tongue to crack Teeho's code. A notable feature of bushmen is their use of the so-called "click" consonants, produced by drawing air into the mouth and clicking the tongue. Because conventional spellings can't represent these sounds, I tried an assortment of imitations. A minute later, a local sitting at the end of the bar chimed in, "Means lion."

Before the sun rose, lying on my back gazing at southern constellations, the significance of Teeho's message came to light. As he stared through slats in that fence—the symbol of the private property alienating his people—he imitated a detained lion pacing back and forth the way caged animals do in zoos the world over. Imprisoned people do it too.

∞ ∞ ∞ ∞ ∞

If someone else's barricades confine you, don't surrender the lesson connected to it. Unsettling things happen. Move on. For lucky animals, and a few lingering migratory people, staying really means having the freedom to go. The handful of nomads, human and otherwise, wandering across an increasingly partitioned planet must rely on strong instincts to endure. It's okay to struggle, and occasionally slip, on the path you know is right.

∞ ∞ ∞ ∞ ∞

"It's all about free will." —Prophecy suggested to young traveler entering Zambia … "Is *Will* okay?" —Rookie traveler's reply

"The moment the slave resolves that he will no longer be a slave, his fetters fall. He frees himself and shows the way to others. Freedom and slavery are mental states." —Mahatma Gandhi

DIRECTION

MAKE LAUGHTER THE SHORTEST DISTANCE BETWEEN STRANGERS (Britain)

A broken clock is still right twice a day. —*Polish proverb*

Sometimes people who have nothing have everything they need. Near a North Sea oil port, I came face to face with unrehearsed survival. Speed walking through a gritty quarter of Hull, England, I nearly tripped over a rhetorically blessed drifter, living in an urban lean-to, adrift in reverie. After sharing a few canned ales, our conversation swayed to the contents of his tattered olive rucksack.

As he fished each item out, he surrendered multi-colored histories of his worldly possessions and arranged them on the sidewalk, exhibiting and professing the import of rope, tarp, a risqué magazine, airline eyeshades, his "idea registry," and an antique army mess kit.

Lastly, he produced a damp, hulking dictionary. Holding it high and with eyes widened he swore, "Mate, this book's got everything."

∞ ∞ ∞ ∞ ∞

"We need the tonic of wildness." —Thoreau

DIRECTION

KEEP IT SWEET (Bermuda)

When the ego speaks, the truth winks—and then ducks for cover.

B ermuda is a quintessentially British island of palms. It was there in 1999, an eccentric self-styled Bermudian traffic supervisor taught me something about crafting a singular life mission.

Located far enough off the coast of North Carolina to forego NASCAR fanaticism but close enough to New York City to attract weekend warriors, the breezy 21-mile fishhook island showcases pink sand beaches separated by limestone cliff-rimmed coves—and wealth. Churches and colorful stone and cedar buildings distinguish the rolling landscape, while convoys of white-collar tourist duos live out biker-couple fantasies on mopeds.

Bermuda is more than a refined, secure haven for wealthy folks stashing money and living off the interest. When I visited, local celebs included a Guinness Book of World Records kite flyer, Ms. Universe 1976, and Johnny Barnes—a then 70ish retired school bus driver who dedicated his life to transferring smiles to everyone transiting around the island's busiest traffic roundabout. Every day from 5:00 to 10:00a.m. Barnes performed by waving, smiling, gesturing, and preaching love to all passersby. The island dedicated a life-sized bronze statue in his honor just down the road from his roundabout. So, soon after passing the real Johnny Barnes you encounter the iron version; Johnny frozen in his traffic-greeting glory, bestowing an evangelical salute, smiling, with arms extended above his head. He apparently loves everything and doesn't keep it a secret.

When I asked him how to stay married forever, he replied with a grin of sin, "Keep puttin' honey on it, to keep it sweet, or you'll be in trouble." Barnes has been blissfully married since 1951.

Here, in the midst of semi-tropical nowhere, an island never visited by war or fast-food franchises, the oldest British colony remains a fresh-air paradise for visitors, insurance corporations, undeclared riches, heroic moped pilots in training, and one chipper, immortalized bus driver.

Sweet.

DIRECTION

LOOK OVER YOUR SHOULDER—BUT DON'T ALWAYS TURN BACK (Gotham)

Do we spend the first half of our lives trying to figure out what to do with the second half of our lives or do we spend the second half of our lives wondering just what the heck happened in the first half? Tough call, but traveling can help us figure it out.

G oing it alone can be lonely. Sometimes, during trying times, we need help from other people to help us rediscover the bright side. Which is why, in my late 20s, in the true spirit of neurotic Manhattan, I went to see an Upper West Side shrink masquerading as a career counselor. I was living with a girlfriend at the time when my résumé began to resemble vomited spaghetti. My addicted traveler pattern of working in sales for a year and then traveling for a year was—in the traditional career mindset—tattooing a hazard sign on my forehead. Freshly dismissed from a soulless job, I announced to my girlfriend that I wanted to write books and give presentations about world travel. She, sensing unsteady grandiosity, suggested that I seek professional help.

So off to Barbara Allen I went, a healer who had reinvented herself as a career counselor after spending 20 years working as a death and dying counselor; a saint who reached out to terminally ill people and their families facing their worst moments. Time after time, Barbara observed that it typically wasn't until people were courting death that they realized what a pity it was to not have identified their passions and migrate toward them fearlessly. I should have. Why didn't I? What was I afraid of? They'd all wonder, what did I have to lose?

Searching into my eyes, Barbara said, "After 20 years of dealing with people who finally realized what they were meant to do with their lives after it was too late, I committed the rest of my life to helping vibrant people like you to realize their dreams while they still have their health." Barbara—60 bucks an hour, holy cow that's a lot, I need to get better quick—started asking questions.

Her first question: "I'm going to give you a million dollars right now. What are you going to do with it?" I began to divvy up my bounty with a third going to a cabin in the woods, a third invested, then I'd travel the world until the rest vaporized. She got me fantasizing about those three scenarios for about five minutes until suddenly asking, "Is your girlfriend in that picture right now?" I swallowed hard, shook my head, and whispered a solemn no. She peered from beneath a lowered forehead, "Contemplate who is and who is not in your dreams."

I went back to my apartment, schemed a crusade, hit the road, wrote a book, and began giving travel seminars. My kind of therapy.

∞ ∞ ∞ ∞ ∞

There are exemptions to every decree—sometimes backtracking rediscovers bliss. Nobody ever forgets visiting Japan. Fresh out of college and backpacking with no expiration date, I hitched

300 miles from Tokyo to a rural village outside Osaka and unexpectedly ended up living with the Doi family for a month. An unofficial babysitter and English-speaking influence for a one- and three-year-old, I relished time with an extended family where four generations lived under one roof.

Twenty-five years later, I returned to Japan and reunited with Emiko and Rieko as adults. Although they didn't actually remember me, I left behind audio and written English lessons to keep that ball rolling, and their parents documented our time together with photos. The stirring reunion was like finding long-lost family in another land, and a reminder that life is sweet.

After humorously reenacting some of the poses from the photos when they were toddlers, we spent another day together, shed a few sappy tears, and hugged one more time. In a country where being on time means being early, I realized that although you cannot be in two places at once, your spirit can. Later, solo again, I bowed to no one in particular, and boarded a plane.

DIRECTION

MAKE THE CULTIVATION OF THE FARMER—NOT THE CROP—A NOBLE PURSUIT (Bolivia)

Some of us don't know beans about romance.

As I walked along the shore of sea-like Lake Titicaca, I see people loading huge white sacks into Chañi's lone church through the vapors of a sunrise. The ordinary building is the centerpiece of a 200-person Bolivian village set between the great lake and an imposing bank of parched mountains. The church is fronted by a rusted, drooping basketball rim, its court separating the shrine to Jesus from a classroom. Nearby, drowsy llama herds graze while cows sip from the trout-filled lake.

Watching them work, I'm reminded that it's been decades since I've done back-breaking work. Bolivia has the largest Native American population in South America. Although less than 10 percent of Bolivia's land is suitable for growing crops—flat and fertile is rare—farming is their primary occupation. Talk about plowing the odds.

A man with a sun-wrinkled face told me they were storing sacks of *habas*, large dried bean pods, an Andean crop staple that's typically exported and baked, likely ending up in richer parts of the world as tortilla chips. Mingling with this subsistence farmer, who maintains cultural links to his 3,000-year-old ancestors, the ambiance changed when his sturdy wife moseyed over to stand by his side. We all paused at 13,000 feet as the wind blew off the Andes. Her searching eyes and unforced smile were shimmering ornaments—more than a rusty grin sharing tooth with metal.

It seemed as if the woman was asking me if I was married by squinting at me while pointing back and forth between us, and then between her and her husband. I shook my head no. A neighbor with an alpaca on a leash strolled by. Echoing an unraveled relationship back home, I gently knocked my fists together to demonstrate a quarrel. Gazing into my eyes, she touched her hand to my chest. Most Bolivians are Roman Catholic, but their beliefs are often mixed with olden tribal beliefs. I'm not sure what type of sacred moment this was. People of the earth spend most of their lives living. She reached into one of the open sacks and put a handful of beans into my hand and squeezed it closed.

There was a time, not long ago, when many in the U.S. shared the view that to be unmarried was unfortunate, even shocking. As the three of us stood there, Bolivia had had 192 governments in 180 years, so it was easy to assume that the current *presidente* on the Bolivian stamp didn't have much time left. Yet this couple had all the time in the world for each other, and now me.

∞ ∞ ∞ ∞ ∞

Many moons later, at a Bridgeport, CT, outdoor music festival, a telling proverb magnetized onto a camper jumped out at me. It finally resolved that forementioned relationship bomb, and parked that Andean hand back on my heart…

"A quarrel is like buttermilk—the more you stir, the thicker it gets."

DIRECTION

GIVE GURUS A CHANCE (New Delhi)

Despairing in the doing...thrilling in the telling.

I've engaged Indian *babas* of many varieties, including Fire Baba, who refuels disposable cigarette lighters; Cow Baba, who helps cows navigate through impossible traffic jams; and Harmony Baba, an expert in inexpensive, pirated music.

"Suitcases, trunks, and backpacks," the Indian-accented man behind me whispered. I turned to see a grey-haired fellow with a sideways-wobbling head. He was peering at the pile of baggage stored in the corner of a busy guesthouse lobby.

"Only significant for what we pack into them?" he inquired. "Or for what they conceal?"

This is the fifth New Delhi-based spiritual guide—likely another self-proclaimed *saddhu* holy man—that's accosted me today. These wise men, informally called babas, peacefully wander without possessions, or worry. Some of them seem keen on exchanging a revelation for a tip.

This wise man caught me staring at a heap of luggage representing every packing option. He seemed to be onto something, so I offered him a seat and tried cajoling him towards a quicker epiphany. We continued looking at and discussing baggage. From petite backpacks to colossal trunks, they're inevitable fashion statements—declarations of the value travelers invest in portability versus flash.

"Their shapes go beyond the familiar," he continued. "No surprise their boring existence easily goes unnoticed."

He seemed satisfied that I agreed with him, though I wasn't yet inspired to fork over any *rupees*.

"Is this true for you?" he asked, head still bobbing from side to side.

"Sure," I say, while reaching under my chair to show and tell my backpack. That's when shock sparked into rage—my backpack was gone. I looked at the old man who calmly nodded toward the door, where a teenager was running out the open door with my pack. I barked and sprinted after the teen, who dropped my belongings in the road and disappeared into a thick crowd of people, cows, and rickshaws.

After rescuing my backpack, I returned to the guesthouse to thank the mindful man, intending to buy him a treat. But he was nowhere to be found. Ten minutes passed, and there was still no sign of him. So I sat down in the same chair, looped my leg through my backpack strap, reaffixed my gaze on the pile of baggage, and resolved that my luggage's boring existence would no longer go unnoticed.

An hour later, I asked a waiter about the stranger who rescued my backpack.

"Luggage Baba," he said, adding a mini head-wobble.

DIRECTION

THE BEST WAY TO KEEP A SECRET IS
NOT TO HAVE ONE (Peru)

*When asked to revisit where you've been, we tend to assess
where we are.*

P ersonal resolutions often fail. We know that. Why is it so
hard for us to change? My New-Age-dweeb guard was up
when I hit Cusco. Way up. With a little help from a sacred vine
and a chanting married couple who sang in a dying Amazonian
language, I seem to have reprogrammed my way of life.

I'm a recovering naughty man. Yikes, a conscience?

Imagine doing everything you can to avoid clichés, and then
merrily becoming one. An assignment to report on the 'newly
discovered' third highest waterfall in the world sent me to baffling
Northern Peru. From there, I drifted south to Cusco, the gateway
to Machu Picchu, where out-of-body experience shopping led
me to question my consumption. It generally takes the boys a bit
longer to grow up than the girls—some lads require a frying-pan
whack on the head to tilt it toward the light. But first I had to
navigate a jungle of New Age frauds.

Touristy but likeable Cusco is the axis of trendy South American spirituality where transplanted con artists posturing as healers routinely swindle flocks of—many newly divorced—gullible faith-seekers on vacation. After mingling with these bogus gurus, a number of tourists tote a few tattered drums, rattles, and overripe mantras home. This enlightenment is often sanctified by a corny personal name change...How ya doin, Santosh? Partly aware and still skeptical, I tiptoed through that poser minefield and bumped into a life-changing, bad habit-busting all night ceremony with a master shaman and his curative jungle juice, *ayahuasca*.

Ayahuasca is an ancient medicinal recipe that blends the extracted liquids from two or more Amazonian vines. Mixed and proffered by shamans, the concoction first quiets the users' ego and then inspires mental breakthroughs via visions that pave the way for insight. A vision quest described by some as "five years of therapy in one night," vice-ending testimonials included people who'd quit cigarettes, cocaine or heroin on the spot, and others who declared war on sexual-abuse wounds and chronic depression immediately following their rituals.

Modern chemists are amazed that this complex synapse stimulator was discovered centuries ago by tropical forest dwellers with no written language. Ayahuasca's benefits are gradually enlightening some American mental health specialists (hola Marin County) who recognize this potentially more sustainable and possibly permanent way to upload serotonin than by gulping unpredictable antidepressants. Celebrity advocates include Sting, Paul Simon, and Tori Amos. Back in the beat 60's, William Burroughs' Yage Letters to Allen Ginsburg documented his trials with Ayahuasca in Peru. In 2004, the U.S. Supreme Court, keeping the government's thumb off the church, ruled unanimously that a New Mexico congregation may use Ayahuasca tea as part of their rituals intended to bond with their God.

Considered remedial, not recreational, a reputable facilitator of sorts is typically required to locate a shaman-led "vine of souls" ceremony. Authentic Amazonian shamans rarely speak English and may not even speak Spanish, and there lies the first challenge. In addition, 'agent' sincerity, knowledge, and prices vary. Upon meeting ascended masters Don Antonio and his wife Rosita, a curing team in their 60's from Pucalpa, I knew I'd found my conduit. Decades ago, Rosita's father, also a master, was reluctant to let his daughter pair off with then 21-year-old Don because of his alcoholic path. This led Don into sobriety and inspired his career choice.

After meeting the healing duo again two days later in Cusco at the same bohemian guest house, we hiked up a dark mountain road that wound uphill and outside the city to a secluded home encircled by an eight-foot stone wall. Inside, our group sat in a circle upon futons on the floor of a candlelit room. Don individually blessed each one of us, two Americans and six Peruvians, by spit-misting an aromatic substance over our heads. We each drank a three-ounce shot of the auburn, woody-tasting Ayahuasca. Twenty minutes later, a dizzy euphoria encouraged us to all lie down on our backs in the shadowy room. The dizziness soon subsided and my first vision leisurely wandered in.

The dreamy series of visualizations launched with a self-propelled flight—me clutching a flightworthy two-by-four wing and flying through an infinite illuminated cave teeming with indented half-dome shelves. Each domed ledge in the hallowed emporium comfortably roosted groups of the important people in my life. I visited dozens of ledges, exchanged greetings, laughs, or memories with comrades, received reassurance from my parents, and nods of approval from my two older brothers. When the breezy voyage landed on the shelf propping up the ex-girlfriend, I said, "Sorry." She tried to reply but couldn't find words. We both cried until I flew away. The tears were real, both in and out of the dream. My flight pattern circled back for a few extra visits to mom and dad, just to validate the spectacle.

Somewhere in the cave the beautiful singing began. A vital element in this ancient ritual are *icaros*, the shaman's power songs, chants, and whispers that cultivate communication with the spirits of the natural world. The icaros help to flush out mental and physical illnesses and nurture relevant visual displays in the minds of the Ayahuasca-medicated. Trained by both a maestro shaman and the spirits themselves, Don and Rosita's harmonizing icaros sustained and steered the entire five-hour odyssey. Their version of world music kaleidoscoped harmonies from India, Africa, Southeast Asia, Peru, and somewhere indescribable.

One predictable outcome of an Ayahuasca ceremony is the literal purging of bad energies, a chance to mug your personal demons. An exorcism, in the form of literally dry-heaving out unhealthy spirits, occurs at intervals after you process unfortunate, unpleasant, and repugnant things stuck in your past. In this shamanic forum, my first confrontation with my unsettled history concluded with the vomit-style purging of that broken relationship. Something stronger than us insisted we finally move on. Other baggage best not remembered was later evacuated in stages. I was free of it, at least for a rapturous moment, maybe longer.

The easy-breathing resumption of another glide through my acquaintance-lined cavern was, in due course, interrupted by a series of visions associated with alcohol, the drug I'd been sipping—and occasionally misusing—in recent months while my fourth book remained unsold. Partying without a reason to celebrate had been on my mind. The 3-D documentary-style shorts debuted with the image of a van-sized stone block monument declaring POWER. I stood at its base, with a buzz and a beer parked in a holster clipped to my belt, and used a chisel and hammer to splinter the monument. The ensuing revelation portrayed me, with beer can in hand, standing above a collage of written statements declaring my life goals. These affirmations of my dreams were arranged on the ground below an elevated arc of sidewalk that arched over skyscrapers, traffic, and noisy pedestrian chaos. As I strolled over the sidewalk-bridge, I urinated upon my dreams. Curtain.

Next: The big-screen flashes to my favorite East Broadway bar consumed in roaring flames while a steady stream of drink-in-hand patrons, also on fire, casually stumbled out the front door and toddled down the street, remaining aflame. Whoa. The climax apparition depicted me seated in a chair in the midst of a sallow, cell-like room illuminated by a bright bulb hanging on the end of a wire. I sat there with my head tilted back to smooth the progress of swilling from a quart-sized beer bottle. Suddenly my exact clone materialized, armed with a butcher knife, and began stabbing me repeatedly in the torso—while I kept drinking, failing to notice.

Not exactly subtle metaphors, especially when the unstoppable movie appears on a stories-high monitor in your mind.

The smell of alcohol then materialized and abruptly made me sit up and gag. I threw up (blanks) again until a mood shift in Don's chanting and Rosita's singing coaxed me back into the flying buddy cave. A few of my unconscious psychological gargoyles, human and non-human enemies seated upon a few shelves in the cave, were waving for attention but I snubbed them. There's nothing predictable about Ayahuasca except the lifeguard role of a good shaman. Their olden insights exist on borrowed time in the modern world.

As the sun rose, the group simultaneously landed back in the material world and discussed their visions with Don and Rosita via the facilitator. The rounds of rib-wrenching dry heaves made me feel as if I'd pulled muscles in my torso, but otherwise I felt fine. The freestyle group discussion, where everyone shared their personal journeys, reminded me of a corporate weekend feel n' heal workshop. After sharing my visions, Don and Rosita had a brief exchange using gentle voices. Then Don looked at me and said, "Your best teacher is your last mistake." A minute later, I readily vowed to the group that I'd be giving up alcohol for a year. After the ceremony, I hiked back into Cusco, lost in thought, curious about a new frontier.

I arrived back in the States a seemingly changed man and enjoyed that clearheaded year without any chest-beating regalia, pining, or month counting. With little drama, the rebalancing was akin to taking on a new hobby by dropping an old one. I had to get clever about entertaining myself: the strolling into any bar and playing Bad Company on the jukebox option expired. I used to peer into ice cream stores, croissant cafes, and coffee joints and wonder, what *are* they doing in there? Energized and more patient, I slept less and woke up focused, putting pen to paper. My newfound patience inserted a few reflective time zones into my conditioned impulse to flee dilemmas.

Years later and imbibing moderately, a relationship is now a breeze because apparently, if you discipline yourself, nobody else has to. I now calmly settle most disputes that might have skyrocketed into war. I escaped the trap that cripples many couples: when drinking together, men tend toward less sensitivity while many women become moreso. If wine swings someone into a warrior stance, delay that conversation until the next morning, when it's oft forgotten.

No nag, shrink, friend, or pill could have led me to this happily altered state. Did this native folk medicine spawn a random psychotropic movie reel in my brain? Was the imbedded hush-hush in my subconscious unlocked? I may have had a subconscious agenda, but as far as I know none of those images had been previously installed. Perhaps I just tripped upon a reason to change. Regardless, the mystical result wedged the first sturdy interleave of discipline into my life since my phase as a collegiate wrestling caveman.

Another lasting impression of this flush of the warring foes ratcheted into my psyche is a restored intent to "ruin" my life, so to say, interpreting ruin as leaving a meaningful legacy— not a statue, but at least a few cool books. *Celestine Prophecy* cuteness aside, Peru inspired me. My heart signed a contract with my head, and I reclaimed my power.

And I'll never forget this: While hugging Shaman Don and Rosita goodbye, Don whispered… "You've got to have try."

DIRECTION

DON'T LET YOUR MIND FORGET WHAT YOUR HEART HAS FELT (Nicaragua)

Assess your coordinates of wonder.

When the sun rises in Costa Rica at least two things happen. Hardcore bird lovers set out on rainforest rambles, and San Jose's gamblers and naughty night owls call it a night. After sampling both, I took a chicken bus to Nicaragua, which in 1999 was slowly limping out of a war. Days later, as the sun rose over Managua, I met a thought-provoking toddler, the youngest of foretellers.

He was barely two years old, living on the rim of dusty Managua in an airport-bordering slum. Walking down his dirt lane, flanked by shanties, he carried a squawking chicken that nearly outsized him. At times, the chicken was at peace with the boy's cuddling intentions, other times rebelling with scratching claws. My thoughts transformed into an open letter and a few suggestions for a boy and his country about hanging onto things that really matter.

Dear Nicaragua Chicken Boy,

Knowledge is portable. In your case, it was an official Republic of Nicaragua chicken that you carried. From afar, the daunting hodgepodge of corrugated steel and random billboards jointed into scrapbook housing looks inescapably dismal. Yet a random dirt-road stroll guided me to you, your enigmatic chicken, and a full cycle of emotions.

While you wait on domestic justice, chicken boy, envision life from a juggler's perspective—maneuvering five airborne balls symbolizing friends, kin, health, occupation, and your higher power. Keeping all these balls in the air becomes an overwhelming yet worthy chore. Understand that the occupation ball is made of rubber—if dropped it bounces back. The other four—friends, kin, health, and higher power—are crystal. If dropped, they are usually irreversibly damaged, never the same.

Vie for balance in your life, despite corrupt strangleholds on your national harmony. You live in a country where the disparity between rich and poor accelerates. Embrace what is closest to your heart. Without passion, life pales.

After discovering you, Nicaragua's future, I retraced my inbound steps, leaving the neighborhood with one more thought for you. Remember that earthquakes and war have erased most of the physical relics of Nicaragua's cultural heritage. So talk to your grandparents—when they pass, libraries burn. Carry that knowledge amigo, and remain inimitable.

Your pal, Bruce

DIRECTION

NEVER UNDERESTIMATE YOUR ABILITY TO CREATE CHANGE (Estonia)

A country's history is discovered in its songs.

M usic mobilizes mortals. Estonia lacks military might and has always been surrounded by much larger countries with intimidating armies. Russia, Germany, and Sweden all vied for its control, creating a tug of war that lasted centuries. Tough times. Inspired by the fall of the Iron Curtain, Estonia symbolically overcame its final suppressor, the U.S.S.R., when country-wide choir jam-bands launched their Singing Revolution. A Baltic Woodstock. Here, choirs outrank sports as a national pastime—some attracting as many as 30,000 singers. Song festival fairgrounds, with their signature bandshell arches, are everywhere.

After 50 years of Soviet repression, in August, 1989, two million Baltic citizens, including people from neighboring Latvia and Lithuania, created an unbroken 350-mile human chain linking the countries in their call for freedom. The likeminded people clutched hands, and changed their destiny. Estonia, where medieval meets modern, sang itself free. The three original flags of the Baltics had been outlawed with possession punishable by prison and torture. Swiftly, these flags—hidden inside walls and ovens for decades—began waving all over the country. The keynote battle-charge song, *My Fatherland is My Love*, has since become an unofficial national anthem.

We're all hooked on songs. While in Estonia, I asked several street-strolling locals to sing for me, and true to form, they obliged. One woman sang the entire unofficial anthem as we stood on an empty sidewalk. This fallout of the Baltic Singing Revolution made me wonder, what would the U.S. choose if it needed a new anthem to sing its way out of a real jam? *Won't Back Down, Born in the USA, American Woman, Highway to Hell, Don't Stop Believin'*?

Healing conflict with music, now that's a concept. Follow your melody.

∞ ∞ ∞ ∞ ∞

Estonia's national bird is the barn swallow. It's no pin-up like the bald eagle, nor a chart-busting singer—but, aptly, an agile survivor for all seasons.

"We are the music makers, and we are the dreamers of dreams."
—Willy Wonka

DIRECTION

LET THE NAKED TRUTH BE (Irian Jaya)

*Recalibrating fashionably late in a place where nudity
neutralizes class lines.*

S ledding to the Poles, summiting Everest, rowing across an
ocean…it's all been done before. However, in an age when
earthbound pioneer glory is virtually unattainable, I slid into
a premiere—playing naked Frisbee with Stone Age natives.
Someone had to do it.

Simplicity died when fashion was born. What is it about modern
culture that feels the need to impose a foreign language, a way
of life, and a religion on a people that live in communion deep
in an impenetrable forest? The well-intended but often genocidal
influence of outsiders continue as Irian Jayan highland tribes,
guilty only of nudity, succumb to an alien oppression. One
force driving this Aboriginal extermination is that frontiersman
psychology.

Irian Jaya makes up half of New Guinea, the world's second
largest island. This Melanesian holdout is Indonesia's least
populated territory, and *nothing* like Bali. Torrential rivers plunge
from the peaks into gorges and lush lowland rainforests before

flowing out toward the coastal plains. Even today, representatives of tribes unknown to the outside world periodically emerge from the forests. In 1990, a previously unidentified group surfaced. Ambassadors of the tribe, evidently shocked by what they saw, immediately disappeared again.

Accessible only by air or after a month of hacking through a steamy jungle with a machete, the Baliem Valley was my launch point for a month-long trek into the region's highlands, requiring a blend of valley walking, high-endurance climbing, and cliff scaling. The rugged terrain isolates intimate Dani tribe villages, which are segmented by stone fences and surrounded by sweet-potato vine gardens, canals, and steep, terraced mountainsides.

The walking routes are the natives' prolific trade trail system. Occasionally, I pull over to let trios of bow-and-arrow toting hunters pass. Mud abounds. You haven't officially trekked until you've had a boot sucked off by a foot of mud—never a concern for the barefoot Dani. In fact, the dark-skinned Afro-resembling Melanesian Aborigines still wear only penis gourds, an early model jock strap made from petrified yellow squash shells that are fitted over their genitalia and fastened skyward by thin strings tied around the waist. The old-style way to rock it.

Ruuf, my Dani guide for the first leg of my trek, led me, calm, wise, and barefoot, leaping nimbly from slippery log to log. When I lost him, I tracked his mud prints. A long, grass-mesh billum bag slung around his forehead and draped across his back contained sweet potatoes, compressed tobacco, leaves for rolling cigarettes, and a small bag of salt. His primordial briefcase also toted a palm-leaf mat doubling as a rain poncho. Upon his head, it resembled a nun's habit.

Unsuspected downpours are common and one monsoon shower was especially enlightening. Betrayed by flooded boots and soaked by sweat inside my raingear, I caught Ruuf smiling under his temporal teepee with not even a drop of water on his petrified squash. Pausing there in the downpour, I contemplated my departure from the essential laws of human survival. Darwinian perfection gazing at a mail-order misfit; a defeated poster child of Western survival gear. I was seduced into surrendering to my innermost nomadic calling—the contents of my backpack later becoming gifts. Luxuries are often not only hindrances but also dispensable.

En route, we encountered 20 local men resting on a bluff overlooking a terraced valley and the thundering Baliem River. The shoeless posse was hauling supplies to their village 30 miles away. Suddenly, they broke into a three-part harmony a cappella, an ancestral call to unite and energize the group. Their simple spirit-lifting chant reminded me of the feeling you get when a bird or other animals hop over and sits by you in the forest—date and time momentarily wait. Sublime.

Ruuf and I shared many bowls of rice. We nibbled small fingerfulls, caveman-like, and peered about the forest. I heard birdcalls, Ruuf heard food. I showed him a photo of a girlfriend. Mixing pantomime with intonation, I attempted to inquire, "Have you ever seen the sea? He shook his head no. "What is your favorite food?" He pointed toward sweet potatoes. "What do you dream about?" He glanced down at the photo of the blonde woman and grinned wide. Archetypal humor.

People are usually more complex than what initial impressions may convey. Frequently, one of the first questions upon meeting someone is "What do you do?" for "what you do" is often misconstrued as who you are. How would Ruuf answer this question? We'll never know. The man for all seasons and I parted with a prehistoric handshake, lasting a minute, graduating to a mutual bicepshake, adjourning with condoning nods. I headed for a nap in a village dwelling, and he ran off, in the buff and into his boondocks.

∞ ∞ ∞ ∞ ∞

Indonesian officials have failed in getting all of the inhabitants of this *wild east* to support "Operation Penis Gourd," which is designed to get them out of their traditional getup and into Western clothing. When these seniors pass on, this sartorial tradition and much of their old way of living will be history. Wave goodbye to the Stone Age and hello to naked shame.

It's difficult to process the rugged, simple beauty of these formerly fierce headhunters and cannibals who discarded stone axes for steel in the mid-1900s. Clock time remains irrelevant here. The small, wiry women do most of the chores, such as raising the children, pigs, and sweet potatoes. They often lug up to 80 pounds of potatoes, and a baby, for miles up and down steep mountain trails. Women work the fields while the men generally walk around, chat, pose for photos, and smoke cigarettes. Intrepid prototypes indeed. The men also tend the squash-to-be-gourds, which they manipulate to grow according to the shape of the manhood sheath they fancy. I tried on a few gourds in various villages, which eventually led me to a new level of embarrassment.

Living in tidy, wood-thatched, grass-domed huts called *honays*, men and women sleep and pass time in separate two-story huts. I was permitted to sleep, and reflect, in honays after receiving consent from a village chief. Certain bungalows are the privilege of men who've established themselves as warriors. A tad rustic, if you focus on the fleas and mice, these alpha-male sanctuaries are fertile pastures for the imagination—superstitiously invested shrunken animal heads, spears, weaponry, and charms hang from the roofs.

The Dani converse in soft tones, if they speak at all. Illuminated by a well-tended fire, we sat in a circle, puffing clove cigarettes, noshing on warm sweet potatoes, enveloped in smoke. Imitating the dudes, I inhaled the clove deeply and achieved a serene cannabis euphoria. Knee-deep in nomadic caché, I accepted the silence as meditation, in a corner of the world where safety pins were once fair trade for a shrunken human head. Meanwhile, the reigning thought in my mind during the interlude was Einstein's prophesy about not being sure about the outcome of a third world war, but asserting that the fourth world war would be fought with sticks and stones. Surely, these vanguards would endure, in spite of pressure to get online with the global economy.

I spent the next morning in church, a wooden cabin with a corrugated tin roof, packed with quasi-clad worshipers. Women and girls sat on the left side, men and boys sat on the right. A lonely dead-battery clock loomed above a makeshift wood box altar, behind it the rambling missionary preacher was the only other person wearing clothes. Seated beside me was a man wearing only a chunky beige gourd, a band of greasy chicken feathers on his head, and a clove cigarette stored in his earlobe piercing. Patiently waiting to interact with the preacher, he inserted a quarter-moon-shaped pig bone into his pierced nasal septum. Although lost on me, their discussion enraptured everyone else. The women sat quietly with net-like billum bags slung around their heads, bulging with provisions and babies. An unsympathetic gatekeeper declined to let people leave before the service concluded.

During prayer, all eyes were closed and heads lowered. Interestingly, they cover both eyes with one hand during prayers in fear of going blind. First came the peek-a-boo glances at the peculiar albino, then the restrained library chuckling. When the service ended, the women passed me to exit the church, their handshakes missing digits. I learned that the older women cut off one or several finger joints as part of a cremation ceremony when someone in their immediate family passes on. Some women I met were missing most of their fingers. Severing a corner of the earlobe is the corresponding practice for men.

Bartering also enthuses the Dani. Safety pins remain a prevailing souvenir trade item. They have become their all-in-one toolbox: surgical implement, fishhook, necklace ornament, wood etcher, earring, and so on. Velcro also makes a splash. Purchasing six-foot-long hunting arrows was one task, getting them through airport security and onto eight different connecting U.S.-bound planes was another. I still use the custom-fit gourd I smuggled home as a prop in my keynote presentation.

In *Walden*, Thoreau speaks of a "realometer," a raw, instinctive gauge to rate the wow-factor of our individual convictions. Here, my realometer stayed pinned to the max. Likewise, foreign visitors can astonish these natives. My icebreaker was also my contribution: a Frisbee. They were riveted by this simple aircraft, a pie-tin cum UFO. The flying saucer captured their imagination and made them belly laugh. Initially, I was concerned that by introducing this game, I was further adding to the ruination of a traditional way of life that deserved to be preserved. My first instinct went against introducing a non-neutral item into their culture, but unanimous child happiness cemented the verdict, and it isn't difficult to replicate a disc using preexisting items— their circular rattan "place mats," we discovered, also flew. At this time, there was still a standing back-flip in my public entertainment arsenal, and each village ranked it up there with making things fly.

While other tradition-defying forces impose religion and outlander value, I tossed my neon-blue flying disc into the last primeval frontier, and they rejoiced wildly over it. Upon entering a small village, I'd stroll into an open area, usually the courtyard in the midst of the hut complex, and spin the Sputnik so it hovered and descended gradually into the waiting huddle. Some ran to it, some ran from it and kept on running. It was perhaps the biggest single event to hit these villages since the first invader donated matches. Now that's Ultimate Frisbee. The Papua natives, having developed for millennia in isolation, have many unique traits including a hunting talent for throwing and launching spears. Straightaway, many of the younger Frisbee throwers advanced from having never seen one to being able to wing it 200 feet—using unconventional gripping techniques, or launching it upside-down.

I played sort of nude, too. At first my gourd was a discomfiture; some of us wage a continuing struggle against fashion. The string tied around my waist failed to hold up the hardened vegetable case that kept fumbling downward, and it itched. I didn't like sprinting barefoot across rocky fields, and I was paranoid about injuring my exposed nutsack. I concluded that some of them intentionally tossed the Frisbee astray, so I'd have to run for it. They laughed at that too.

∞ ∞ ∞ ∞ ∞

Clothing optional might be optimal. The Dani, former cannibals, seem like the most gentle and hospitable people on earth. Thoreau suggested that people are rich in proportion to the number of things they can afford to let alone. Too bad we can't let this final pristine refuge be. In a surge of serendipity, a culture that doesn't bother to keep track of its age adopted one harmless result of the times—flying plastic.

It will be some time before Frisbees rival the importance of pigs in this quiet corner of the world. Near the end of my sojourn back in time, I entered a village and pitched the flying disc into another curious horde. This village chief had difficulty catching, throwing, and comprehending it, as did some of the other elders. His discontent with the game grew when the disobedient aircraft drifted into the pigpen, spooking the priceless swine. The chief abruptly disappeared into the men's honay.

As the sun was setting and the Frisbee fanfare was winding down, the chief reappeared. Strutting erect, bows and arrows slung across his back, he paused in the center of the village and drew an arrow. Focusing, he aimed skyward at the hovering disc.

A second later the Frisbee's heart was punctured. Crippled, it wobbled to earth. Justice. My realometer flared. Game over— the chief retrieved the impaled UFO and retired into his hut.

The wind whistled through my gourd.

∞ ∞ ∞ ∞ ∞

"It is an interesting question how far men would retain their relative rank if they were divested of their clothes." —Thoreau, Walden 1854

DIRECTION

SING YOUR WAY OUT OF A JAM
(Fiji ~ Nunavut)

Get round-wound-sound.

I roamed Fiji's mountains for weeks just before a military coup in 2000 ousted the elected government and spooked international tourism for a year. Politics aside, these isles remain a divine setting to go to church, regardless of your spiritual status.

Worldwide, missionaries provide a doorway to Christianity, with an irresistible doorknob being music. Efforts to establish the faith in the Fiji Islands began in 1825 by the London missionary society and was successful, as the mission lingers. Even those who have sidestepped organized religion find gospel singing a worthwhile reason to visit the churches built in nearly every settlement.

If the Fijians treasure one thing they inherited from the missionaries most, it is the music, sacred song that they infuse with stirring magic, especially in the rural chapels. The church may be an unpainted weather-beaten building down a remote and rutted road, but through the doors and windows on a Sunday morning, angelic voices and curious, beaming children beckon.

I sat in many of Fiji's five denominational churches, listening to soulful harmonies reminiscent of the deep American South. In Navai's Adventist Church, a village elder reads a psalm, and then the worshippers sitting near the altar transform into the choir. With no musical instruments, these men and women lift untrained voices in glorious three-part harmony, praising the heavens with a pure beauty European cathedral choirs cannot match—deep velvet from ages long past.

Navai's gospel serenade lured me into this holy shelter, an agreeable, muggy Kiwanis-style lodge flanked on all sides by Venetian windows. It was the humanity that kept me there. After the children stopped sneaking peeks at me, they refocused their attention on the preacher. There was a message on the blackboard behind him: God has a plan for you.

Below that, in reference to the blessing line of snacks available: "Banana Cake," "Stone Buns."

Sometimes it's nice to know what the plan is. I asked the only other visitor in the church, and in this misty mountain range, if he believed in a god. "Not very much," the traveler answered before peering back toward the choir… "But not very little either," he added in a livelier accent.

∞ ∞ ∞ ∞ ∞

Nunavut, Canada

Nunavut is a High Arctic territory comprising one-fifth of Canada's total size. Only 35,000 people, mostly Inuit, call it home. I can see the homes of 35,000 people outside the window of my urban dwelling. Up here, houses are built high on stilts to avoid snowdrift buildup. Each cube-ish home has two external tanks, one for potable water and one for waste, imported and exported by trucks. This setup makes residents ultra-conscious of usage and disposal. If you had to carry the amount of water you probably use taking one shower you wouldn't make it up a flight of stairs, let alone budge it.

Gjoa-Haven, far north of the Arctic Circle, receives no more than three foreigner ship visits per year. Lucky to be there, I met two teenagers, Aglukkaq and Keknek, who were keen on continuing an Inuit tradition called throat singing. Keeping a tradition traced back to Mongolia, these young women created multi-layered supernatural cadences. Haunting, but also beautiful and mesmerizing, its eerie harmonies resembled guttural, breathy electronica music. As a duet mixing throaty growls and soaring repetitive rhythms, they stopped the clock. They'd been training for four years for a performance that lasts about five minutes. In a culture where centuries-old survival skills are now sadly taught as arts and crafts, Aglukkaq shared that they had received a grant to go sing in Scotland. Then she adjusted her wool hat and said, "We hope it's not too hot there."

∞ ∞ ∞ ∞ ∞

The national anthem of Honduras resulted from a 1904 contest won by a Honduran poet and scored by a German composer—so their battle-hymn sounds like college football halftime music.

"Poland is the only country to elect a professional musician as its President." —Krakow street troubadour

DIRECTION

CREATE YOUR OWN RITES OF PASSAGE
(Borneo)

*Remember what you have seen, because everything forgotten
returns to the circling winds —Navajo chant*

The few still living as unshackled Aboriginals in this world remain puzzled over why city people do not wander. Ancient societies, a few lingering native cultures, and determined cultural holdouts provide rites of passage that graduate their kinfolk into new levels of awareness. In generalized Western society—namely in the United States of Generica—there's getting a library card (well, more like a first website password) and a driver's license, concluding prom with naughtiness, turning 16 or 21, entering the military, graduating college, and getting married. Religion aside, Western culture rarely provides spiritual signposts. You must go out and find them, or create initiations that suit you.

Borneo's Aboriginal highlanders call their rite of passage a *peselai*. This long hike is also a spiritual journey that enhances knowledge of other ways of life and a sense of self. It's an initiation to test their resolve in new places, in this case by trekking hundreds of miles from their mountain homelands to visit and work in coastal towns. In such places, they're hard to miss. Even along wide streets, these men walk in single file together, just as they do on narrow jungle trails.

This rite of passage is also a way to acquire wealth and social status. Before embarking, these highlanders must receive specific omens from the jungle—calls and movements from certain birds and hawks, along with a *woof* from the barking deer. Waiting for the departure signs from these animals can take more than a month.

You may not have noticed them, but your personal signposts may already be there. It's hard to get lost when you pursue passion, a gift you usually give yourself. If a misaligned antennae has been leading you astray, shed it, or at least bend it in a new direction.

Woof. Time to make a move.

∞ ∞ ∞ ∞ ∞

Do you remember the first time you got to stay home alone without adult supervision? That's a mini rite of passage. Doing your first charitable act for a stranger is another. Riding your first bicycle without training wheels, attending your first slumber party, and experiencing your first kiss are a mix of public and private ceremonies. How about your first solo trip outside your state, or state of mind? Realizing you don't know everything and that your parents aren't fools is a less celebrated rite. Consider observed customs, such as, letting your child drive for the first time—or having to take away your parent's driver's license. Observing others' rites of passage during our adult years can be powerful because we see a bigger picture than we did in our youth and become more aware of our humanity.

I'm mildly shocked when fellow North Americans, who claim to be worldly, admit to never having driven across their motherland from coast to coast. The Atlantic to Pacific manifest destiny tour should be a standard righteous passage rite for all of Uncle Sam's kids. After doing so, you develop a patriotic appreciation for its space, human variety, and geographic diversity.

∞ ∞ ∞ ∞ ∞

You can always adopt another culture's rite. Throughout East Asia, Buddha is everywhere. I've been visiting Buddhist countries for decades, not because I'm Buddhist, but because I cherish their scenery, food, climate, and people—their warm, mellow, and extremely tolerant nature is wonderful. The core philosophy of this 2,500-year-old way of life pretty much bewildered me until a special Burmese monk put it like this:

"To love someone is to suffer; to hate someone is to suffer."

I think we can comprehend that frame of mind.

∞ ∞ ∞ ∞ ∞

Borneo

In years past, I've found it handy to occasionally rent a real man to guide me into otherwise untried ways of life—and gather insight from his rites of passage…

Sometimes, the toughest thing I do in a day is snap dry spaghetti in half before boiling it. It's not the stuff of an outdoorsy Renaissance man, but I'm betting that—off camera—the survivalist stars occasionally define their daily workouts with spaghetti cracking. In Borneo's jungle, an unsung survival master named Belansai made me re-examine my mojo and wonder if I'd gone soft.

Belansai's talents included *bamboozling* (cooking hand-caught fish in a campfire-heated bamboo tube), machete-hacking jungle foliage and transforming it into a shelter, and chatting with wild orangutans. Initiated into surviving in the rainforest by his grandfather, Belansai not only used the machete fastened to his hip to chop trees and fashion open-air shelters, but he also used it to finely chop garlic. He was late 50ish—his Iban tribe doesn't keep track of ages so it was only a guess. He was also trim and ripped without ever doing a crunch. Standing back and watching him do pretty much anything begged the question: "What can I *really* do?" Well, translating Belansai's advice for the modern man does come to mind. A happy partner in an arranged marriage, he offered up his thoughts on women: Fight as long as you are still alive. Wait, that was his *overall* advice.

Although watching Belansai tinker around our camp was better than an action movie, it was time for a hike. Frequent pit stops were required to yank blood-sucking leeches off of our bodies. At one de-leeching rest area, Belansai put his finger to his lips and pointed up at an orangutan glaring down at us from 40 feet above. Tourists visit rescued but still captive orangutans in Borneo's zoos, but this tree-swinging fellow was all wild and a bit crabby. He first challenged our neighborhood raid by aggressively shaking limbs and throwing broken branches. Then, after swaying nimbly between five gigantic trees, he yelled at us. That was Belansai's cue to converse. The ape mellowed-out and we trudged on. Surely aware of the decimation of the orangutan habitat to make room for more crops, a minute later, Belansai said, "Ape mad, maybe sad."

Before leaving the jungle, Belansai waltzed out of the Jelia River with freshly caught fish and frogs in both hands and then brewed our final tea. After a few sips, this Gandhi amid survivalists pointed at wild boar jawbones hung in a tree like trophies and invited me to go hunting. Instead, I promised to stay in touch. My urban-numbed psyche got its knees dirty. I'd soon be back online, while the only way to communicate with Belansai would be calling a regional radio station DJ who'd send him a one-way message over the airwaves. Pretty neat for a guy who has never driven a car. That's *rite*.

DIRECTION

LISTEN WITH A THIRD EAR TO WHAT'S NOT SAID (Egypt)

When someone shows you their true colors, believe them.

The redefining English language noun—once limited to persons, places, and things—now includes ideas. As English evolves, the ancient writing system of Egypt, hieroglyphs, remains set in stone, but not without a few puzzles.

Hieroglyphs, with more than 2,000 characters, were chiseled in rows or columns that can be read from left to right, right to left, or top to bottom. Try that, English or Portuguese. The key to reading hieroglyphs is noting which direction the animal or human characters on the sidelines are facing. If they face right, you read from right to left. If they face left, you read left to right.

While musing over a hieroglyphic patch on a temple wall in Luxor—the Nile-side open air museum—a sentence starting with a face looking to the right dead-ends with a face looking left, and therefore, creates an ancient staring contest. Does that mean this line can be read in both directions, or that it should be reread? Primitive 10 foot-long sentences whittled into rock have a way of drawing you in, so I stood beside the ruin wall and accosted passing tour guides. None of them could answer the question. It seems like they can only reference from the prerecorded tour-group scripts banging around in their heads. Egyptology schmology.

I had abandoned my quest to solve the scripted face-off until I crawled deep inside the Great Pyramid of Giza through a crude tunnel carved out by eighth-century Arab looters. Rising 460 feet, it was the world's tallest human-made structure for 3,800 years until it was surpassed in 1300 by England's Lincoln Cathedral (where, by the way, my dad and I once argued the semantics of how the absence of tipping affects food service). The Great Pyramid's 2.5 million blocks weigh between two and 70 tons and are cut so precise that a credit card still can't be wedged between any of them. However, *you* can still wedge into their midst.

One of the three known chambers discovered inside the pyramid is the King's Chamber, a dorm-sized tomb. Crawling up the narrow refrigerator-sized passageway from the base of the pyramid into its core rouses mild claustrophobia. The claustrophobia factor explodes if the person shimmying ahead of you panics and suddenly insists on back-pedaling like a spooked horse down a narrow section of the tunnel where it's impossible to bypass anything bigger than a rabbit.

Indeed, the guy in front of me snapped, and the procession of crawlers behind us all had to frantically reverse-crawl back to the constricted passageway's entrance so he could escape. I re-entered and reached the tunnel's top end where I sat in a corner of the dimly lit sarcophagus and welcomed the meditative vibe. Being metaphysically sandwiched between a hand-holding, trance-moaning New Age couple and a gaggle of babbly, flash photo-snapping Frenchies renewed my appreciation for ventilation. Once again, I puzzled over the ancients' batty hieroglyphic face-to-face trick at Luxor. My ping-ponging contemplation jogged the breadth of the chicken and egg riddle as the French holidaymakers left. The temporary silence was broken when New Age gal whispered to New Age guy: If vegetarians eat vegetables, what do humanitarians eat?

So, now I'm engaging two brainteasers within the confined, geometric center of six million tons of limestone sitting upon a 13.5-acre footprint—same land area as the Louisiana Superdome, and, oddly, a similar locker-room aroma. Basking in The Great Pyramid's inner ether, I wonder if that long-gone prankster from Luxor chiseled a bit of backstory for how modern politicians interpret the writing on the wall. Meanwhile, because the New Agers still didn't notice me sitting behind the King's red granite coffin, they feel safe notching up their cuddle to another chakra...naughty energy.

Just like a boomerang, which, fittingly, was invented by Egyptians to hunt birds, our personalized hieroglyphs (mantras) can loop one back to where he or she started—another opportunity to be humbled. The lack of fresh air fogged, yet accelerated my thought process. The personal Rosetta Stone continuously being chiseled in my mind uncovers three private pastimes—rescuing overturned horseshoe crabs, scanning the horizon from atop white pine trees, and writing through nights of wild weather. I need air.

It's time to go, but not before the couple's Egyptian Superdome climax. As I exit the chamber and slink back into the descending tunnel, another group of tourists enters the musky King's Chamber. A shiny-headed, bespeckled British man stands up and tells his companion, "Silence is golden, if you haven't the answer."

DIRECTION

FOLLOW YOUR COLORBLIND HEART
(Ground Zero)

All inclusive means all exclusive—even in a
New York State of Mind.

I grew up on Long Island, twice. Moving between bordering towns when I was 10 provided my first lesson in racial inequality. Hempstead, then a predominantly African-American town suffering urban ghetto-like struggles, and Garden City, a comfortable churchgoing village with a strong Irish-American heritage, might as well have been separated by a Berlin-style wall in 1972. As the Black Power movement raged into full swing, the Hempstead school system was in a state of nearly constant chaos. Racially charged in-class student fighting also victimized teachers; class disruptions were the rule. As a third and fourth grader, I feared telling my parents that I was being threatened, bullied, spit on, and literally pissed on at school. In the final months there, I was secretly terrified. The daily mayhem got so bad for my older brothers during our final year in Hempstead that they had to enroll in the Seaford school system a few towns away, where my dad taught.

After moving, I morphed from one of the best-dressed, smartest, and obedient (in school anyway) students in troubled Fulton School to becoming advantaged Stratford Elementary School's chief mischief maker. I immediately taught my new preppy friends—fresh out of choice summer camps—how to shoplift, kiss girls, turn classes into game shows, and break into the school at night. What a difference a mile can make.

I didn't grasp the value of formal education until college. I was an average high school student, but one junior high school teacher stands apart as making an enduring difference— because I feared her. Mrs. McCauley, my eighth-grade typing teacher, could have manhandled any surly inmate. She knew all the adolescent tricks and would flash venom from her eyes to diffuse them. Because of her no horseplay rule, I learned to type on a hulking 50-pound typewriter faster than I could think. Thanks, Mrs. McCauley. Tough love works.

∞ ∞ ∞ ∞ ∞

Decades later, I landed alongside the East River on Manhattan's Lower East Side, two miles from Ground Zero, but in a neighborhood having no connection to the financial district. It was another example of an invisible wall separating haves and have-nots. We all know what happened downtown in September 2001, but what people outside of the region don't realize is that it took 18 months for most conversations there to stop being about 9/11, until returning to the more trivial things people tend to talk about with strangers—sports, television, movies, fashion, etc. During those 18 moon cycles, tri-state conversations were real, heart-to-heart, and of the essence, just like they are when you travel away from the comforts of home to underdog communities without electricity. As one, post-apocalypse New York City's enduring binges— materialism, neuroticism, workaholism—came to a screeching halt. Listening and caring was back in vogue.

∞ ∞ ∞ ∞ ∞

We all go through phases where our sensitivity to others ebbs and flows. Sometimes we don't notice the gatekeepers of our culture, because they're camouflaged by the ruins of ghettocracy. A year before 9/11, I was in vagabond mode when a public radio station played Martin Luther King, Jr.'s "I Have a Dream" speech. It gave me chills, as it always does. Minutes later, beneath the lower East Side's badlands on a then decrepit subway station platform, I spotted an African-American homeless guy who'd been camping out that week on a bench. I'd been avoiding his space in anticipation of body odor. He sat there among four overstuffed, ripped garbage bags, his sleepy eyes observing. Ready to hold my breath and slip by, a notion stopped me in my tracks. The man had a story that deserved to be heard.

I paused and offered a hello, which made him blink at the dim overhead lights like a mole prematurely sprung from hibernation. We'd just struck up a conversation when the train arrived, so I let it pass and sat down beside him. Most of us would be devastated if we had to spend just one night like this. With drugs not a factor, he was lucid, just way down on his luck and avoiding days of rain.

"Got a nice pair of corduroys in there if you want," he said, pointing to one of his bags.

Joseph favored the East Broadway station, because the cops were lenient and the trains arriving from Brooklyn through the long tunnel under the East River "pushed in a kind breeze." I asked him about camping out in other subway stations. Taking on a professorial tone, he said, "Cop stations have, like, halos, safety rings around the precincts that are patrolled big time. Down here, we a long way from a halo." Trains continued to pull in and out of the station.

I forgot we were buried beneath badlands. Our duty-free discussions revealed we had more in common than what met the eye. I was then homeless, too, just fortunate to have family, friends, and strangers applaud my continuing nomadic jaunts around the world. That fine line between us made me realize my fortune. Chance was the difference between me donning clean clothes that day and setting up camp next to Joseph. Remorse shot into my heart as his situation dawned on me. He sensed my despair and tried to cheer me by offering a slice of rye bread.

A dozen trains stopped and churned on. Another rumbling train's tunnel breeze pushed in from Brooklyn. I stood up and prepared to say goodbye by presenting my hand for a clasp, and we both grinned again. Like wild seeds scattered by the wind, our lives had taken us in different directions. However, I was grateful that our paths had crossed. We slowly shook hands, frozen right at the moment of a revelation. Blending Yankee flair with underground wit, he forecasted, "It's all about feeling free to stay."

I stepped into the northbound subway car. Before the doors closed, Joseph waved big and recapped, "Don't forget ta' dream…and, if you lose dat dream, just remember where ya' hid it."

If you take something special from someone, you'll eventually give it back to them, or someone else. I still peek around for Joseph when I'm on that platform beneath a now gentrifying neighborhood. A candle loses nothing by lighting others. He re-lit mine. Talk to strangers, regardless of their station in life.

Many souls are saved by saving one.

∞ ∞ ∞ ∞ ∞

Fear Is Not The Only Force At Work In The World Today — banner perched above Manhattan's smoldering Twin Towers.

"I have decided to stick with love. Hate is too great a burden to bear." —Martin Luther King, Jr.

DIRECTION

ENERGY FOLLOWS THOUGHTS: PICK GOOD ONES (South Korea)

My only daily routine while visiting South Korea was to find a place to rest my head as the sun set. While traveling solo, open agendas frequently lead to shared dinners with new friends and overnight homestay invitations. This alternate lifestyle also makes you a keen eavesdropper, and keener to befriend a translator who is also drawn to overhearing public conversations.

Sitting with a bilingual student in the shadows of a small town recreation hall on the outskirts of Kwangju, I read him an article about how U.S. Reaganomics were stirring the international pot. Opting for something lighter, we listened in on a discussion between a local elder who was playing ping pong with his pre-teen granddaughter. As they volleyed, the grandfather announced, "Two tigers are arguing in my mind."

"Arguing about what," asked the girl.

The man caught the ball and suspended the volley. "One tiger is unhappy, the other tiger is happy," he said. "...and the same argument is going on in everybody's mind, all the time."

The volley resumed until the young girl grasped the ball to inquire, "Who wins the argument?"

"The tiger you pet."

∞ ∞ ∞ ∞ ∞

Words have no wings, but they can fly many thousands of miles. —Korean proverb

"Ahh, many factories…very beautiful." —Jeong Lyle Lee's optimistic reply to my inquiry, "Is Kwangju (a Korean city) beautiful, or are there many factories there?"

DIRECTION

RECOGNIZE PRIDE NEEDS NO FLAG
(Caribbean ~ Cambodia)

Grace over race.

In 1635, two Spanish ships transporting African slaves to the West Indies shipwrecked near the Caribbean island of St. Vincent. The escaped slaves were welcomed and protected by the native Carib Indians. Their intermingling formed the Garifuna people, who remained on the island and eventually traded with the French. In 1797, sugar-planting Brits took control of St. Vincent, defeating the pro-French Garifuna and deporting them all to Honduras.

There, those Garifuna refugees merged with displaced South American rainforest-dwelling Arawaks and African Maroons. These chance meetings mixed bloodlines, created a new language, and gave birth to the proud and funky *yancunu* boogie. Imagine booty shaking in triple time to bongo beats.

After watching a group of dancing locals body quaking on the beach, I strolled along the shore of Honduras's north coast and saw a Garifuna elder standing knee-deep in the water. He was wearing a dapper cap, balancing a little fishing pole upon his shoulder, and toasting with a canned beer toward the sun as it dipped into the sea. I introduced myself, and he removed his cap with the pole and raised his brow in a way that I assumed meant he was game for a brew-slanted story swap if I was.

We settled in for a happy-hour chat, and the stars emerged. Down the beach, a group of foreign visitors began bickering. The fisherman slowly hummed his disapproval, "When two men fight over a woman, it's usually the fight they want, not the woman."

An hour later—when the argument finally fizzled and the distant sound of bongo beats restarted—my newfound Garifuna friend summed up the nature of battling: At high tide, fish eat bugs—at low tide, bugs eat fish.

∞ ∞ ∞ ∞ ∞

Cambodia

I'm sitting outside on a mini stool in northern Cambodia where my bent knees don't fit under the table. A three-course meal arrives from the nearby food stall—a hard-boiled egg served as a delicacy with three additional finger bowls presenting spices, limes, and mint. *Egg vendor #7*, Chantheaea, giggles when she returns with a tiny long-handle spoon. Meanwhile, I watch two guys, Narit and Ponlok, shoot it out on a makeshift outdoor pool table. It's 2003, and this jungle-encased village, Cheabb, probably won't see electricity in the lifetime of these two pool sharks. Cambodia's capital city, Phnom Penh, has just built its first shopping mall with an escalator that has become an instant tourist attraction. I realize later that Chantheaea was chuckling about my inside-out T-shirt. I haven't passed a mirror in weeks.

I've flown 15,000 miles by plane, over-nighted on a bench of a chugging riverboat, spent a day in the dusty cab of a puny Japanese pickup crammed with 10 riders, and then 10 hours on a wobbling motorbike sputtering on rutted, meandering jungle trails. The trail, barely worthy of foot traffic, frequently requires crossing rivers on slimy log bridges. It becomes impassable during the wet season.

My brother Basil and I were repeatedly warned not to venture into this isolated region that's supposedly rife with landmines and holdups by teams of bandits. However, our reward for forging ahead was a spontaneous night that fused a wedding and a bizarre theater odyssey. The first thing we saw in Cheabb was a mobile PA system announcing what later turned out to be a play. The PA system involved two guys on a motorbike rigged with a large horn on the handlebars connected to an amplifier sitting in the drivers lap. The rear passenger held a mike to a Walkman that made the announcements.

In this off-the-grid destination, the wooden box houses are raised on six-foot stilts. In the shade below, black buffalo, pigs, and chickens reside. The people, mostly rice farmers, steal naps in hammocks slung between stilts under the houses or between the trees. Everyone we pass waves hello. My hunch is that once war-ravaged, perpetually destitute Cambodia had a lighter side, and I wasn't quitting until we found it. Landmines, civil war, and genocide dominate many associations with Cambodia, but life has returned to a new version of normal, even in Preah Vihear Province, one of the poorest and most isolated.

There's no way for an outsider to know they're crossing between the neighboring villages of Cheabb Lech and Cheabb Kart (Cheabb east and west). But that's where we were invited into the soul of this village with zero tourism. In one magical night, we attended a wedding reception, which later segued into an outdoor theater performance, and then slept on the top cop's porch.

The wedding highlights included proud toasts ladled from a 35-gallon jug of homemade milky-fermented booze, dancing to insanely loud Cambodian pop, eating bugs, and listening to the best man speech in which he noted that the bride's premiere hobby was jumping rope. The groom, dressed in a frumpy, oversized suit, couldn't stop snickering during the should-be solemn slow dances. Our go-to-guy, the only one in town who could speak English, told us about the local pothead, a little girl who wears a red cooking pot as a hat.

After the wedding reception, the group marched across town to join 200 people already seated on the ground before a stage that was amplified by a lone microphone hanging from a wire. The wooden stage set was draped in billowing, silky tarps. The performance, hours and hours of short bits, were punctuated by the manual closing of a dainty pink curtain. A flash photo (Basil's) started a tizzy that startled the entire audience and made actors modify their act and speak in even higher pitched voices.

Where there are no televisions, traveling troupes are still the stars. Within the crowd, several campfires were maintained to combat the 70-degree winter chill. At one point during the six-hour Khmer epic play, half of the audience suddenly stood up and gasped—a reverse domino effect that didn't seem like a standing ovation. It wasn't. A six-foot-long heat-seeking venomous snake had crawled into the audience. Once the snake was hacked in half by someone who happened to have a machete handy, the show resumed. Basil suggested that the snake's demise might be a metaphor for what happens here when someone threatens married life.

After the marathon performance, we feasted with the wedding gang, but passed on the cow stomach and dried blood patties that resembled black tofu cakes. After waking up on the hospitable police chief's front porch, we visited several schools, all raised 12x12-foot platforms either under a home or outside covered by tarps. The blackboards were black paint on flat boards and the instructional guides were laminated posters, one for math and one for language. After Basil donated hordes of pens and notebooks to these makeshift schools, he also stepped in as interim teacher, which routinely inspired more laughter than learning.

Despite the forewarnings about landmines and holdups, we ventured to Cheabb where the people, like most Cambodians, exemplify warmth, grace, and pride, which is incredible when considering the unspeakable horrors many of them have endured in their lifetime. In these more prosperous times, some still manage to survive on one dollar and 1,000 calories per day. The Khmer capacity to overcome extreme adversity and still welcome unannounced travelers with smiles and respect *is* humanity. Being the first foreigners to visit a place where they've never seen any is a traveler's cliché—but when you unearth the last remnants of virgin turf in Southeast Asia, dignity and joy is what you'll find.

As my brother and I prepared to roll out of Cheabb, we enjoyed a final hard-boiled egg at the food stall. The newly married couple rode past and waved to us and all of the food stall workers. They were honeymoon bound—a visit to the other side of the village— which made the staff cheer wildly. That's when it dawned on us that the bride was #7, our previous egg vendor, Chantheaea.

DIRECTION

GO WITH THE FLOW (Laos)

Why knot?

Finding your way in Laos can be a challenge. Street addresses are rarely used. If they are, building numbers match the order of construction. Lao transit often means huddling in the back of a family-size tuk-tuk. These oblong, bald-tired trucks make room for three lucky ladies riding in front with the driver, while 20 others cram into and upon the dingy pickup's tarp-roofed bed. Because many villages can only be accessed by foot or boat, one mode of river travel presented a do-it-yourself option with two choices: sink or swim.

In northern Laos, 6-foot 9-inch travel-writing cohort Brad and I inherited a recently commissioned green bamboo raft valued at $12 to float a stretch of a river that originates in China and faces pending multi-dam destruction along its entire course. Semi-buoyant, slightly navigable, and gradually sinking due to waterlog, our 10-by-2-foot craft was also coming apart from collisions with various rocks. When night fell, we floated in nearly waist-deep water as the baleful purr of another set of rapids seemed to foretell our doom. We were weekend warriors in primetime.

The backstory of this unplanned water voyage is a lesson in international bargaining. From the last road in Nong Kiaw, we took a motorized longboat upriver to Muang Noi via the River Ou. When navigating headlong into rapids, we crashed into rocks and had to totter to the riverbank for repairs. Little did we know what an omen this would turn out to be.

Accessible only by boat, our destination, Muang Noi, is an idyllic village on an elevated riverside plain cradled by large mountains. A refreshing departure from Southeast Asia's earsplitting transport madness, the little town remains blissfully devoid of motorized vehicles. There was only the drone of periodic generators creating electricity. The biggest currency note, 20,000 *kip* ($2), went a long way for frugal globetrotters seeking spectacular hikes and river floats. Here, the backpackers were starting to coexist with middle-aged European couples, likely revealing the future of this place. The predictable tourism cycle starts with backpackers flocking to an out-of-the-way gem, a decade later come the guided groups, and another decade brings the resorts.

Every town has a go-to guy. In Muang Noi, it was Kao, who for a fair wage, made many travelers whimsical daily dreams come true. On a professional level, he would be called an expediter or a fixer. We called him the magic man. When he offered to build us a boat, Brad and I clashed. I voted for continued freewheeling hiking and local riverboat tripping, as we've all heard foreboding maxims about boat ownership. Brad, however, saw a grand adventure brewing. I eventually convinced Brad to wait another day to decide.

A few hours later, I found myself sipping a beer in a thatched-roof establishment and wondering how to stave off Brad's boat dream. That's when a British guy I'd befriended stumbled in with one hand clutching a paddle, and the other a banged-up rifle. "Oh my god, they're coming for me," he stammered. "What did

I do?" He dropped the rifle on the table and slapped his forehead. Come to find out, he'd gone "into business" with an Israeli guy to purchase a handmade boat for the market price of $12, but when they showed up to board and float their craft, the builder requested two more dollars for a pair of handmade paddles. The Israeli wouldn't budge and demanded the paddles be inclusive of the $12 they'd already forked over. The Laotian bamboo craftsman wouldn't negotiate. Harsh words flew, prompting the Laotian man to strut home, paddles in hand. The Brit and the Israeli trailed him through town and into his house, a hut really, and grabbed the only paddle they could find. And to make a point, they also snatched an antique rifle that was hanging on the man's wall. While the argument over $2 paddles may seem incredibly petty, when ultra-thrifty travelers are on the road for a long time, a few dollars can make or break a budget—and possibly someone's sanity.

After 10 minutes of consoling the sweating Brit, three calm plainclothes Lao policemen arrived at the restaurant to fetch the gun burglar. Coming to his defense, I pleaded with the cops to accept the Brit's apology (invented by me), which included an offer to buy dinner and drinks for the boat maker and the police. With faces frozen, they weren't interested. I couldn't help but feel sorry for a nice guy who'd gotten in over his head. Off they marched with the Brit. Before exiting the restaurant, he thanked me for defending him and handed me the disputed paddle sighing, "You can have my boat."

Soon after, Brad strolled into the restaurant, and I told him the full story, minus the gifting of the boat. He caught me off guard when he pointed to the paddle leaning on the table and asked what it was. Immediately after confessing that I now owned a boat, Brad lit up. "Let's go!" he said. In a mad scrabble, we checked out of our huts, commissioned Kao to find us a second oar, and ship our backpacks downriver on the next local transport boat. Then we set sail.

Not 10 minutes into our downriver excursion, the raft began doing a wheelie since big Brad commandeered the back. Because we had warm beer on board and were careening off rocks, we agreed to name our craft *Bamboozler*. I knew we were in over our heads when a two-ton water buffalo swimming across the river gave us a steady warning look I interpreted as, "What the fu*k are these dorks doing here?"

Like two wagon-pulling seven-year-olds attempting to run away from home, we puffed out our chests and rowed on. Keeping pace with that mindset, we became the afternoon entertainment for children on the shoreline by echoing various animal sounds. Brad mimics a great cow. Later, we docked on the shoreline for our first of several random village visits. Kids arrived and laughed with us, and then the elder men waltzed up and chuckled at our boat, and us. Let the buyer beware. As opposed to dried brown, buoyant bamboo, our freshly cut green boat was cumbersome and basically unsteerable. Regardless, we still got credit for arriving by homespun boat and celebrated our dockings by buying all the kids pencils and writing pads from the lone shops near the makeshift marinas.

Eventually, our time on the water took its toll. "I have a feeling someone's not rowing," I accused Brad, forgetting there was a 240-pound guy back there who wasn't smiling. And one oar, mine, was more likely to be used to fan myself. Both oars were two-foot long sections of bamboo sliced on one end to insert a chunky leaf. You could hardly call our floating logs a boat. When a father and son paddled by in their slick dugout canoe and ogled us with confused wonder, we gawked back at the harmony of their smooth, silent glide.

The sun set behind a cliff and the nocturnal jungle animals began to stir. The distant hiss of another run of whitewater roared louder and louder. We took swigs from our beers and braced for impact. Inexplicably, we clunked through the whitewater series like an underwater toboggan. Weaving like an unmanned magic carpet ride, we ran into rocks that spun our boat out of control, submerging it deeper underwater. Somehow, we eventually righted it, but not before the sound of cracking bamboo was heard competing with the gush of the rapids. Our limping underwater raft now set the waterline above our waists. In this part of the world, they call foreigners *falang*. The Falang Navy drifted on.

Having survived our brush with drowning and discovering that our sack of beer was still tied on, we discussed lighter issues. Then it occurred to us that neither of us had any idea where Kao had actually forwarded our backpacks. I yelped "wait," to a deaf river deity. Still happily helpless and barely floating, the jesting continued...

"Brad, our raft is a bit of a lemon."

Brad responded, "*Your* raft."

Now in total darkness, we continue navigating blindly until a passing motorized passenger boat pulled up next to us, and the elderly pilot waved us into his boat. Upon boarding, we pointed to our raft, and he nodded a slow no, dismissing it with a backhanded wave. Emergency hospitality at its best. The kind, calm, and graceful Lao people make it hard to comprehend that Laos remains the most heavily bombed country ever. In a nine-year undeclared war, the U.S. dropped half a ton of bombs for every inhabitant.

Rescued at sea, we docked another mile downriver and discovered that our packs were on our rescue boat. Our good fortune multiplied when we re-encountered the apprehended Brit in that village, where he was taken, questioned, and released. After paying the apologetic would-be felon an honorarium for the stipulated boat, we shared a few laughs, and I realized that it was the first boat I'd ever bought—and for that matter, abandoned—albeit in the span of a day. Bucket list check for boat ownership.

Weeks later, back home in New York City, I found patches of reddish River Ou mud on the shorts I'd worn on the raft. Surprisingly, many of the world's most daring pathfinders never discovered what they were looking for—riches, renown, and new trade routes to the Orient—but they all fearlessly cast searchlights into the unknown. Collectively, they mapped and helped merge the globe's peoples and ways. Although at first reluctant for this particular adventure, I can't imagine missing it. Brad and I didn't exactly obliterate navigating presumptions that had endured for ages, but after smelling that Lao river again, I felt equally fulfilled and pitched my shorts into a washing machine.

∞ ∞ ∞ ∞ ∞

Don't bargain for a boat not in the water." —Brendan Lake, Maine boat builder

DIRECTION

FIND A LIGHT IN THE DARK (USA ~ Asia)

Contemporary cavemen can still find their way.

A Long Island Sewer

M y interest in caving started in seventh grade when various pals and I used the rainwater drainage tunnel system to explore the otherworld beneath the streets of Garden City, New York. Jim, now a civil engineer, long ago invited me to view sumps—gritty rainwater holding basins—as suburban ponds. One such sump, conveniently located behind Jim's house and parallel to our high school's athletic field, made entering the tunnel easy. He connected a BMW car seat to the base of a baby stroller, attached a few truck side-mirrors for style, and we were off. With one of us pushing and the other one seated and holding a flashlight, we explored endless miles of interconnected, convoluted tunnels leading to streetside sewer compartments.

Sometimes losing our way on account of too many bends, compartments, and intersecting routes, we'd eliminate the risk of not finding our way back by exiting skyward through various manhole covers. This was also a possibility when our flashlight batteries died, and we were rendered completely blind. We soon learned to distinguish between manhole covers in the middle of roads and those under sidewalks. Needless to say, we learned quickly not to attempt an exit from a manhole cover when speeding cars were rolling over it.

Jim eventually outfitted anyone invited to venture into our town's innards with rubber boots and what he termed "smoking jackets." A traditional smoking jacket is an overgarment designed to be worn while puffing pipes and cigars. Jim's version used thrift store suit jackets as mud and odor armor. Every mission explored further into the unknown. Self-appointed spies delving deeper into the cool down under, we discovered that by placing truck side-mirrors at key intersections, we could illuminate and see around corners. I'll never forget the thump the carriage made bumping over the tunnel's section seams. Though the dank, decomposing odor was assuredly offensive to most, it smelled like adventure to us. It was all about conquering the next compartment, the next bend in the cave. And we were never deterred by the hollow glow of rats' eyes as they stared into the beams of our flashlights.

One eighth-grade afternoon, when we were nearing the end of this stage of subterranean delinquency, we emerged, resembling gnarly coal miners, from the manhole directly in front of the high school. There were four of us, as Jim had since built a second tunnel-rolling explorer. The entire cheerleading team, which was practicing on the lawn 20 feet away, froze and stared at us in our rubber boots and smoking jackets in a state of fear and confusion. Underclassmen to say the least, our fated 1975 arrival at the ankles of the Garden City High School cheerleaders would be a preset for how certain women would view me for the rest of my life.

That spirit of exploration and camaraderie was not forgotten. Decades later, I was nominated to plan Jim's bachelor party. That night, I invited him, supposedly in advance of a gathering happening elsewhere, to meet me for a beer in the grandstand overlooking our high school's athletic field. As we sat there casually chatting, I arranged for his pals (some former tunnelers) to emerge one by one—at first inexplicably—from a hole in the fence that surrounded *that* nearby sump.

∞ ∞ ∞ ∞ ∞

A New York Subway Tunnel

Big city caves were not lost on me either and remained beacons of discovery. When I was 22, I lived briefly in Queens, New York. One night at 3am, I was returning home from an indulgent Manhattan debutante ball. Waiting on the station platform, sporting a tuxedo, beset by impatience, and duped by a robust Champagne buzz, I jumped onto the subway tracks and ran beneath the East River all the way to Queens in the surreal tunnel. I eluded a passing train by pinning myself against the dank wall. Upon arriving at the next station (Queensboro Plaza), I climbed up onto the platform, straightened up, and nodded to the captivated passengers waiting there for the next train.

∞ ∞ ∞ ∞ ∞

A Cave in Borneo

The caving continued in Borneo, the world's third largest island and one of the Earth's lingering green patches. Sarawak's Mulu National Park is a miracle of epic caves. Deer Cave, spacious enough to house a mega stadium, has several heavenly 1,000-foot waterfall spires draining from the cave's roof. Half of the falling water becomes mist. As the sun sets every day, this ultimate bat grotto becomes the stage for millions of hungry, darting bats emerging from the cave's mouth to gobble tons of insects. As the bat storm darkens the sky, all flights into and out of the nearest airport are canceled. This daily event is also an aromatic experience. The ammonia-scented bat guava offends some. Surely it means something else to the rare, remaining Aboriginals still managing to live off the grid in Borneo, and the guide who was following me.

Emerging from the cave back into the sunshine-baking rainforest, a local guide, the one I wasn't able to shake, promised, "We're racing to turn our rainforests into parks rather than chopsticks." Impressed, I asked him what he liked best about the cave, and he pulled a tattered wad of laminated index cards from his shirt pocket. After flipping past a few cards pasted with bat images, he stopped at one bearing only a one-sentence quote, and read aloud:

"If there hadn't been women, we'd still be squatting in a cave eating raw meat, because we made civilization in order to impress our girlfriends." —Orson Welles

∞ ∞ ∞ ∞ ∞

A Cave in the Philippines

Most guys have been shot down for merely acting like cavemen. That sort of rejection is universal. Evidently, caves can be good places to ponder such heavy thoughts in another part of Southeast Asia. On Sabang, an island in the Philippines, survivors of Magellan's fateful expedition restocked supplies on their way back to Spain. Here, I rowed three miles upstream into the world's longest underground river. Flowing from beneath a mountain into the sea, the river cave's ceiling is a continuous faultline, and my handheld lantern hunted an infinity of its stony Rorschach hallucinations. This burrow of brackish tidal waters meanders through a submerged passageway and visits several massive rooms, including an eerie but stunning 200-foot-high cathedral with sculpture-esque outcroppings.

Floating motionless in the midst of the cathedral, my outrigger canoe's guide and rear oarsman, Danilo, clicked off his headlamp, so I followed suit. Amid the pitch black, he admitted that his attempt to serenade his first love, old-style by singing outside her window, was a failure. She didn't show. Seems the courting stakes are higher in a country where divorce is still pretty much nonexistent.

"She may not even have been home," Danilo mused aloud.

As the gloom of his confession sunk in, bats and swifts audibly swooped past. I paddled back toward the entrance, and my adjusting eyes took pleasure in the stalagmites, stalactites, and quivering patches of napping bat swarms that hung from the walls and ceiling. Reemerging into daylight near the cave's mouth—back in the humid domain of lizards and macaques—Danilo suggested in soft tones, referencing flying things, or women, or both, "All bird, like all human, is individual…and some birds only mate once a year."

That's when the other previously silent guy in the boat, the other expat, chimed in, "Sorry honey, I've got a headache…and I've got one next year, too."

Resonating that metaphor, Danilo nodded coyly ahead at the waiting throng of new customers, mostly female. After loading them into his boat, he paddled back into the cave. Before fading into the dark, he peered back at me onshore and pledged that he's "learning to play the guitar." Seems a classic Indo-Pacific pickup songline is brewing.

Be your own searchlight.

DIRECTION

GIVE THE HUSHED A VOICE—BY LISTENING (Rwanda)

Making everyone equal has no equal.

One mode of leaving goodwill footprints outside your motherland is voluntourism, whereby vacationing tourists and travelers give back by mentoring those in need. Hoping to make a difference, I volunteered two months to a non-religious charity in Kenya and Rwanda in 2008—first as a media liberator, second as a business consultant, and also as an ally. A revelation was how many unpaid, unnoticed hours and fundraised dollars go into presenting the simplest staples and gifts to those in need. Because more than half of Rwanda's Gross Domestic Product is donor money, most career-bound graduates—engineers, journalists, and academics—gravitate toward Kigali's non-governmental organization (NGO) money as opposed to following their intended career tracks. Engineering graduates can earn more money working for an NGO in accounting mode than as an NGO engineer. This rerouted talent pool nearly drained Rwanda's trade and middle classes. As a result, the craftspeople inventing, manufacturing, and fixing things come from neighboring countries.

In Kigali, Rwanda's hilly capital city, the mission was to transform an existing but overlooked journalism-mentoring program. I soon comprehended that teaching Rwandans to tell their own story is a complex challenge. Because I've been dancing on the freelance-writer tightrope for decades, I partially understood their pain. In America, an incessant stream of aspiring writers attempts to break in, and the odds remain stacked against them. In Rwanda, poverty and lack of opportunity dash many writers' hopes, but since a major thrust of the 1994 genocide was orchestrated by government-controlled print and radio, most Rwandans still justly fear all media. This added a huge hurdle to mentoring journalists here, but we tried. Our collaboration resulted in several students publishing their debut stories in *The New Times*, Rwanda's leading daily newspaper.

The world media tends to report only when Africans are either taking or losing lives, but there's more to the story. We began encouraging the students to find a story. Their riverside facility was near a hillside neighborhood called Cyahafi, which survived without electricity or a fresh-water delivery system. None of the students had ever ventured into this neighborhood, so we led eight journalism, photography, videography, and filmmaking students into their school's backyard to discover story lines. I shadowed a 20-something guy named Cadeau, who emerged as our lead writer.

During this time, a team of workers was busy restoring the banks of the Mpazi River, which meanders alongside Cyahafi, by meticulously placing stones in the riverbed to ensure its smooth, uninterrupted flow. The eroding riverbanks' periodic flooding had claimed several houses. Plus, the river had pooled into a series of malaria mosquito-breeding ponds and infectious swimming holes that were an enticing danger to children. We saw it as a storyline, and indeed, while roaming and discussing title development, story color, and clever interview questions, several local issues came to light, including the fact that dead bodies used to be dumped in the river, and children often drowned in the contaminated pools. Random residents thanked the government for sponsoring the nearly complete project. Other interviewees included local shop owners, the oldest resident, and a mother of six, whose house had collapsed into the river.

It wasn't long before the aspiring journalists learned a life lesson. You don't have to travel far to uncover news. Vital stories are often right next door. In this case, Cadeau, a liberated reporter, adopted the philosophy of don't hate the media, become the media.

The traditional media does a fine job of covering bad news. Help shine a light on good news, however small, to give hope some legs.

∞ ∞ ∞ ∞ ∞

My voluntourism group also focused on reshuffling a T-shirt printing project to sustain and educate genocide orphans who live together in Kimironko, a government-housing community in Kigali. For me, the crowning moment in Rwanda was a particular gift with wings. My friend Brian Steidle, whose experience as an unarmed military observer in Darfur in 2004 led to his global policy-changing book and movie *The Devil Came on Horseback*, was assigned to mentor a Rwandan anti-genocide freedom fighter in photojournalism. After working side-by-side for weeks, Brian gifted his camera—the Canon he discreetly used to inform *The New York Times* and the world about the Janjaweed-fueled genocide in Sudan—to his student. "That camera was born in Africa and deserves to remain here and continue informing the world through a fellow warrior's eyes," Brian said. Although the Canon was like one of Brian's appendages, and he seemed unarmed without it, his Rwandan comrade's proud grin was his reward for paying it forward.

Soonafter, the aforementioned aspiring Rwandan photojournalist debuted with a project about why most of the Rwandan war veterans were hooked on heroin. Unfortunately, he then got hooked himself and sold Brian's $7,000 camera for $500. While the outcome in trying to help others isn't always storybook, all we can do is continue trying.

Hope endures. Freddy Mutanguha, the lone genocide survivor of his family and an enthusiastic employee at Rwanda's Kigali Memorial Centre—a museum campaigning to prevent genocide worldwide—reinforced that virtue when he said, "You have to work on the heart of the people."

∞ ∞ ∞ ∞ ∞

"Due to genocide, postcards are in short supply" —on handmade postcard sent from Rwanda.

DIRECTION

HEAL A BROKEN HEART BY MENDING OTHER'S (Tompkins Square)

Those who hunt two loves, catch none.

Metropolises are handy for legally snooping on other people's chats. In my home city of more than eight million people, I leaned against the East Village fence surrounding Tompkins Square Park and tuned into the odds and ends of a few conversations between strolling twosomes. In the time it took for a cunning squirel to smuggle a cache of peanut shells into hiding, I overheard...

"Perhaps he needs to focus a bit more on his *shelf* awareness."

Soonafter, a line stolen from a duo marching in the opposite direction...

"Women with headshots are usually trouble."

Cities can also strain relationships.

A moment later, I saw a woman working her way along the north rim the park, randomly stooping to place what I thought were quarters on the sidewalk, fire hydrants, lamp-post bases, car fenders, and whatever else looked like it needed adorning. Curious, I trailed her.

"Are those for good luck?" I inquired. "A peace offering... Charity?"

"Thank you for reminding me," she smiled. "All of that."

Strolling on with a loaded backpack, giving out *change*, she mused, "Go have one."

I retrieved one of the gold coin tokens that had hearts and words on both sides, soon discovering that every token she placed shared the same contrary messages. One side showed 40 hearts crashing to the ground and was dually inscribed: I Can Seem To Forget You and Trust No One. The flipside of this token contemplating another side of love showed 21 cheerfully organized hearts with the top of the coin face reading: In You I Trust and Your Wind Song Stays on My Mind. Mint(ed) advice about gambling on love—flipping the coin come to life.

As she continued south along the park's eastern rim, I stood on the corner revisiting the coin's messages until I came within earshot of two passing cell phone yappers, both in heated discussions. One—presumably referring to a puzzling male—sang out into the night, "You can't break a wild horse with feathers!" The other, in a milder tone, "You're going to have to talk to your God about that."

DIRECTION

INVENT YOUR OWN CONSTELLATIONS
(Long Island ~ Goa)

We all see the same moon.

Hempstead, New York

It's important to recognize wisdom when we hear it. Think about it, sometimes we don't even realize our favorite moments until they've passed. When I was young enough to still trust in Santa Claus, my dad and I took late evening walks on a golf course that, without exception, he'd never step foot on in the daylight. Reclining on the cool greens, we'd gaze up at the compelling starscape. Lying perpendicular to dad and using his stomach as a pillow, I remember my head rising and falling slightly with his inhales and exhales. We discussed astronomy, the rebel moon, Fudgesicles, and my older brothers' ritual of tickling me into convulsions. When I reflect on these perfectly calm times, I can recall his voice and his poetic flair that could make reading an insurance policy sound like a JFK speech.

Our discussions wandered as high as the sky. Medieval times were dominated by faith and mysticism that helped paint the zodiac dome. We wondered, astrologically, who said we have to

125

buy into what's up there?

In that hour of darkness, we lay on the earth, erasing bias and realigning the star patterns to symbolize whatever we wanted. We discovered a "woman opening a door for a chipmunk," a "grasshopper dining with chopsticks," and even a "little boy helping a blind person across the street." My dad taught me to make the sky mean something personal.

Family and friends rewriting astrology will endure, or at least reclining together on the planet for a while. Surely, my dad didn't invent this—who knows how many ancient fathers laid with their children discussing the nighttime skies.

"What do you see?" I asked my father.

"Wishes. My hopes are in the stars."

∞ ∞ ∞ ∞ ∞

Goa, India

Decades later in Goa, India, in the midst of an early 90's all-night beach dance party, all 50 partygoers laid on their backs on the sand to behold the sky. This type of revelry set the stage for the massive Full Moon parties that eventually took hold worldwide. As the moon mimicked high noon, the sky-gazing intermission during this gathering became an international forum on shifting perception.

"What would you say if you could stand on the moon, looking at the Earth?" someone asked in a British accent while pointing skyward.

A moment of silence.

"Some questions are more informative than any answer," a Scandinavian mused, opting to alter the query.

A local Indian woman who'd been transformed by this expat hippie colony told the Scandinavian, "Your statement is not clear to me."

"Clear, like the weather on the moon?" chimed in an American.

A ski-lift attendant from Jasper, Canada, had the final muse: "Bad weather *is* good weather."

∞ ∞ ∞ ∞ ∞

"Two men looked out through prison bars. One saw mud, the other stars." —Oscar Wilde

DIRECTION

DON'T JUDGE YOUR RIVALS
(Bosnia-Herzegovina)

*Those with whom you compete may be more in step with your
values and goals than you think.*

Sarajevo—the other Jerusalem and the tipping point for
the start of WWI—symbolized religious crossroads and
crossfire through the ages. Headline-hungry media specializes
in images that disturb, the case here for decades. Locals share
stories about Bosnia paying the bulk of the 1990's Balkans
War toll when nearly constant artillery fire from the mountains
surrounding their beautiful city killed thousands, cut power, and
blockaded the delivery of vital supplies. Imagine years of bullets
and bombs raining down on your crippled town. These people
know hard times and how to cautiously greet good times.

Unlike the other Western Balkan countries I visited, Bosnia
seemed to have a macho element I didn't encounter elsewhere,
probably a reflection of hard living. Nightlife is typified by
throngs of chain-smoking dudes minus the necessary female
balance, so I explored other options.

My apropos Sarajevo finale was attending a football match with Bosnia's most popular sportswriter and his seven-year-old son in the stadium where the 1984 Winter Olympics opening ceremonies was held. It was Sarajevo versus Celik, another team from Bosnia-Herzegovina. The crowd was 99 percent guys, all with raging fan fever.

The crazed fan momentum kept building until it felt like a riot was on the menu. At full volume, the maniacal Sarajevo fans behind the opposing team's goal never seemed to take a breath. Suddenly, they began screaming even louder, in horror, and scrambling away from tear-gas bombs that were ignited in their midst by a killjoy fan from the opposing team. The mania sent hundreds of fans either tumbling over high fences or onto the playing field to escape the wretched gas, which quickly drifted our way. The scene resembled a panicking ant colony exploding outward. People everywhere were choking and scratching their stinging eyes. My otherwise affable host suggested we leave immediately.

Running to the parking lot, we found we couldn't escape the cloud that followed us. Changing tactics, we sprinted back into a stadium hallway. Everywhere, people were crouched on all fours, covering their faces. One guy was handing out wet napkins to cover people's noses. Eventually finding our way to the car, we drove away leaving behind a mist of poor sportsmanship. Is this what happens when the guys are out after dark without the girls? At least this battle stayed pretty much on the field.

Driving back into a calmer part of Sarajevo, the sportswriter said something to his son, which made him laugh. I asked him what he'd said. Translation: "That was pointless, like snakes fighting in a sack." The sportswriter then certified his take on the unsportsmanlike conduct, and life in a place taunted by war…

"Root for the name on the front of your team's uniform (the team's name)—not the name on the back of it (the individual player's name)."

∞ ∞ ∞ ∞ ∞

No Gentle Ride, Man —U-Haul "Gentle-Ride Van" revised with black tape at *Burning Man* peace festival, Black Rock City, Nevada

Get a grip. —Golf lesson metaphor

DIRECTION

TWEAK YOUR IDENTITY WHILE TRAVELING (Aruba)

"Inspector of snowstorms." —Henry David Thoreau's self-appointed title

C hoctaw Indians communicate using two past tenses: one for giving confirmed information, and the other for passing on material taken without verifying the source. Consider a tense that pardons fleeting impersonations.

Traveling creates a divine opportunity to reinvent yourself. I've been roving the international traveler circuit for decades. In the days of my youth, I'd occasionally find it necessary to beat a would-be heckler to the punch using a little bait and switch. Socializing while traveling abroad, especially as a rookie, can be an uphill battle to overturn stereotypes. If you need a break from this patented scenario, throw the crotchety one off course with a fib or two. Embellish. Be someone else for a day.

When one asks: "Where are you from?"

Consider replies in this vein: "I'm a professional pogo stick competitor." "I'm scouting local talent for the next edition of the

Guinness World Records." or "I'm here to invent this country's new tourism slogan." I've also claimed that I was a "Beer sommelier." Most effective is whispering, "I can't talk about it."

Also consider toying with an invented alias. Your parents chose a name for you that suited their mood at the time. Sometimes you may be more in the mood for a pen name. Pick one that suits your future aspirations, hints at an emerging talent, reflects your life experience, or might help you gain entry into an otherwise private function. You update friends on your relationship and occupation status. While roaming, why not entice strangers by stating those statuses with a twist.

Reflective of achievements and aspirations, name changing was, and with any luck will remain, common among Aboriginal tribes. Here and now, how about naming things (like you) in conjunction with a visual equivalent? One of the prevailing clichés of contemporary art is that it serves as a mirror of its time. Inherit your new self by way of an interim stage name. Examples: Colt, Wit, Emmy, Chairman, Dare, Dog-God, Dynamode, Stellar, Aide.

Until the 1990s, American collegians were still flocking exclusively to Europe in droves while young Europeans, Australians, and New Zealanders were discovering Asia's charms. Ronald Reagan and Bush, Sr., weren't exactly popular with those said backpackers, who partied in packs and made their political annoyances known to the rare, roaming American. If you think today's young Canadians are tough on Americans while abroad, triple it before Bill Clinton.

At first, I stoutly defended my homeland, falling into its traps—"Rambo good, right?" Down the line, I assisted the natives of these mostly socialized countries in surrendering to a few of America's many charms: blues and jazz, ZZ Top, Michael Jordan, ethical vigilante Charles Bronson. Station wagons, even. As the years of socializing with the quick-to-judge became decades, I realized that it takes time for *all* of us to separate citizens from politics—something very clear to most travelers you'll meet once they cruise past age 30, maybe 40. You really can't judge folks by their nation (unless you've been a waiter who has served certain French people).

Feeding into anger further propagandizes it. The next step in the ceasefire process presents an intersection of options. One route is to gang up on your home country along with its critics, which derails the sourpuss, then spin the slagging around and eventually make them sit back while you help them pick on *their* homeland. A more sustainable option is erasing the trite labels some people embrace by sharing your truths about your birthplace. It's more fun, too, but that's another story.

∞ ∞ ∞ ∞ ∞

Isla de Long

In a related vein, here's a ploy for rerouting tribe-sensitive discrimination occurring in your own country. When people ask me where I grew up, my patent answer is, "Isla de Long." This throws anyone prone to generalizations off the stereotypical lampoon about heralding from New York's Long Island: "Strong Island?"…"You mean LawnGuyland?" The list goes on. Anyone from New Jersey has also been down this road.

∞ ∞ ∞ ∞ ∞

Aruba

Question overheard while riding in van past Aruba's Outback Steakhouse: *Can I talk English here?*

Answer, provided by random stranger while slowing down for Aruba's Hooters: *Sure, but you'll need to learn it first.*

DIRECTION

RISE ABOVE IT (Athea, Ireland)

One way of diminishing slander is by imitating the hawk. When battered by crows or other pests, it doesn't return battle, opting instead to fly higher and higher in ever-widening circles until the pests bother elsewhere.

My grandmother Mary was born out of wedlock in 1904 in ultra-Catholic Ireland when there were few greater sins than birth before marriage. Then 14, her mother was not allowed to marry the equally young father because the shamed families wouldn't allow it. Thus, my great-grandmother was soon banished to Australia, and her daughter Mary was raised by relatives in Athea, a tiny Irish village.

Some of the people in Athea regarded Mary with disdain. Although she was a happy child, the gossip in the countryside community made her the target of rumors, and some classmates and their parents snubbed her. When her mother married and settled in Australia, she wrote to Mary repeatedly, asking her to join her there. However, the letters were intercepted and destroyed by relatives to prevent her from leaving.

During their childhood, Mary's neighbor and friend, who decades later became my grandfather, James O'Sullivan, was sympathetic to her plight and thought of her as a lovely lass. James served as an Irish Republic Army Captain in the 1916 battle for Ireland's independence. He sailed the Atlantic Ocean in 1922 to lay railroads in Canada, and then lived in Montana to experience the cowboy lifestyle.

Eventually, my grandfather settled in New York City and opened O'Sullivan's Chophouse, a tavern and restaurant that became northern Manhattan's off-the-boat Gaelic Mecca, and featured the longest mahogany bar in the city. Never forgetting his first true love, James reunited with Mary once the bar was up and running. As their courtship blossomed, the 19-year-old beauty with a heart of gold was liberated. They soon married and raised six daughters and a son on Long Island.

It wasn't until she was in her seventies that my grandmother confessed to one of her daughters the grief she carried alone for all those years—never burdening her children or feeling sorry for herself. Being a wonderful mother and wife trumped all. She was loved and admired by everyone who knew her; no one ever knew of the longing she must have endured for her own mother. During her triumphant 1980's return to Ireland with her children, she was warmly welcomed by the surviving members of her mother's family. She never knew her mother, but that didn't prevent her from creating a love-filled life.

Your truth is what you do with it.

∞ ∞ ∞ ∞ ∞

Adversity makes things stronger. There is a 5,000 year-old bristlecone pine hugging Nevada's side of the White Mountains. It's the oldest known living tree on earth. The tree grows on the north-facing slope of the immense peak, which when compared to its south-facing slope, faces much harsher environmental conditions, including less sun, more wind, more snow, and longer winters. That's rising to the occasion, in tree-speak.

DIRECTION

SHOP OUTSIDE THE SHOP (Thailand)

Bring home something that is a part of the place you visit.

A 1992 courier flight set the stage for my first visit to Thailand since being a mid-80s five-bucks-a-day-budget backpacker. A solo motorbike safari in Thailand's northern mountains was an existential escape from another job attempt requiring dry-cleaned shirts. Just like Homeland Security wiped out the courier flight, Thailand's wholesomeness was being trampled under the weight of mass tourism. But you can always find a pure heart if you know where to look.

On excursions abroad, I try to acquire one unforgettable keepsake and gift. Often, things that are not officially for sale become those gems, and the tale of the transaction becomes a souvenir itself. I'm routinely on the lookout where there are no price tags. Worksites—factories, mills, home-based workshops, ports, mines—are replete with handmade tools, hunting paraphernalia, garments, and such that might complement your desk, wall, or reputation as a gift giver.

In Thailand's misty mountains, I encountered a group from a local hilltribe returning from a day of river fishing. Along with baskets of fish, they each had fish traps slung around their shoulders. The traps fused lobster-trap utility with bamboo ingenuity. Created from one section of bamboo sliced into segments and enlarged into a vase shape, the trap's inner bamboo-stick corkscrew entraps the fish who are lured inside by bait. I bought one for double the offering price.

I knew the fish trap—tied to the outside of my backpack while transiting Bangkok on foot—was a winner when scores of elderly men accosted me to admire the functional artwork recalling their youth and a fading way of life. Another sign was the perplexed stares it earned on the New York City subway ride home from the airport.

You'd think that savvy shopping in an out-of-the-way village defined by coconuts, hogs, and woven baskets would be a misnomer, but by focusing less on how things look and more on how they work, you can end up with a real crowd pleaser. People look at the fish trap, are puzzled by the bamboo marvel, then cave into admiration.

When buying things that aren't officially for sale, be sensitive to cultural rape. Make sure the economically stressed are parting with possessions they can easily replace with your payment. Don't be swayed by politeness regarding an item they will really miss. Acquiring not-for-sale genuine parts of the places you visit necessitates sensitivity, fair compromise, and bargaining with the right individual.

"Like playing flute to a buffalo." —Thai expression about bargaining falling on deaf ears

∞ ∞ ∞ ∞ ∞

Consider also shopping off the beaten path in post offices and further amusing your friends back home. Along with cashing tax refund checks, another enjoyable civic interaction can be purchasing stamps around the world. My strategy probes past the single standard tourist stamp that is automatically offered to mail international post cards. Once you know the price of that lone international stamp, ask the postal clerk to see their collection of domestic stamps, and mix and match your favorites to equal the international value. You can create a collage of four or five domestic stamps, making the unsung side of postcards a mosaic of imported art. Consider sticking such a postage collage on the back of a photo you've taken on a trip.

∞ ∞ ∞ ∞ ∞

By the way, less developed country workplaces are great places to throw spontaneous parties. On my daily wanders, I visit bike repair shops, laundromats, bakeries, and other more physical businesses. I'm not shopping, but instead, screening them as places to return to later in the night bringing gifts of food, notebooks, or, what the heck, a case of beer. The unsuspecting workers are incredibly grateful, and they'll likely be the last type of local you'd meet in a tourist-fueled establishment. Try it.

DIRECTION

FIND A BEST FRIEND WITH FOUR FEET
(Russia ~ Cyprus)

"Every life should have nine cats." —*Cat fan, Lesotho, Africa*

To err is human. However, full forgiveness might only possible from a pet. I begin this animal musing with *the end*, among Moscow's tombs. Hundreds of Russia's most famous artistic, literary, musical, and political figures are buried in Novodevichy Cemetery. On a stirring stroll through Russian history, I discovered that this hall-of-fame memorial collection stages not just gravestones but row upon row of elaborate images and sculptures depicting the buried legends in telling poses. Famed comedian Yury Nikulin sits relaxing next to his dog, while the nearby ex-presidents' monuments portray less lighthearted souls.

There's also a tribute to chemist-extraordinaire Dmitri Mendeleev, who, with mixed success, attempted to make everyone *Absolute*ly lighthearted. Vodka was stumbled upon 500 years ago when grain was distilled into what became Russia's state beverage. Today, there are no fancy drink mixers at these parties that define normalized immoderation—a straight vodka shot seems to accompany every celebratory occasion, including

139

meals. Mendeleev, who tortured us in high school with his creation of the periodic table of the elements is better known among Russians for purifying and pegging vodka at 80-proof.

Strolling on in the cemetery, I eventually circled back to bronzed Yury and his dog. It occurred to me that a likeness of my childhood dog, Ben, had certainly earned a spot on my plot, if I end up with one. Right then a buried sense of pet guilt overcame me. I'm not unfamiliar with surging tangential thoughts, but it seemed odd that Chelsea, my childhood cat, also leapt into my mind. Though not because a bronze Chelsea might sit upon my plot in a graveyard campus.

Our globe teems with cats that survey everything and supposedly lick themselves clean (I argue this popular theory. If you pay attention, you'll notice they tend to lick and re-lick the same spot, usually tonguing a specific patch a few inches below one armpit). Some cat people regard their cats above their offspring. They know that mistreating a kitty even once can invite a feline karma imbalance that will spy on them for life. Granted, one or two of us at age four may have swung a cat by the tail helicopter-style, but putting one in the clothes dryer to see if they make the same sound as tumbling sneakers is unspeakable. Luckily, I'm in a country that forgives foolish youth. "The first pancake you make is never perfect." —Russian saying

Confession. I am not hardwired to vex cats. But, early in my second decade, armed with an idea and little else, I mildly electrocuted Chelsea, ironically a Russian Blue breed. Most of us discover at some point that a brisk shuffle across a carpet amps us with a static electrical charge sufficient to create sparks when we touch metal or another human. It also works on cat noses, prompting a shock-sneeze-hiccup. You can get cats to fall for this once or twice, but they won't fall for it ever again unless your lightning-rod finger is tuna scented. Chelsea, have mercy.

I exited Novodevichy Cemetery, pondering mortality and what I might pack for my final journey. I also imagined my beagle Ben, again, trotting beside me and honored his legacy. The genuine Moscow Circus is simply being there—an apt place to testify that we should celebrate pets, wherever we stray.

∞ ∞ ∞ ∞ ∞

Cyprus

Cyprus also has a way of reminding us that we're all somehow connected to animals. This island nation has remnants dating to 5000BC left behind by a dizzying succession of conquering empires. It has been invaded more than any other country in Europe—and possibly by even more cats. It has, not surprisingly, a Cat Monastery. The monastery was founded in 327AD when the island was blighted by snakes that overran after a 17-year drought. The cats were first gathered to eliminate the snakes, and throughout the centuries, their descendants moved into this holy cat orphanage.

Roaming through the Cat Monastery, I was stopped in my tracks when one of the cats stared me down and maintained a pensive gaze that lasted minutes. She may have sensed my part in Chelsea's shock sneezes. You can run, but you can't hide. I turned to one of the passing nuns and inquired about kitty's pensive nature. "Does that cat always look like that?" I asked. I think she read my question as one about the cat's appearance, not the way it was squinting at me, and answered, "Yes." Then, because I'd asked such a harebrained question, the nun appraised me sympathetically and moved on.

I continued pondering the staredown until another nun passed. I asked her about the feline who seemed to have my number. "Dogs may believe they're human, but cats know they're sacred," was all she said.

∞ ∞ ∞ ∞ ∞

"Catnip can affect lions and tigers, as well as cats." —Romanian donkey-cart pilot, suggesting "we're all in this together."

DIRECTION

IF YOU DON'T KNOW WHERE YOU'RE GOING, ANY PATH WILL LEAD YOU THERE (Jordan)

If you feel this bad right now, it's probably because you were capable of feeling that good at another time. —*Bedouin camel driver*

A visit to Jordan featured a world wonder but starred a camel pilot named Walid, who I, at first, considered an annoyance. Petra means rock in Greek; the name of its much visited World Heritage rock city formed inside a rose-red slot canyon. This hand-carved metropolis was etched 2,000 years ago to fashion a long-distance-traveler's stopover. A primeval desert complex of chiseled apartments, stores, banks, and tombs flanks a winding, descending road that evolved from a dry river bed. It's a stony trading post blended by Greek, Roman, and lastly Aboriginal Nabataaen craftsmen.

When the neighborhood was abandoned by the Nabataaens, it was reoccupied by nomadic Bedouins, who still provide hospitality today. I climbed atop the clifftop flanking this widening valley, garnering a better look on this archetypal caravan toll road,

143

where the ancients performed human sacrifices to appease their gods. From there, I could also see what I believed were tourists being hustled by the likes of Walid.

As the setting sun flushed Petra from rose to gold, I descended down to the valley floor. Back amid the hubbub, I again encountered Walid, the patient Bedouin camel-taxi pilot. After a few innocuous exchanges, I asked him why warlike humankind hasn't been kind to itself. His answer, in between sips of tea, came slowly.

"Sometimes when you throw a stick for a dog to retrieve, the dog can't find it. The silly dog stands in front of you looking at your pointing finger instead of where you're actually pointing. The same thing happens in politics. The people point in the right direction, but the politicians stare in the other."

Shifting with the ages, Jordanians, like most Middle Easterners, crave peace and quietude. After a sober pause, we both thought about his words. Then, as Walid and his camel started to lope away, he closed his eyes, pointed skyward and confirmed, "We wait for peace to break out."

The U.N. should employ such diplomats.

∞ ∞ ∞ ∞ ∞

"Stones decay; words last." —Samoan Proverb

"War *is* terrorism." —Danish stump speaker in Christiania, Denmark's self-proclaimed autonomous neighborhood.

DIRECTION

FEEL THE STRENGTH OF THE LABOR OF LOVE (Cotswolds)

What a difference a walk makes.

L ong-distance walking veterans, my father and I tackled the renowned 240-mile, coast-to-coast trek across Northern England's rugged terrain in 1996. Two years later, shortly after dad endured life-saving surgery, we tackled Offa's Dyke, a 200-mile long wall built in the eighth century to keep the Welsh on their side of that giant fence.

On our third walk across the Commonwealth, my father, then 76, and I rambled the width of England's Cotswolds region, a country paradise defined by enchanting drystone walls dating back hundreds of years. The region has a woolspun history and is picture-postcard flawless. And, one benefit of undertaking an exhausting itinerary is that it left us no energy to recycle any debates about my tenth-grade car-crashing spree.

The Romans laid out this part of Europe in ten-acre plots. Don't dare suggest it was the French. Today, these plots have matured into showcases of a fading way of life. These serene river valleys of sheep pens on soft rolling hills with limestone buildings and outcroppings remain out of harm's way from developers. It endures as a haven of trout-filled streams, quaint stone hamlets, stone walls, and romping horses.

Unfolding our map and our sense of humor ensured that we had a grand time losing our bearings, never a long way from a stone wall or a friendly character. Our route from Burford to Stow-on-the-Wold started on a forgotten, car-free single-lane road that visited woods, farms, cottages with window-sill flower boxes, tiny medieval stone villages, bounteous wildflowers, and rare fellow walkers. Roaming 10 to 20 miles per day, sort of with a plan, we slept in archetypal English inns. Predictably, these accommodations were made of stone with low-overhead medieval-era doorways. We become aware of separate hot and cold water faucets, uber-creaky stairs, and twin beds so short that our feet were left dangling.

On the trail, my ears adjusted from urban car horns to ewe-speak. The footpath broke into farms divided by stiles; turnstile gates allowing ramblers to pass but not livestock. Dad had no trouble covering our daily distances, or hurdling the older five-foot-high wooden stiles.

Minutes before sunset, we encountered a stone wall and the man working to preserve it. Today's stone-wall builders preserve an ancient tradition that both pays the bills and safeguards the Isles' uncommon landscape. The hardworking stone mason, a chap with meaty hands, massive forearms, and steady phrasing, assured us his art form couldn't be mechanized. A dry stone wall uses no mortar, only limestones, gravity, friction, and a talent for made-to-last jigsaw puzzles. A symbol of national pride, this typically inherited craft merits prestige; wall building is to Britain what gourmet cooking is to France.

Dry stonewall architects obsess about their materials, describing shades of limestone as passionately as interior designers might salute skylights. They wax eloquent about subtle hues from specific quarries, renowned builders who left unmistakable signatures, and how an able mason can dismantle and rebuild—stone by stone—an identical wall. Like radiance passing through a prism, stone walls share ancestry and imagination.

As the sun set behind us, the wall builder chuckled, "The last ramblers passing this way asked me 'What I made building walls'…and I told them I make people heave a sigh."

Dad then asked about optimum stone sizes and which stone position in the wall was the most vital for longevity. The Englishman rested a hand on the wall, looked at the ground, and then slowly raised his head to trace his eyes along a mile of accomplished stonework behind him. Turning his glance my way—but slyly gesturing at my father—he mused, "Just don't pull that card, or the whole thing collapses!" After that wily epiphany and another chuckle, my dad and I trekked on.

On our final day, we strolled through a retired nobleman's digs with miles of hilly lawns and well-spaced chestnut oak trees, some 800-years-old with trunks having 24-foot circumferences. We paused at a 13th-century water mill and agreed that we were in an outdoor museum. In the final mile, we climbed a steep ridge near a two-house settlement that wound past friendly miniature ponies, another hundred sheep, and led to a bench set on the high point.

I sat on the bench and watched as my dad walked slowly with a slight limp up the steep path toward me. He was puffing a bit, scaling a mountain once summited by Alexander Cromwell. I thought again about the cunning dry-stone wall builder who had said—speaking about his wall's hidden power—but also I think in retrospect, about parents everywhere…

"What you don't see is the strength of the wall."

It was then that I vowed to keep discovering the charms of life with my dad—that vital card in my familial deck and a stone wall of love—one step at a time.

∞ ∞ ∞ ∞ ∞

"Wallers do it in all weathers." —Drystone Waller's credo on a bumper sticker

DIRECTION

IF YOU DON'T FIT INSIDE THE BOX, CLIMB ON TOP OF IT AND HAVE A GOOD LOOK AROUND (Ecuador)

Create your own calendar.

S et two miles above sea level, Inga Pirca is the northernmost outpost of the Inca Trail. It was a thriving religious temple, military fortress, political settlement, and a solar calendar for discerning planting seasons. Viewed from high above, the complex depicts a puma. Started in 1150, the settlement was finished by the Incas in 1500, and thereby, inherited the Inca code for living: Don't lie, don't steal, and don't be lazy. The penalty for murder meant, in addition to continuing to do your own job, undertaking the murdered person's workload for life.

As I was hiking down from this mystifying ruin, a dusty trailside shop's Inca calendar caught my eye. It was a multicolored tapestry of geometric symbols corresponding to the Incas ancient but sophisticated lifestyle. The shopkeeper helped me decipher a recurring Quechua symbol on the calendar that represented a record of a marriage proposal. The image revealed young lovers united at the lips with nearby parents chaperoning so nothing wayward would occur before the wedding. The complexity and mystery of the Inca calendar is diluted by modern calendars, and the fact that today's parents generally have no idea what their kids are doing while on dates.

∞ ∞ ∞ ∞ ∞

We all interpret calendars with varying degrees of urgency or insurgency. Unlike impulsive men, women viewing erotica are stimulated in a part of the brain linked to planning, which must be why they love to plan, often meditating events that are months, even years away. Most men, on the other hand, can barely contemplate the fog clouding the next weekend. Feel free to diminish these planning disparities by reinventing your own hot spots on a calendar, because many mandatory landmarks on our calendar were drafted into service by Madison Avenue. On appointed days, we're obliged to fawn over national forefathers, Christ, Menoras, Muhammad, turkeys, trees, candy, moms, dads, partners, or bosses. Can't this just be instinctual, or waivable?

Do we really need to be instructed on when and how to express gratitude to our key allies? Let's hope not. Consider reorganizing your calendar around lucky coincidences, moon phases, random sunrises or sunsets, and custom-made anniversaries—like the day you got fired from a job you hated anyway, or the days you think your children's DNA was fashioned. Prioritize dates that reflect the way you enjoy life and avoid traffic jams, peak-priced gift shopping and flights, and crowded restaurants. Fashion your own darn holidays.

In the new tradition of adding personally patriotic states of mind to our calendar, ponder an annual Detour Day, where we all intentionally take different routes to school, work, grocery stores, or wherever our hobbies, virtues, or sins lead us. This reroute should include random stopovers in previously undiscovered playgrounds, eateries, bars, woods, stores, and places of worship. Breaking routines increases awareness and longevity.

Let go, sometimes it takes a while to get things right. Walt Whitman devoted 37 years to writing his masterpiece, *Leaves of Grass*. It evolved, from its birth to its finale, to encompass nine different editions. I'm betting that he wasn't chained to a calendar. Alas, datebooks can also provide perspective. It took the first man to walk around the world four years, three months, and six days to complete his journey—about the same amount of time it takes for keen students to graduate college.

∞ ∞ ∞ ∞ ∞

I waltzed out of the Ecuadorian shop, *new* calendar in hand, and resolved to delay my flight home.

∞ ∞ ∞ ∞ ∞

"Move that calendar away from the fan." —Guam bartender's solution "to stop time from flying."

"When you happy, you no hear clock tick." —overheard in Turkish bathhouse

DIRECTION

HIRE EDUCATION (Kenya)

Know your worth.

Acting with a voluntourism guerilla taskforce from the USA, I worked with the Kiseryan Girls Senior Academy, a Maasai boarding school for young women in the Ngong Hills beyond Nairobi. The school awards scholarships to impoverished Maasai girls, aged 12 to 18 years. The scholarships are vital, as most have no education options and are likely given into arranged marriages by age 14, or worse.

We sprung into action with a Nairobi-based teenage newspaper to initiate a speech-writing competition for 200 Maasai girls. I challenged the girls to express their personal views in a 250-word speech aimed at their newly established and polarized coalition government leaders. After introducing the pen as a tool of change, I dared the students to imagine themselves presenting these petitions, live, to help foster peace in Kenya. After all, Kenya's national anthem is a Swahili prayer. I emphasized that powerful essays can double as moving speeches, and reminded them that the leaders of Liberia, Argentina, India, Israel, Pakistan and the Philippines are now or have been women.

My team and the teen newspaper editors reviewed the speech entries and selected three writers to read their speeches at a theatrical awards ceremony and crowned the winners for their courage to speak out. Reading the speeches sent shivers down my spine, as each was firmly handwritten so you could feel the pen's ridges on the backside of the paper, creating emotional Braille. I imagined each teenager pondering and then inscribing her will. With post-election violence still a daily threat and thousands in Internally Displaced Person camps, the speeches plead to stop the senseless bloodshed that also devastated tourism, Kenya's economic jackpot.

We completed this month-long project barely two months after Kenya erupted into savagery in December 2007. The country's youth took center stage, bearing the brunt of the unspeakable slaughter. With half of the world's population under 23 years of age, educating and inspiring them has never been more critical. Otherwise, they become ticking time-bombs.

The speech contest winner, Ann Muiruri, and two runners-up had their speeches published. And, so their voices were truly heard, the press clips and videos of their speeches were delivered to the dueling leaders in Kenya's Parliament. Did a troubled hybrid government listen to these sage teens?

Inside the stark cement shell of the school's largest room, we showcased making dreams come true. When Ann finished presenting her speech, Give Peace and Dialogue a Chance, her vision stirred a proverbial pot of common sense that, apparently, had been beyond the adults running the country. These young ladies—Kenya's future—spoke for the world.

Maasai Ann's prophesy...

Your Excellency, President Mwai Kibaki and Honourable Raila Odinga, I take this opportunity to share with you my thoughts on how to stop the skirmishes in our country. Kenya has been a haven for refugees and everyone until 31st December 2007 when all hell broke loose, and this was no longer the Kenya I knew.

Innocent blood was shed, many Kenyans were displaced and their homes burnt to ashes, which led them to be refugees in their own country. Surely, is this the Kenya we have been building for all these years? Urgent intervention is required to save Kenya before it subsides and sinks into the abyss joining other war-torn countries like Somalia, Rwanda, and others.

We entrusted you with the responsibility to lead us, respecting our national flag together with our national anthem, which states that we should live in peace, love, and unity. We request you as our leaders to embrace peace and negotiate together to restore the glory for our land.

Two things have led to this unpleasant situation: Hatred that lies deep in many hearts brought about by the disputed election. Secondly, the lamentable state of our institutions. Therefore, we request you to visit the affected areas, offer a hand in building homes, schools for the affected, and viable institutions that will address their grievances.

Development of a country takes a lifetime. Destruction takes a moment. You have the power to change Kenya if only you commit yourselves to it.

DIRECTION

UNITE THE NATIONS (Taiwan)

Anger is contagious—don't get infected.

When I wandered into Taiwan in 1987 as a glorified drifter, my first vision was of a shirtless guy on a muffler-free moped needling through gridlocked traffic while carrying a king-size mattress and a box spring tied on his back. He was oblivious to the noisy chaos that was Taipei, a sooty, avoidable, industrial metropolis where scooters doubled as mini-vans.

Twenty-five years later, from the window of my hotel, I hear only classical music playing in the street. Recycling is now compulsory, garbage and recycling trucks announce their arrival by playing classical music. Taipei is dancing to a new tune.

In the *remade* Taiwan, 15 million scooters—now with everyone wearing helmets—share the roads with 10-million four-wheel vehicles. But it works. Rude drivers and honking horns are now rare, and the air is clear in what is now a vibrant, livable city. I even saw a scooter carrying a dog wearing her own helmet.

The Taiwanese are soft-spoken, sensitive to social graces, and patient. Inspired first by SARS and the Japanese, people wear surgical masks so they don't get sick—and even more often, when they are sick, so as not to infect others. Nice.

While Taiwan feels like an official country, China continues to claim it as its own. Although its status is also not recognized by the U.N., Taiwan is officially recognized by places such as Belize, Costa Rica, El Salvador, and Honduras—faithful Central American hospitality. The U.N. should ponder an inherent play on words: Unite'd'Nations.

Officially sacred, Taipei's Lungshan Temple serves as a U.N. of the spiritual world. This rousing Buddhist and Taoist *God-Mart* features an enshrined wisdom guru (students pray here before exams), a fertility deity (use your imagination), and a love/matchmaking God. The Money Prayer Guru, however, seemed to be on break, as the world suffered a recession. All tolerant Gods have free passes to be here.

At the end of the day though, sometimes all the guidance you need is found waiting on a random street corner. I moseyed into a convenience store where a Taiwanese news channel talking-head was ranting about his country's enduring territorial standoff with the Chinese government. Unable to understand the tirade, I stared at the TV until the shopkeeper, a slight man with an ecclesiastical demeanor, quietly suggested, "He who angers you…owns you."

…*Well* Made in Taiwan.

∞ ∞ ∞ ∞ ∞

"Anger, with any luck, is a brief madness." —Amsterdam morning-glory-seed guru

DIRECTION

LET INNER BEAUTY BE THE PRETTIEST THING YOU WEAR (Mozambique)

"She a-look-a-like-a 'Dolly Lama' who-a put on her makeup on a bumpy road." —*Italian Casanova, pointing at disembarking Milan bus tourists*

Mozambique is a Portuguese-speaking country in southern Africa where, as in Portugal, dancing registers just below food and shelter as necessities. I found the celebratory spirit of Mozambique's dance scene to be a freeing departure from the dance club scenes of my youth, which featured dozens of drink-clutching men surrounding and peering hopefully into flickering strobe-lit dance floors swimming with women whirling around piles of purses at their feet. This was a hit or miss approach to desire, rendered more futile by deafening music. As if it wasn't hard enough for men to control what inspires them to lurch toward certain procreative signposts.

After a few turns in the flashing lights as a club kid, you figure out that dancing doesn't require someone else's permission. In Maputo, Mozambique's worn metropolis, any plot within earshot of music can inspire dancing—and overstated hairstyles and makeup are not required to participate. It's freelance beauty in plain light.

There has been a lot of ink and tears spilled on the roads in and out of romance, a life force more complicated than advanced chemistry. When female baboons are in heat their bottoms swell up and turn crimson. Women announce the arrival of their fertile days by naturally unleashing changes in skin tone, fragrance, lip size, and pupil size, thereby unknowingly telegraphing fertility signals. This beautification comes free of charge.

Today, in a world conned by beauty marketing, it seems unadulterated loveliness can't compete. I had a gorgeous revelation in Hollywood when I first beheld makeup giant Max Factor's world-changing gadget, the beauty calibrator. The man behind the company, the cosmetic engineer of Hollywood's original pretties, built a high-tech halo apparatus to measure the cranial feature characteristics that proved to rouse the masses. Factor then used makeup and lighting to replicate the features on other women. Meanwhile, this calibrator, designed to make all women look alike, resembles what patients wear while in traction after breaking their necks. Somewhere between the inventions of the steam engine and the search engine, we have to ask what happened. Is beauty science, art, or neither, and must it really be gauged? Remember, no matter what you look like, somewhere, you are beautiful.

Taking a dance break in an after-hours Mozambique restaurant, I sat next to a local guy who was also catching his breath. We looked at a frowning man who'd been standing, arms folded, in the same spot all night long. The guy next to me put his hand on my shoulder and said, "Never lend a gun to a man who can't dance."

∞ ∞ ∞ ∞ ∞

What constitutes beauty varies by culture. In Fiji, men love women with bouncy afros and ample padding on their bones. In fact, I brought a fit girlfriend there, and all the local women nodded in sympathy because they thought she was ill. In Japan, intentionally chiseled fang teeth were once the rage. In Jamaica, men love women with generous butts, similar to the way Americans loved big cars in the 70s. When a Jamaican guy saw my dates' small behind, he sorrowfully referred to it as an Isuzu.

∞ ∞ ∞ ∞ ∞

I discovered another telling take on beauty when I met Yardley Jones on the suburban fringe of Edmonton, Canada. An internationally syndicated, award-winning cartoonist for Canada's major newspapers for four decades, his résumé includes live portraits of LBJ, JFK, and Trudeau. The Liverpool-born artist spotted early in life the humor, irony, and sadness that surround us as we make our way through life. He arrived in Canada in 1957 by boat and never stopped painting portraits of passing pedestrians. When I asked him about the difference between drawing men and women, he revealed that when the portrait is done, men glance first at their face and nod with approval while women's eyes flash immediately to their portrayed body size—always stick figures with boobs—and immediately glow with satisfaction.

∞ ∞ ∞ ∞ ∞

She is like a road...pretty, but crooked. —Mozambique Proverb

"'T'was a woman who drove me to drink...and I never had the decency to write and thank her." —W.C. Fields

DIRECTION

IN ANY WAR, REALIZE TRUTH IS THE FIRST CASUALTY (Germany)

I was in Berlin in August before the 9-11 terrorist attacks. It was there I came upon an underground omen—small, neatly scripted graffiti, barely decipherable in the dusky crimson glow of an underground nuclear fallout shelter beneath the city streets. "He who shoots first, dies second," it read.

The Cold War-era shelter was outfitted with its own air and water purification systems. Only 50-percent of our typical oxygen intake would be available so as to safeguard against panic. The thin air is meant to tranquilize the 3,500 people, the shelter's maximum capacity, into a slumber.

When I stepped into the fallout shelter's in-house morgue, I joined an elderly English woman who was staring into a corner, deep in thought. After two moments (hers and mine), she whispered that she'd lost her home to a Second World War bomb. Another moment of silence ensued before she said, "In any war, truth is the first casualty."

Broadminded non-political solutions to the continuous warfare creeping into every shade of our planet won't see the light until more travelers meet. It's time for a widespread outbreak of tolerance.

DIRECTION

PENGUINS ARE HAPPIER THAN
CLAMS—DISCOVER WHY (Antarctica)

Quack means howdy in penguin.

I keep an inventory of the things I've seen that were, at first, nearly impossible to comprehend. A few of these dimensional milestones took seconds—even minutes—to process: the Grand Canyon, Angkor Wat, the Taj Mahal, Ethiopia's underground rock-hewn churches, Canada's Quetico lakes, Miss Brazil flipping her hair at a pool party, Machu Picchu, my daughter's face, and the glacially wrapped Himalayas. After trekking through Nepal's mind-bending rock and ice, I predicted that sensory overload as matchless. Then, I beheld Antarctica.

The earth's polar underside—a crystal otherworld—overwhelms with sculpted baby-blue icebergs slowly drifting past skyscraper-height glacial palaces. Whales breach, seals snooze, and penguins return your stare. This perpetual winter wonderland gives new meaning to finally hitting bottom, *way* down under.

Antarctic penguins, upright birds that can't fly, are as playful as puppies. The UN-sponsored 1959 Antarctic treaty mandated that this continent only be explored with peace for all in mind:

no to hunting, fishing, industry, exporting, oil drilling, or weapons testing. Mingling with penguins, penguins willing, is permissible.

On a solo hike, I met three thousand Gentoo penguins quacking like an army of trumpeting kazoos, all flapping their wing-fins merrily. Their kazoo/quack soundtrack melded with whimpering seals, yapping gulls, pleading terns, thundering glaciers, and the air-releasing *phishes* from whale blowholes.

A few would-be guards in this colony of Gentoo penguins seemed to be spying on their ever-present foe, fur seals snoring on nearby boulders. Keeping a respectful distance, I sat on a rock, and a few penguins began spying on me. The curious group waddled within a foot of my roost and returned my ogle. After a five-minute staring match, the foursome in the front row tilted their heads, quacked, snapped their heads back to the other shoulder, and quacked again. Interpreted hospitality.

Letting them be, I watched penguins passionately tackling issues, like tag. In Darwinian terms, these games of tag are actually parents running away from two or three of their hungry chicks to see who is stronger and faster (or likely hungrier), and therefore more likely to survive the winter. The reward for determined tag victors—winners of natural selection—is mom or dad regurgitating a semi-digested snack into their mouth. Sometimes waddling parents and chicks trip and fall forward onto their belly and immediately initiate a paddling motion to maintain their running speed as toboggans. Mother Nature's least remunerated entertainers are also the ultimate survivalists.

In their first summer of life, these black-and-white suited comedians wait for their new suit to arrive while they shed fluffy baby feathers and grow into their waterproof skin. They stand around seemingly shooting the breeze, accepting your decision to do the same thing. Photographing penguins is similar to shooting a moderately amused child; you lose them if you break the spell.

Visitors are required to maintain a respectful 15-foot distance from all wildlife. Seated and partially honoring this, I didn't shoo away the curious penguins who wobbled up and stood before me. The more territorial fur seals—the penguin's nemesis—would first bemoan my presence by whimpering like cold puppies. Fur seals, hairy, puppy-faced dolphins with big flippers, reek of low-tide musk. Penguin tag, in both waddle and toboggan mode, roused the sleeping seals, which was like waking up hungover linebackers. The seals' protest mounted with throaty, menacing growls and culminated with mock galloping lunges. I'd witnessed several snarling, biting, and head-butting wrestling rituals between fur seals. When one of these 500-pound beasts initiated a few thumping charges in my direction, I ran. (Sprinted.)

My hike continued for hours along a wide black-pebble beach sandwiched between a soupy bay of iceberg bits and a towering glacier wall. There, I discovered another penguin theme. Antarctic shores are littered with whalebones, the disturbing legacy of a merciless, now outlawed whaling industry. Often, you see several penguins holding court, majestically upright, next to colossal whale vertebra. Once you develop an eye for it, you notice what seems to be penguin tributes to remains of departed whales. They stand guard by the bones. So, I sat there among the penguins, some safeguarding whale remains, others umpiring games of tag or anticipating seal awakenings. It dawned on me that this coexistence between penguins and seals resembles rocky marriages, where, kids in tow, parents barely tolerate each other's company.

There's no one to stamp your passport here. The White Continent lingers as an example of how our faultless planet intended on enduring the eons. Your mind wanders during your time amid the ice. Making the best of being utterly vulnerable among relentless challenges, the penguins reminded me that pining and whining wastes precious time. Wedged in this survival argument for the ages, I whispered "please" to no one in particular. At that, the penguin before me nodded to his pal, quacked in my face again, spun on a heel, and waddled away to resume holding court by a stack of whalebones.

DIRECTION

DON'T GET HITCHED TO BAD NEWS
(Japan ~ North America)

CNN Ruined Hitchhiking

The Japanese are, for good reason, known as incredibly trusting people. Hitching, though not encouraged, is still not frowned upon in Japan—a nation where maybe means no. A truck driver once gave me a lift from Tokyo to Osaka, bought me soup from a vending machine, and tried repeatedly to illustrate the immensity of Mount Fuji. The only word we had in common was Madonna. Arriving in Osaka after midnight, I had difficulty explaining to him that I needed to find a cheap place to sleep. The confusion continued until he drove me to the police station in search of an interpreter. After a momentary exchange with the police, he waved farewell and walked back to his truck. A policeman then set folded blankets and a pillow on a cot inside one of the jail cells. He motioned me into the cell, returning with biscuits and a glass of juice. With a fatherly nod, he pointed to a clock to indicate he'd be back by morning before closing the cell door without locking it.

∞ ∞ ∞ ∞ ∞

North America

As you may expect, career travelers are often good at—or at least insistent upon—holding court, especially around tables of food or drink. When assembling groups of such personalities, this can also be a recipe for clashing open-road philosophies. A revelation occurred to me while attending a Canada Media Marketplace trade show in New York City. After being busted for eavesdropping on a conversation, I met two gentlemen about my age who were new members of the famed Explorers Club. Located on Manhattan's Upper East Side, The Explorers Club knows how to celebrate the old-style hardcore adventurer—pre *Gore-Tex*. But my sense was that these members had never experienced the lost art of hitchhiking, which has been a rite of passage for many road warriors. Mark Twain, Jack Kerouac, Tim Cahill, and Paul Theroux are just some of the greats who come to mind. I asked the guys if they'd ever hitchhiked, and they said never.

Although I now believe that it's possible to find adventure while toting rolling luggage, it's hard for me to look another man in the eye and consider him a genuine adventurer if he has never had to make a hitchhiking sign and use it. Understandably, hitching is less popular with women who are similarly on track to see the world.

Because hitchhiking has earned a bad rap in recent decades, it now, unfortunately, only limps along as a way to make new friends, discover new places, and spawn authentic encounters bred on instant trust. And it still won't cost you a penny. Between the ages of 15 and 35, I made hundreds of hitching signs that took me through every state, 10 Canadian provinces, and dozens of other countries. Hitching a ride defined my entertainment.

Debuting in 1980, CNN quickly drew an audience with its 24-hour newscast. Prior to that, the dissemination of bad news was limited to what a few antennae-fed networks could exaggerate regionally during their half-hour time slots. The ever-present news cycle, a contagion further escalated by CNN clones, soon became unavoidable. Until then, hitchhikers were still unannounced messengers of freedom, but the minute-by-minute news tsunami eventually insinuated—based on scant events—that hitchhikers were thieving and murderous types. The paranoia directed towards hitchhikers compounded as the armed robbery in the Southwest or the murder in the Northeast was now on everybody's doorstep. The art of hitching a ride got an F and was forever changed.

But hitchhikers forged on, even as the explosion of 'no hitchhiking' signs along highway entrance ramps merged with the widespread policy of truckers' insurance being voided if they picked up random riders. But, I managed to feed my hitching habit until the wheels fell off after 9-11. I hitched long distances a few times after that, but it was never the same. I loved that open, trusting America…and I miss it, still.

Enjoying a freestyle childhood, I began hitchhiking in seventh grade, which eventually led me across America and the world. It was my first entrée into travel. At 16, I played hooky from school while bluffing my parents about a fictional ski vacation, so I could hitchhike from Long Island to the Florida Keys, twice. That's when I knew that my life would unfold outside the mainstream. I would no longer be able to resist the instant rapport you can have with strangers while traveling. Free therapy—anonymous conversing—is often the best kind.

One memorable sea-to-shining-sea hitchhike was a late 80's month-long odyssey from Los Angeles to New York City that followed a year in Asia. Drinkable tap water and french fries were highlights. No longer experiencing this sort of freedom, I found such rolling rites of passage to be one of the few things that make me pine for my youth.

My long-distance style of hitching relied less on sticking

out a thumb and more on wooing gas station customers. By approaching the top guy at a gas station with identification in hand, I'd fib that my car had broken down near the exit and that I was hoping to politely catch a lift from a customer, without hassling anyone. Easy. Then I stood back and picked out my preference of license plate—vital to knowing from where they were coming or going—vehicle, music style, gender, coffee or soda. Later, I'd always come clean about the so-called broken-down car.

Just to prove that I could, in 1997, at 35 years of age, I hitched the U.S. coast-to-coast once again. The next summer, further averting a mini mid-30s slump, I decided to shake things up again by thumbing rides from Maine to Montana via Canada. Both odysseys reconfirmed that most people have a heart and don't want to harm anybody. That hitch well into the 'no-hitch' era was an unintentional public-service dispatch, at least for me and the people who paved my way. The last ride of each day typically ended up turning into a party or an invitation to sleep on their couch—in that land of the free and that home of the brave.

∞ ∞ ∞ ∞ ∞

Disclaimer: Hitchhiking can be dangerous, you probably shouldn't try it. But, if you must hitch, remain clever. Occasionally, I'd create signs for a destination that was in the opposite direction of my actual destination, and display it while thumbing in the direction of my desired destination. When a concerned driver pulled over to correct my blooper, I'd explain my tactic and request a lift. Other disarming sign options: *Please, Harmless, Free Beer, Mountains, Hello, Mom, Trees.*

Ps, In the day, hitching was also a great way to collect trivia. I've always been disturbed by celebrity worship and was amused to hear an example of monkey-see monkey-do from a trucker, as we crossed the New Mexico desert in the middle of the night.

Apparently, in 1977, Fonzie, star of the television show Happy Days, got a library card. In the following week, library card applications increased 500 percent in the U.S.

DIRECTION

MAKE DANCING YOUR SHORTCUT TO HAPPINESS (Nova Scotia ~ Venezuela)

"A front got no back." —P-Nut, a Charleston,
South Carolina, street-poet

D ancing and lovemaking are two lingering quarters where humans can still be the animals they are by design. All other animals (well, perhaps not groomed poodles) are instinctively what they are: natural. But, prevailing human instinct is often diluted by self-consciousness, so we're not impulsively cooperating with what our DNA screams to us. Whatever you do, don't change the way you dance unless it's for a contest offering a big prize to do so.

The summer following my freshman year in college, I hitchhiked from Long Island to Nova Scotia and back. In Nova Scotia's capital, Halifax, I found my way into a very large bar with a stage. On the stage, a local rock DJ hosted a twist-on-the-waterbed contest to Chubby Checker's tune, *The Twist*. Performing the twist in your socks on a wobbly, sheetless waterbed was somewhat of a challenge to the participants, and a chuckle for the audience. To raise the stakes and win the grand prize—the waterbed—I twisted for a bit and then, tapping into my gymnastic roots, kicked into a handstand and walked around the wooden frame of the bed on my hands. With that highlight, I won. During the ceremonial interview, the DJ asked, "Who are you going to sleep with on your prize?"

"I hitchhiked here from New York, so I can't claim this prize." I said, adding, "I'd like to donate my bed to a local charity, or the runner-up."

Applause immediately followed, as did the telling expression of Nova Scotian hospitality, in the form of dollars and coins thrown onto the stage. Enough currency flew my way to buy my own waterbed back in the States. This was back in the day when waterbeds were still competing with beanbag chairs for the top of the cool pyramid.

∞ ∞ ∞ ∞ ∞

Venezuela

Economic prudence once led me to a traditional Caracas, Venezuela, dance hall. In easygoing local joints on the 'wrong side of town,' your chances of encountering English speakers diminish—where the upside is limited Spanish skills make your search for a dance partner a bona-fide challenge.

On such dance floors, fanatic freestyle boogeying is an option, but you might scare the ever-present grandparents. Other options are persuading one of the more experienced señors or señoritas to familiarize you with the hand and foot placements, or watching other couples' moves until you get the hang of it. Even the language-impaired visitor soon realizes that dancing, like eating, is routine here—a national pastime. Albeit festive and immediately intimate for the visitor, the Venezuelan faces remain unreadable as torsos mesh. It's their reality, not a *show* about it.

Dancing endures as a hedonistic life force that's neither illegal nor unhealthy. Contagious dancé zones remain indifferent to status and worry. So join the party. Maybe the hokey pokey *is* what it's all about.

∞ ∞ ∞ ∞ ∞

"The one thing that can solve most of our problems is dancing."— James Brown

"Put a man and girl on stage, and there is already a story; a man and two girls, there is already a plot." —George Balanchine (on dance)

MODERN DANCING and IMMODEST DRESS STIR SEX DESIRE: leading to lustful flirting, fornication, adultery, divorce, disease, destruction and judgment. —San Francisco bar sign echoing Victorian ethos

DIRECTION

DON'T LET OTHER PEOPLE'S OPINIONS BECOME YOUR OPINION OF YOURSELF
(Sweden ~ Bahrain ~ Abu Dhabi)

Don't hook your fate to someone else's drab drama.

I visited an elementary school in Gothenburg, Sweden, where a friend was substitute teaching. I sat in the back of the classroom while his students took part in a geography lesson. They were learning that a compass needle points toward Earth's magnetic north and were shown that a magnet nearby causes the needle to spin without bearing. When the magnet was removed, once again the needle points toward its true bearing. The students were next introduced to explorers who used compasses to find their way.

After class, walking into town, my friend likened human wisdom to a built-in compass, as it points the way and gives us direction. He suggested that magnets represented confusion and negative influences. Remove the bad magnets—ill will—and our instinct continues guiding us on the right course.

Goodwill is the currency of humanity. Never allow anyone, who doesn't truly care about you, to attempt to define you.

∞ ∞ ∞ ∞ ∞

Persian Gulf

"That is the Arabian Gulf, *not* the Persian Gulf." —correction made by Bahrainian air-conditioner repairman gesturing toward Gulf concealed by a desert sandstorm.

"Don't attack other people's plan in defense of not making your own." — Abu Dhabi airport employee to stuffy Brit being forced into checking luggage

DIRECTION

BEAR IN MIND THAT YOUR FAMILY NOT ONLY PUSHES YOUR BUTTONS BUT ALSO INSTALLS THEM

"Frankly, I'm fed up with politicians in Washington lecturing the rest of us about family values. Our families have values. But our government doesn't." —Bill Clinton

My first advocate for wandering was my oldest brother. Basil, Jr. taught me to keep one eye on the road and the other on reasons to detour from it. Before I'd turned 10, he set me loose with the skill sets required to hitchhike, sneak out of our house at night without parental detection, sprint away from police cars just to invite a chase, crawl invisibly for blocks through the continuum of hedges separating suburban backyards, scale any building in town, and permanently borrow things from department stores. He also coached me on enduring and resolving disciplinary interrogations from crabby adults, like the golf course greenskeeper who begrudgingly failed to expose my golf ball reselling scam, or detect my tree house looming in pine a tree hovering over a putting green. Doable anarchy.

Although Basil and I get along like best friends most of the time, that's not the case when he decides to pull rank. That's when we go silent for a spell. An observer once asked me if he pushed my buttons. "Push them?" I asked, "He installed them!"

The first indication of Basil's preference for alternative transport was his passion for navigating the entire length of the rusty chain-link fence surrounding the Hempstead, N.Y. golf course without touching the ground. Mock rock-climbing decades before it hit gyms and malls, his always clinging progression along the miles-long eight-foot barrier required a full day of plotting routes through or around vines, bushes, and honeysuckle blossoms. There were also tree branches that were either overhanging or enmeshed into the fence. As I trailed him on these odysseys, we'd often find ourselves gripping a listing fence with our backs to the ground. Falling and touching the soil once meant total failure, and a return to the starting point.

Five years my senior, Basil was touring the world far and wide before I graduated high school. Bathing in mischief's cologne bonded us and launched my life on the road. It also put a new spin on getting lost, just for the heck of it. He continues encouraging nearly everyone he meets to follow that unsigned dirt road—metaphorical or actual—to discover their own set of rat-race exit blueprints.

∞ ∞ ∞ ∞ ∞

We all have countless tales we can share about siblings. My middle brother Bryan's permanent move into Manhattan at 19 made him a road warrior of another sort. An actor's actor, he melds Robin Williams's zaniness with a gift for imitating global accents and dialects. His myriad impersonations range from a flamboyant Puerto Rican hairdresser to a repressed but naughty British Royal.

In the 1980s, Bryan drove a horse-drawn carriage in New York

City. It was a lawless era citywide, when carriage drivers were solely in command of their routes, horse and customer safety, and unstructured whims. During this unregulated period, Bryan's always evolving comedic act featured two sidekicks, his pets. Jerome was a capuchin monkey—the hyper sort that assist paralyzed people—which he rescued by buying him off a homeless crack addict. Jerome then took up residence in Bryan's Hell's Kitchen railroad apartment. His other companion was a young goat (named Bruce, after me, something about him doing whatever he wanted) he adopted in Pennsylvania's Amish Country who was then raised in a horse stable on Manhattan's West 38th St.

Bryan would bring both Jerome and Bruce with him while driving the carriage. Needless to say, the spectacle was attention-getting. Mesmerized tourists would stop and gawk, jaws agape, then slowly begin asking carefully worded questions. While touring Central Park or the city streets with customers, the peppy monkey and the impish goat sat astride Bryan, on opposing sides of his carriage driving perch. En route, Jerome would occasionally turn around and stare at the customers, silently at first, and then emit a blood-curdling scream that sounded like an angry baby in distress. Meanwhile, Bruce, sleepily looking on, would pitch in an intermittent high-pitched "maaah." When the stars were correctly aligned for an animal chorus, the horse would pitch in a neigh, snort, or whinny.

While parked curbside and waiting for customers, Bryan fed carrots to his horse. Meanwhile, Jerome, now perched upon his shoulder, would nibble bits of the banana protruding from his tuxedo jacket pocket. Keeping the entire crew happy, Bryan also fed apple slices to the goat, who patiently observed from his roost upon the carriage. You don't see this sort of thing in Manhattan anymore.

Bryan is not all about clowning and Dr. Doolittling. Since arriving in Manhattan in 1977, he's been volunteering in homeless shelters and soup kitchens. Without sermonizing altruism, he taught me that you accomplish nothing in life until you make another person happy—and that it doesn't hurt to make them howl with laughter, either.

DIRECTION

COMPETE WITH YOURSELF (Grand Canyon)

Water can be habit-forming.

M any vacationers peer over the rim of the Grand Canyon into its overwhelming river gorge, gasp, and then return to their cars to hunt for a burger. After doing just that, I returned years later to explore the guts of the God of all Gullies on a 150-mile rafting trip. Even when you're a mile deep in the earth's reddish crust on a raft drifting the length of this colossal culvert, you can't escape sibling rivalry and city-slicker spite. Down there, the Colorado River has gargantuan whitewater that delineates life or death if played wrong. One set of rapids— really an angry waterfall—forever changed my inner tide.

Joining my brother Basil and his posse of Idaho rancher pals on day three of a 21-day private trip, I hiked down from the canyon's south rim in the dark and found myself waiting by the river until they floated by the sandbar upon which I stood. I smelled the motley crew, most of whom run a few hardcore rivers every year, before I saw them. I was a New York City whitewater rafting rookie joining a bonded posse way after pecking orders had been established. Needless to say, finding training time to navigate rapids on my own wasn't easy. Wanting to make sure I made the most of the experience, Basil committed me to a secret challenge before I arrived. This was typical and in the spirit of our childhood dares. After all, he was the one who familiarized me with suburban delinquency and shoplifting patchouli-scented candles years before my peers were allowed to cross streets by themselves. This test was rowing a raft solo over Lava Falls, the most dangerous stretch of the river and one of the country's most difficult navigable rapids. I had about two weeks to train for it. Initially, a set of oars in my fists made my raft no more versatile than a buoy.

To prepare, I stole training time on the raft in the evenings while everyone else was enjoying happy hour after breaking camp on random sandy beaches. I spent most of this time spinning the boat with sharp alternating paddle movements in one direction and then suddenly turning it in the opposite direction. Every evening, I'd go out and twirl myself into a sweat, which made Basil's Idaho cohorts chuckle about how the city boy needed to find his gym. By day, the brotherly dynamics of being taught how to run unforgiving rapids involved much screaming and frequent reminders of how expensive it is to repair a smashed boat. There was also a repeating bit about how pissed-off our parents would be if I died.

As the days in this geologic miracle passed, I began navigating ripples and smaller rapids. Basil and I shared a tent where we talked about the looming challenge every night until we fell asleep. He decided not to tell anyone else in the group about our secret until the morning of Lava Falls for fear they'd vote the idea down. There was no escaping my city-folk pigeonhole.

When the day arrived, half of the crew was unsupportive of the idea of my solo run. After I agreed to pay for any damages to the raft, it was stripped of everything except the oars, and I was finally given a green light. This gamble would not have been possible on a commercially organized trip, which is propelled by boat engines and signed waivers. Everyone scouted the waterfall from a nearby cliff, and one by one four rafts and three kayakers plunged into the roaring drop. One raft capsized and two others narrowly missed being sucked into the water tornado big enough to swallow a bus.

With a look I hadn't seen in years, Basil patted me on the waist and then floated away on the fifth raft. I scouted my route over Lava Falls's millions of gallons-per-minute froth, which helped center me with an adrenaline rush I only remember from the minutes before a wrestling match. It was the sort of anticipation that sets nausea butterflies free in your stomach. I hiked upstream on the trail toward the raft, discovering a series of large, surly, black ravens standing on the riverbank's boulders and peering at me with tilted heads. I passed one after another, until it seemed I hadn't yet earned a pass from the scavenger review board. Farther afield, I noticed that a pack of bighorn desert sheep had stopped chewing the brush to gaze my way. When I reached the stripped-down boat, a final raven sat on its inflated rim, staring at me gloomily. It slowly cocked its head from side to side. Losing the ability to maintain an internal dialogue, I swallowed hard and realized there was no turning back.

Trembling like a nudist in a snowstorm, I boarded the raft. It was then that the sound of my heart exploding in my ears overtook the thunder of the misting downstream mayhem. Accelerating toward the rim of the cliff, my panic was ultimately subdued by a strange quieting. This was, after all, a dare. I did my best to hit the mark everyone recommended, but drifted left of center, which, after an initial weightless freefall, meant dancing on the rim of that dreaded all-encompassing whirlpool. Balancing on the rim, I rowed furiously while a blinding froth battered my face. Stuck between heaven and hell, I heard the guttural choking sounds of the vortex trying to consume me. I hoped I was rowing in the right direction. Then, time stood still until I spun the raft and was spit out of the mammoth eddy to cleanly run the lower rapids. The deafening jet-engine roar of the plummet subsided, and I docked downstream. The crowd's reaction was mixed. It seemed that a few of the cowboys were disappointed I hadn't flipped. Basil, on the other hand, was validated. We strolled out of sight to celebrate privately. Brotherhood.

Aside from chasing women, the river trench cutting a mile into the parched Arizona desert reset my bar for testing Mother Nature's wrath. It also made me rethink the trials we choose. The worthiest competitions are sometimes an inner journey with ourselves. The red sand embedded in my hair, ears, clothes, and gear followed me for a month after this voyage. The call of Lava Falls and that black raven's gaze still do.

DIRECTION

HORSE AROUND (Arizona)

If your halo wobbles, reach up and right it.

After emerging from a Grand Canyon rafting trip resembling a caveman, a hitchhike landed me at the front gates of a premiere wellness resort where the hot lava-stone massage cost as much as my monthly rent. This was the resort's first backpacker check-in, and I'm pretty sure the only one delivered by a pickup truck with gun racks. Three weeks without a shave and television, I arrived reeking of the muggy socks brewing inside my auburn clay-stained sleeping bag and unaware that President Clinton had been re-elected.

Writing about this chic destination spa near Tucson meant Jacuzzis overlooking mountain-panorama sunsets and white-jacketed waiter quartets presenting roasted fennel, nopal cactus, anasazi beans braised in saffron, and anchovy chili. If anyone here knew where I'd napped the previous night—in a random, unlocked parked car—they'd dial 911. After a decade of exploring the tropics where you sup on a main course of rice in lantern-lit bamboo-thatched huts, I welcomed the merge of luxury and mindfulness to steer me "into the moment." So I washed my clothes in a seashell-shaped sink and then tried to blend in with the affluent clientele, all smartly dressed for cactus climate. Unfortunately, my readiness to mingle was sidetracked by the gurgle of running water. The trickling water features, which aim to soothe in such retreats, are to me no more than irritating gargling soundtracks that make me want to call a plumber.

The next morning, birdcall-led tunes set the tone for a palatial outdoor buffet breakfast, where placecards trumpeted the calories and fat stats of each item. The chirping soundtrack made my head pirouette in search of flying food thieves. I was then whisked away to the nearby horse farm for the Equine Experience, which provided an opportunity to open "a door into the room of self-acceptance." Hmmm, it was time to come clean.

The Equine Experience, a shrink session with a horse, first introduced equestrian ground skills. It is a straightforward workshop for those perceiving it solely as an opportunity to groom a horse and then coax your new pal into galloping in circles. However, it's really a lesson in self-awareness, a chance to identify communication patterns that do and don't work, relying on horses who are amazingly deft at reading those around them. For instance, I can come on a bit strong sometimes and ignore the impact my approach has on people. But when the horse balked a foot sideways to escape my hyper gesturing, I noticed. When I mellowed out, so did the horse. Later, lapsing again and turning up the volume, I tattled to the instructor—who favored being called an equine facilitator—about a bumpy romance and, sure enough, horsie froze. Another energy connection I never would have made on my own.

This brushing and combing session was certainly not my first experience with horses. During my college summers, I drove a horse-drawn carriage and was affectionate with my horse. I know my strawberry roan partner and I bonded, despite the fact that I didn't always "greet him first by gently touching his shoulder." My newfound non-urban perspective, however, made me doubly aware of how sensitive horses are to human emotion. Then came the lesson on focusing through hoof cleaning. My first attempts to lift my horse's hooves were unsuccessful. He wouldn't budge, and I couldn't figure out why. My facilitator correctly observed that I was thinking about 10 things at once. She told me to stand back, focus only on one hoof, approach it with confidence, and pick it up. Yup. I stepped back, eyeballed a hoof, and reapproached boldly. Hooves began lifting into the air.

These Arizona horses may be trained to empathize with the knuckleheaded, and unlike Manhattan's carriage-driving horses, they don't have to worry about steam spouting from manhole covers or garbage trucks roaring like dragons. Then again, nor do these resort employees. On this ranch, the aromatherapy is reciprocal.

The therapeutic finale was the liberty lunge, my bid to encourage the stallion to walk, canter, and then gallop within a pen. With a whip in hand (for visual impact only) and a reproving tone, I marched toward the horse's rear, which convinced him to take off. To keep things moving, I also galloped in a circle, and roused my inner cowboy. I stopped when the horse seemed dizzy—but wait, does that mean I'm dizzy, too?

"Horses will always take care of themselves," I was assured. "You only need to take care of yourself."

DIRECTION

PREPARE TO BECOME AN OVERNIGHT
SENSATION (Philippines ~ Saratoga Springs)

Although I was disappointed when *The New York Times* condensed an involved story I wrote into a 175-word sidebar, I eventually had a freeing realization: Even highly regarded publications can overlook the heart of a story. However, I remain a believer that every headline informs others.

That in-print *New York Times* paraphrase opened with this…

Journey Picks a Vocalist: After performing for 25 years in dimly lighted bars in the Philippines, Arnel Pineda, 40, has been hired as the new singer for the 1980's rock band Journey. The band's guitarist, Neal Schon, was impressed by footage of Mr. Pineda performing Journey covers on YouTube and flew him to California for an audition.

In an effort to dodge routine, I invent a new quest for every place I visit. My third roam through the Philippines, Southeast Asia's only Christian country, vowed to answer the question: Why are the Philippines the rock-and-roll engine for the rest of Asia? From Hong Kong to Singapore and back up to Tokyo or Beijing, if there's a skilled rock band on stage, they're likely

Filipino. Tuning into their soundtrack, which deftly reproduces every Western musical style, forced me to challenge Emerson's declaration that imitation cannot go beyond its model.

The Spanish colonial era that began in 1565 introduced guitars, choirs, and the art of serenading. This Eurasian hybrid—linked to the Renaissance—set the stage for a nation hooked on music. Historically, Filipinos have a song for every occasion, such as planting rice, fishing at night, and courting sweethearts. The Filipino serenade was inspired by the old-style Spanish romantic scenario: A guy shows up with his guitar outside his dreamgirl's home and croons a love song. If she opens her window to listen and sings a song in response, he is en route to cuddling. If the window doesn't budge, it's off to voice lessons or another gal's house. Nearly every Filipino man I met born before 1960 had vivid recollections of serenading his eventual wife—or being shot down in flames.

My melody mission first led me to sand and jungle-fringed Palawan, a narrow 250-mile-long island bisected by an imposing spine of limestone mountains. One of 7,017 Philippine islands, it is where I met Bing, a charming mother of five. She was serenaded at 2am by her eventual husband, who wasn't put off by her underwhelming appearance at the window—her face at the time was encrusted with otherwise beautifying talcum powder. It was true love from the get-go.

Music cultivated its way into the Philippine heart long before the Spanish towed in stone cannonballs and religion. Palawan's indigenous lowland Aboriginals, the Tagbanuas, expressed feelings of love in singing poems inspired by the inexhaustible variety of sounds in nature. They imitated the singing of insects and birds and created a bird scale that mimics musical notation. That birdlore vocabulary continues to bond men and women of the jungle.

In the 1980s, karaoke was invented by a Filipino man and then sold to a Japanese investor. It overtook the Philippines and modernized the serenade. Then, jukebox-style videoke began booming from street corners, bars, and malls. While American-style serenades play out as pricey gifts, horse-drawn carriage rides, and scoreboard proposals—most American men sing to their women only to humor them—Filipinos still sing to theirs as if their futures depend on it.

After Spain's rule gave way to American colonization, Uncle Sam did a few things right in this part of Asia. The U.S. legacy included teaching everyone English by building schools in practically every village. Hollywood was also delivered to their doorstep. The Vietnam-era military bases needed entertaining, so Filipino rock, jazz, and lounge bands surfaced and thrived. Base towns became live Western music hubs that inspired many to pick up a guitar and sing. American soldiers also left behind a legacy of vintage guitars. Hundreds of collectors' guitars—mostly Gibsons—found permanent homes in the Philippines. Turkey may have claimed the world's "East Meets West" slogan, but it also justly describes the Philippines's music scene.

Modern Manila, a mega-city of 15 million, is traditional yet faddish, Asian in character, but Western in disposition. Still hunting my storyline there, I was unaware that the irrepressible Filipino musicality was about to storm America until my assigning editor emailed to share a rumor that the iconic 1980's rock band Journey had just auditioned a Filipino named Arnel Pineda as their new lead vocalist, and that same singer was fronting his Manila-based rock cover band, The Zoo, in a few hours. I sat in the front row and introduced myself to Arnel between sets. He sat with me and explained that Journey's guitarist admired his covers of the band's hits on YouTube and flew him to California. Only a few days after his tryout, it was supernatural to witness this still unknown would-be star rock out in a random, smoky Manila bar.

While the decision to hire Arnel had still not been made, I interviewed him after two more Manila shows. His arena-rocking potential was obvious. A month later, Journey announced he was their new vocalist and a world tour. A Filipino fronting a Rock and Roll Hall of Fame-bound band was the biggest entertainment news ever in the Philippines, outshining Filipino Lea Salonga's Tony Award-winning role in *Miss Saigon*.

The enlightened never figure out who is teaching and who is learning. Before Arnel was launched out of obscurity and into the world spotlight, the youthful, unassuming 40-year-old was armed only with standard Filipino politeness. He insisted that his birthplace was "a big sponge that's open to world music." No stranger to smiling, he added, "We grew up breathing music, it's in our veins."

Some may call it luck, but Arnel was well-prepared for this opportunity. His mother, a tailor who passed away when he was 13, began grooming him via in-home performances at age five. Born into poverty, he was competing in local singing competitions by age seven. He went pro at 15, initially showcasing his vocal range in malls and later throughout the Philippines and other parts of Asia. His story was also punctuated by spells of hunger and homelessness.

It seems almost everybody in the Philippines can carry a tune. Women sing to nobody in particular, as they stare into internet café computer screens; a man whistles as he stands before a urinal; cab drivers croon along with their radios, maids belt out while working; a teenaged boy strums a guitar on a street corner, practicing a puppy love song. Like Brazilians and Irish, few Filipinos are performance shy, because music—from liturgical to metal—is bred into their souls. Although karaoke machines are displacing windowsill serenades, my faith was restored as my Philippine Airlines flight touched down in California, and two flight attendants seated in the jump seats facing me began singing to each other. Music celebrates a universal love, and there's no greater invitation to love than singing about it.

∞ ∞ ∞ ∞ ∞

Saratoga Springs, N.Y.

When Arnel Pineda first toured the world with Journey in 2008, he invited me backstage in Saratoga Springs, NY, where he was about to dazzle 25,000 wildly cheering fans. After a hug and a handshake, we reflected on how things had changed for him since our smoky bar-room conversations in Manila. It was a fleeting moment to revel in his rags-to-riches story. It's rare to successfully replace the lead singer of an iconic band. Van Halen and AC/DC pulled it off, as did Journey. Before heading to center stage, he said, "If my mom was alive today, she would have been so proud." His body may have been on cloud nine, but his familial heart was beating aloud. I reminded him that I wanted to write his biography. Walking into the spotlight, he turned around and nodded a yes.

DIRECTION

NOURISH YOUR BELLY GOD (Jamaica)

"What tastes sweet in the mouth can burn the belly." —Rasta priest warning: Fear what you fancy (translated from "Wha sweet ina mout hat dah belly.")

Ancient Greek philosopher Epicurus believed that the greatest good is to seek personal happiness. Today, an epicurean is someone who praises food, and other indulgences. The Greeks would have found much to ponder in Jamaica.

At dusk and in search of a meal, I descended from the lofty Blue Mountains to the edge of Kingston, Jamaica's allegedly dangerous shoreline city. Hungrily eyeing Papine Town Square from a distance, I noticed a tall man leading a group of dancing disciples. Their outdoor Sabbath drumming service was a stationary tribal march to chant-infused songs. Many of the worshippers wore tarnished steel cooking-pot hats and were draped in green, red, and yellow gowns—the Rastafarian's signature stoplight colors celebrating the Ethiopian flag. I drew closer to the cowbell player and three drummers keeping the beat. A follower appeared and led me by the wrist to meet a priest from the School of Vision whose members were from a Rasta community residing in the Blue Mountains. The priest suggested a time-out, encouraging me to step away from the procession so he could share a thought.

For the amateur, comprehending the Jamaican-English lilt can require two or three takes. I took in an hour-long manifesto that was colored by chalk diagrams the priest engraved on the pavement. Sworn claims included a cryptic geometry that foretold of government tracking devices implanted in all of us at birth. This was cross-referenced in Revelations chapter 13. Other Bible-in-hand interpretations were accompanied by surging eyebrows and gestures. He also pointed skyward at UFOs.

The priest closed the Bible, waved off the chalk diagrams, and whispered, "Nuu broom sweep clean mon, but owl broom noe dem cahna." After a few rounds of translation tennis, I understood this to mean "the new broom may sweep tidily, but the old broom knows all the corners." He was on a roll.

The marching-dance beats continued as incense filled the air. Nearing a conclusion, my teacher spoke of the sacramental link to attaining herbally encouraged revelations. Then, with a crinkled squint, he added, "I'm a farmer."

As a blazing sun set behind shimmering blue peaks, I asked the preacher man about food. He looked away from the compass within a pyramid he'd drawn on the ground—the one linking all of his theorems—faced the mist-shrouded mountains, and bowed to them. His lordly stare into the highlands eventually rejoined mine, and then he peered over my shoulder. He gestured toward a dancing devotee, a man engaging in perhaps the fiftieth twirling of his beard, and one of the few in the country with an ample midsection. The Holy Rasta pointed at the plump dancer—who happened to own a restaurant—and slyly said, "Belly God."

∞ ∞ ∞ ∞ ∞

"I'm eating a bag of yard work." —Reluctant Icelandic health-kicker, forking a salad.

"I'm in shape. *ROUND* is a shape." —Romantic Norwegian man, embracing a woman at Berlin's Love Parade.

"The only thing coming between me and her will be my belly." —Argentine lifeguard, at work on Mar del Plata.

"I love my country. It's a beautiful country. I have never left. If I do, it will be for a short time. —Woman on Jamaica's Hellshire Beach.

DIRECTION

TURN YOUR BACK ON THE SHORE TO UNDERSTAND THE SEA (Burma)

Simplicity has no baggage.

I 'm sitting in a kayak in a hidden cove somewhere in the Andaman Sea's Mergui Archipelago. This mostly uninhabited string of reefs and islands extend 200 miles along Burma's coast—an 800-isle Eden the size of Vermont. Since time immemorial, Mergui's waters have been home to floating nomad families, the Moken, who live most of the year on *kabangs*, houseboats made from big hollowed-out trees.

The Moken belong to no country, carry no ID, and speak their own language. The gypsies drift in groups of at least six boats, each vessel housing one family, usually made up of three generations. They wed young, and the community builds couples a boat, wherein the newlyweds can start their own family.

These floating villages migrate between temporary moorings. The Moken use traps, nets, and spears to hunt turtles and collect sand worms, shellfish, and clams. They also swim deep into submerged caves harvesting sea cucumbers for export to China and Japan. Without modern scuba gear, they dive as deep as 80 feet, equipped with only a mask, fins, and a long hosepipe which acts as a snorkel. These houseboaters have no concept of making rent or "meeting you on Wednesday." They have little reason to make or keep appointments.

By kayak, I glided through lush mangroves and into two-story-high sea caves looking for the Moken. It took me, my New Jersey friend, and our guide Tham ("Tom") days to find these elusive people who are born, live, and die at sea. Encountering them on land, we found the invitation to exchange confidences rare, but approaching our first seagoing Moken in a kayak seemed to give us a bit of credibility. I paddled up to a band of very tan families in small dugout canoes. Seated with paddles across their knees, they wait for the tide to go out.

An impossibly beautiful woman with broad cheeks and shiny long black hair sat alone in a tiny canoe. Her smile reveals teeth stained dark red with betel nut. "How's the fishing?" I ask her. Tham translates my question into Burmese, and a group effort translates it into Moken. "Fish scared away—now over there," nods the woman.

I turn to my friend to jest about their sea-bound life being one way to avoid paying rent. When Tham mistakenly translates the quip, an elder glances our way, winces with gentle but searching eyes, and speaks. Tham says something lost or found in translation: "Don't rent space in your head to just anyone." Rewind a few centuries, or advice ahead of its time?

This universe is a medley of mountainous islands, craggy coastlines, desolate beaches cut into steep-sided limestone pinnacles, and conical upthrusts capped by forest and jagged rocks. We paddle around rock-tower islands, their faces tide-chiseled with gurgling tunnels through which powerful surf ebbs and flows. The roller-coaster tidal action alerts mudskippers and rock crabs to scuttle about the stone facades. Flying fish bounce like skipped stones on the propelled current into dense, partially submerged trees. We follow them.

We time ourselves to ride high tide into mangrove tunnels and then exit on low tide through a vine-encased artery. Massive roots, twisting and intertwined around and above us, form a mangrove church, light twinkling through clusters like rays through stained glass. Not having encountered any more Moken for days, I sit in the sand eating a bowl of rice. The only time I've thought about home in a month was having just snorkeled against a fierce tide, colliding with stinging jellyfish traffic.

Back on the move in the kayaks, we approach a kabang, smoke rising from its stove. The boat noses up to my kayak, and a wiry man emerges from beneath the thatched roof wearing a curious glance. He looks at Tham. Tham looks at me but says nothing. The interaction with this seagoer shows there is more binding us than separating us. We are, after all, floating. A gesture is made. Tham decodes it as an invitation to board the kabang. The one-room interior resembles a live-aboard vessel belonging to a boat mechanic—basic but prepared.

Half of all Americans live within 50 miles of their birthplace—the Moken spend their entire lives on it. The kabang is a carved, canoe-like hull supporting a wooden frame secured by bamboo pegs and rattan rope. Thatched palm leaves make the roof and sails. The mini Noah's Ark is as versatile as a studio apartment, with many items serving double duty, such as tables used as chopping blocks and hammocks becoming fishing nets. I point to various items—stove, bed, fishing spear—and mime their uses. Each guess receives a nod. Open on both ends, there is a sturdy feel to the boat.

These ingenious gypsy rigs, balanced and light for their size, are designed to safely carry a family of up to eight through vicious Indian Ocean storms. Though they look rustic, their naval technology has mystified sea traders, pirates, and anthropologists through the centuries. Mokens focus on pride in the face of scarcity. Kabangs symbolize the ultimate clutter-free existence, a formalized "letting go" that uses identical scroll designs on the bow and stern to illustrate the mouth-to-exit digestive process that holds onto nothing permanently. In another era, this sage design announced to pirates, "We have nothing to steal." It's freedom dictated by the whims of the sea.

When the man (who is both a father and a son on this boat) hosting us joins our conversation, he chimes in via Tham, "The sea is the children's playground and teacher." Family activities revolve around the boat, just as western families' revolve around kitchens and TV rooms. Their homes just happen to float. Despite living on the move, they live connected—connected to the water, connected to the stars, connected to the seasons, and connected to each other.

The Moken may be the last link to the indigenous Southeast Asians who survived the Ice Age by taking to boats 10,000 years ago, when the region was submerged in 300 feet of water. The Moken's strong cultural identity, developed on the water, is being forced to adapt to new environments. Some now live in thatched huts elevated on stilts driven into the mud. Still, they seldom venture any distance inland from the beach. Boat dwellers don't have much business on land.

As the world changes around them, the Moken are slowly disappearing. But, for as long as they survive, they seem to be sublimely impervious to the despair occurring in the rest of the world. Many cultures like theirs persist under the gun, seemingly impossibly, because genetically they don't know when to quit. In this lonely dockside corner of Asia, knotty vitality breathes, even on the fringe of a country that's typically at war with itself. As the kabang floats away, a teenager on board turns around, waves faintly, and lends one more Moken moment.

There is no way to harmony. Harmony is the way.

The sunrise is a stronger symbol than the sun setting on Burma's departing sea gypsies. The winds are watching. As the boat disappeared into the horizon, I wonder if life at sea will outlast life on land.

∞ ∞ ∞ ∞ ∞

I first encountered the Moken in 2001. During the 2004 tsunami that devastated the Indian Ocean shoreline, Burma was also flooded. Because Moken teachings hinge on ancestral storytelling, their elders knew that the initial, extraordinary low tide retreat of the sea indicated that a tidal wave was imminent. As a result, most Moken families immediately retreated to higher ground and were spared.

DIRECTION

BRACKET YOUR INDULGENCES
(Grenada)

Nobody gossips about virtue.

A mopey, well-fed stray hound strolls by and faintly sniffs me. I'm leaning against an impromptu beer truck on the fringe of a resort area on the Caribbean island of Grenada while distant Calypso music fills the barbequed night air. I'm fishing for West Indian gossip from the middle-aged guy whom I just gifted another icy brew. He grins and announces the same thing four times, as his songlike accent is lost on me until a fourth translation: "Who have cocoa in sun, look out for rain." This Grenadian proverb suggests minding your own business—as in, it takes six consecutive days to sun-dry cocoa beans, so pay attention to the weather instead of trivial matters. The mellow dog takes the cue and moseys elsewhere, but I stick around.

This lively traffic circle near Grand Anse beach borders a makeshift outdoor marketplace sarcastically named "Wall Street" because the strip-mall parking area is bookended by banks. Along with being a mini-bus hub, the circle attracts locals who gather to buy open-air grilled meat and drink beverages sold from ice chests in pickup beds. At night, cars blare music, creating instant parties. Unlike other over-priced Caribbean islands that are designed so tourists rarely meet non-resort personnel, here I'm dancing in a parking lot with grandmothers, sipping bargain brew.

Strolling away from Wall Street, I follow the sound of steel drums into a palm-tree surrounded auditorium to behold a showcase of senior Calypso musicians. It sounds happy, so I wonder why 500 fans are calmly seated. I find out that Calypso, a West Indies invention, is "listening music" that doubles as delivery for satire and political commentary. Now I understand why the concert-goers are chuckling more than foot-tapping. At this point, I still have no idea how passionate these folks are about their history and politics. A woman looks away from the stage and smiles at me. I'm going to like it here.

Spice Island is an apt metaphor, as all races blend here. Children don't speak about black or white skin, rather brown or peach skin. I stumble upon a new definition for relativity after meeting several men in my age bracket whose fathers had 10 or more offspring, sometimes with as many women. With so many folks related on this small island, everyone knowing each other keeps things safe. Also keeping the peace is their attachment to British Colonial law. One must bow to a picture of the Queen when entering a court. And if you swear, it's not hard to land there. Locals call this a "church state" because cursing within earshot of a cop can warrant an arrest.

A long way from church, I step out onto the beach and wander down to a seaside bar. Nuggets of Grenadian folklore fly at me from every direction. As the sun dips into the water, the wave-crashing soundtrack is competing with singing frogs—a tiny newt-like chorus that sounds like an army of loud piccolos. The bartender leans forward to tell me something arriving via "tele-Grenadian" (meaning, gossip spreads fast here). "Don't let the sun go down on it," he adds, urging everyone there to solve problems with loved ones quickly. There's just something about getting good advice when you're barefoot.

I hail a cab wanting to be delivered to a popular dance joint. My plans rapidly change, however, when my taxi driver pulls over. Also a recreation advisor, Keith gives the bar I'm heading to a thumbs-down and redirects us to a local joint where the upbeat Soca music takes center stage and gets Grenadians up and bouncing. They call it *whining*, pronounced why-ning, a carnal dance demonstration I first witnessed in Jamaica. Think doggie-style dancing couples swiveling for hours, rarely making eye contact with one other.

Five hours later, I ask Keith, "What time is it?" "GMT," he replies (Grenada Maybe Time).

The nutmeg on Grenada's flag is telling, as it's used to flavor many local dishes and heralded to cure everything from colds to infidelity. Taxi talent Keith and I share a few meals in local joints. The national dish is called oil down, namesaked by the coconut-milk oil residue that infuses the one-pot stew of breadfruit, callaloo, okra, cabbage, fish, dumplings, turmeric, and whatever else is on hand. While graduating from a heaping plate of oil down to brew, two schoolgirls in uniform sit across from us. Keith advises them, "Boys and books don't agree."

A few days later, Keith drops me off at the airport. As I walk away from his car, he reminds me, "What you miss ain't pass you." His way of saying, don't worry about anything, it's coming either way. He then retells me that copasetic is a Grenadian word.

A bad attitude is a disability. —Grenadian cabbie Keith

DIRECTION

DON'T USE MONEY TO KEEP SCORE
(Palau ~ Slovenia ~ Bahamas)

"There ain't no shame in being poor. Abraham Lincoln was poor." —Panhandling Manhattan-streetcorner sage

H ow people relate to wealth is telling. While kayaking through one of Palau's mangroves, I asked my guide about Palau's mythical money-bird (a *delerrok*), an archaic but slightly blinged-out dove symbolizing spiritual wealth. The image is everywhere, including dozens of representations etched on the capital building. The bird appears to be ingesting coin-shaped bits while simultaneously eliminating them from its other end. Legend has it that this bird gave birth to the bead money pieces once used for trading in ancient Southeast Asia. Other debated interpretations are "Can't take it with you" and "Eat money— crap money." Palauns' relaxed attitude toward affluence, and pretty much everything else, makes even Hawaii seem stressful.

∞ ∞ ∞ ∞ ∞

Slovenia

One benefit of being poor, a condition most of us will experience at least once in our lives, is that it shows you who your real friends are. The former Yugoslavian states—the Balkans, no stranger to hard times—have always viewed their neighbors in Slovenia as stubborn, hard-working mountain folks. And indeed, they were a vital manufacturing engine for that regime. Separated by only an arm of the Alps from neighboring Austria, mostly Roman Catholic Slovenia shares a Western European view of the world. Although some separate Slovenia from the Balkans, it remains indisputably Slavic and retells what a difference a mountain range can make.

In Slovenia's lake-hugging town of Bled, there's a small island in the middle of a lake that's the perch for the fairytale-come-true Church of St. Mary. Inside, visitors are encouraged to make a wish as they ring the immense church bells. The downside is that the gigantic bells clang all day long. The upside is that people seem to dig wishing for something while making sounds that can be heard for miles. Ninety-nine steps rise from the water's edge to this centuries-old church's entrance. A local wedding tradition urges grooms to carry their new brides up these steps. During the climb, the bride must remain silent—likely a fleeting moment.

I met newlyweds descending the steps of that fabled Slovenian church. I wished them well and then told them about a Bahamian minister who, a decade prior, married good friends of mine. That charming outdoor ceremony in the Bahamas got my attention when the minister looked at the bride and groom and pledged, "If you tell the truth about any problem, your problem becomes part of your past. But if you lie about it, it becomes part of your future."

Hopefully newlyweds everywhere have taken the time to get to know each other's ways, and understand that money stress is the number one cause of marital failure—drugs and infidelity rate second and third. Sooner or later, we all figure out that soul mates trump wild sex dates.

The Slovenian newlyweds promised to spread the Bahamian Minister's words. And the church bells tolled again.

DIRECTION

GET LOST AND FIND YOURSELF
(St. Barts)

Surviving extravagance.

S taying on track with trends can throw you off. When mobile, I seek a melding of culture shock, epic scenery, and goodwill. I shy away from many things French because it usually means plump prices, puny meal portions, and *that look* if you order the wrong wine, or worse, your meat cooked.

Testing this generalization on the French Caribbean island of St. Barts, I discovered that although the eight-mile-long volcanic island is no bargain, there is free fun to be had in the form of off-trail hiking. In a world where most people have limited or no access to drinkable tap water, jetsetter vacations come with some guilt. However, smelling all of the Earth's blossoms— from a besieged Syria to this star getaway in the West Indies—is as telling as it is polarizing.

Driving hilly St. Barts narrow, winding roads in a cab costs five bucks a minute, so my girlfriend Heather and I remained afoot on its less developed southeast coast. The island has 22 beaches—all public—that are interspersed with craggy cliffs.

The interior, which we found by default, is rocky and dry, as it lacks neighboring Saba's mountains tall enough to attract regular clouds. Nonetheless, because of the island's petite dimensions, I figured that any hike would soon meet a beach. Wrong.

The hike from Pointe a Toiny to Saline Beach seemed doable on the trail that leads to the Washing Machine, a cliff-encircled surfers' beach not recommended for amateurs. That's where the path vanished, launching us into a strange land. Trekking the arid ridgeline and bushwhacking beyond that landmark meant navigating cactus colonies and thorny brush while startling packs of wild goats. Dozens of meandering trails were, in fact, mislaid goat tracks, which left us scrambling in circles. "Holy shit, we're lost on St. Barts," I thought. I'm also thinking that this isn't exactly the birthday Heather imagined on St. Barts. And if I'm not mistaken, she's going to miss her spa appointment. "Only you and I would find ourselves bushwhacking our way across St. Barts," she said.

A wayward hour later, what we believe to be Saline Beach, one of the island's nude options, comes into view from afar, and the holiday begins again. There is even a disco soundtrack provided by a bobbing offshore party boat.

But we still had one more batty-goat valley to navigate. In the guts of that final basin, we found ourselves under some shady trees behind a small cove with only a final thorny cliff separating us from victory. Now confident we're going to make it, we unexpectedly spook a colony of camping French families, not surprising since we approached their hideaway from the mountainside and must have resembled thrashed fugitives. Noting their shocked expressions, I call out, "We're lost." At first, they say nothing and only stare in a state of disbelief. Then they break into laughter, and we hear *bonjour*. One of the kids, who is toasting a mini hot-dog on a stick held over a campfire, extends the branch toward Heather and offers to share his snack.

A peace offering from the French, and some realigning of my stereotype.

∞ ∞ ∞ ∞ ∞

"As long as you're trying to 'bridge the gap,' that means there's still a gap." —Wife, overheard arguing with husband in nearby Saint Maarten

DIRECTION

DIVIDE WISDOM

—*Prophetic sign for two towns accessed by Exit 102 on Idaho's Interstate 15*

Pittsburgh

After circling the Asian arc of the Pacific Rim for a year while America got acquainted with Guns 'N Roses, I hitchhiked, in stages, from Los Angeles to New York City. Twenty-five-years wise and a vagabond in full bloom, I visited an unsanctioned, smoldering garbage dump under an interstate bridge outside of Pittsburgh to look for material with which to craft an updated destination sign. In this unforeseen underworld, I ran into some needy people collecting broken furniture to feed the barrel fire heating their ramshackle hideout.

"Hunting wood, man?" one of them asked me.

"No, pal, I'm into cardboard," I answered, getting on my way.

Partly arrived and partly escaped, I stepped up onto the highway's shoulder and flashed my New York sign. The wind from a speeding truck made me stumble backwards. Silence returned until the voice of the man under the bridge shouted, "Bro, it ain't about where you from, it where you goin' that count."

∞ ∞ ∞ ∞ ∞

Poverty was the general rule in the Asia I'd just left, but the astute hobo residing beneath that Pittsburgh bridge was a poignant encounter with U.S. homelessness. The United Nations Human Development Index scale measures social wellbeing by quantifying longevity, education, and standard of living. Imagine graphs and numbers. Add inexplicable contentment to the scale, and this index doesn't do justice to the poor people cracking jokes in the less developed parts of the world. Traveling reveals that the poor inevitably spend more time with their families, and that the separation of children and grandparents is a somewhat alien concept.

It's hard to hear the people who are listening.

DIRECTION

PRESUME SMALL COUNTRIES HAVE BIG OUTLOOKS (Latvia)

Shades of freedom—evolving from red (communist) to green (democracy).

A s opposed to huge countries like the U.S., where some residents can live lifetimes without encountering foreigners, residents of small countries with numerous neighbors have global outlooks by necessity. A tiny country with a big reputation for nightlife, Latvia has been free from Soviet occupation since 1989. Its photogenic capital, Riga, is viewed by some untamed party-seeking Euros as an inexpensive binge getaway. It's not surprising considering that Riga's Old City overflows with inviting and inexpensive bars and restaurants. When inbound weekend warriors let their hair down, it can annoy the locals.

Riga's immense European-style central market is not on the party circuit. There, I asked a local what she thought about the inbound party animals. At that moment, a coiffed Russian sauntered by. Tearing the veneer off any illusion, the local nodded toward the showboat and replied with a twist: "That's what happens when a hairdo becomes a hair-don't."

I stood in that same spot near the seafood peddlers, and it got better. A hardcover book-toting local guy waltzed by, and I asked him about Latvian hairstyles. Lacking caché but logging originality, he predicted, "*Non*-judgment day is near." I remind myself that when you ask the wrong question, you'll rarely get the right answer.

Reborn Baltic liberty in the air, I accosted another local who waved me off with a Latvian slur. A nearby woman witnessed my dismissal and asked me if I needed help. I asked her how Latvian life had changed with democracy, and how Russians, their former occupiers, got along with Latvians. Her offering: Self-praise is not an endorsement.

Happy with that trio of swift informal interviews, I walked towards a doorway and saw an elderly man decked out in an Art Nouveau period outfit. Motionless, he stared contemplatively toward the market's breezy open-air exit. I waved hello, and he flapped a no thank you. The helpful woman I'd just met was keeping pace a step behind me. She saw me gesture toward the sharp-dressed man and again asked if I needed assistance. I said no, but leered toward the Art Nouveau guy suggesting that he might. They had a brief conversation and the man then exited the building.

"What did *he* say?" I asked her.

She pointed at the illuminated *EXIT* sign hovering over the arched stone doorway, and explained that he also regarded it as a starting point…

"Every exit is also an entrance."

∞ ∞ ∞ ∞ ∞

"Ten years ago, we sell all our snakes to China. So now we have many more rats. The rats are very tasty." —Deckhand, during float down Myanmar's Ayeyarwady River

DIRECTION

TAKE (HUMAN) WILDLIFE OFF THE
ENDANGERED SPECIES LIST
(Alberta ~ Costa Rica)

...But save the animals.

B e open to interspecies communication. Alberta, one of Canada's ten provinces, sits above Montana and shares its loathing for human herding. Alberta's vast mountain ranges and plains enable people and wildlife to coexist. Pretty much. The hearty people, boundless elk, and the resolute bull moose—cowish giants with antlers and street smarts—are all trying to coexist.

But, as human domains expand, moose inevitably roam into towns. In autumn, in hip places like Banff, they rub their antlers against itch-cordial objects to help shed winter velvet. Hammocks and swing sets are popular choices, but their antlers often become ensnared in them. The result is uprooting and parading hammocks and swings around town like jewelry. This mobile cargo easily entangles with trees and brush and endanger the animal and people. Then they need to be tranquilized while their antlers are detangled.

Perhaps these moose are trying to tell us something. We assemble societies replete with recreational objects, like hammocks and swings, but sharing the fate of most in-home exercise machines, we ultimately desert them for fancier gadgets. These patient beasts, losing territory to pavement and deforestation, challenge our progressing inertia by marching our abandoned self-indulgent paraphernalia down Main Street.

∞ ∞ ∞ ∞ ∞

"Having respect for the Endangered Species Act is admirable, but acting like an endangered species also deserves merit." — Chilean research scientist sighting a humpback whale

∞ ∞ ∞ ∞ ∞

Elk, by the way, share a similar recreation ethos in Alberta's Jasper National Park, a heavenly showcase of Canada's version of the Rocky Mountains. Jasper Village is a conscious exception for residential and business settlement within the massive park. A persistent dilemma in this long-term rental community is the "elk problem." Elk not cognizant of public indecency codes—those who breed next to restaurants and occasionally hip-check locals—involuntarily enter the 500-mile relocation program, a wilderness work release program with three strikes. After two relocations to the wilds, an elk's third lip-smacking gaze into a brew pub might be its last.

Jasper built a fence around its elementary school playground to keep male elk out during mating season; a spring break barricade of sorts. Wisely, bulls seek out spacious fields to ogle as many cows as possible, not unlike restless dudes trawling dance floors full of women. If you also take the long view, this bullish outlook suggests rediscovering the spirit of playgrounds, and your inner wild. Be a voluptuary.

∞ ∞ ∞ ∞ ∞

Costa Rica

One night in San Jose, Costa Rica, I was woken at 4am by an earthquake gauging 7.0 on the Richter scale. Crumbling ceiling plaster fell on me, and I anticipated my bed tumbling through the crackling fourth floor. After 30 seconds, the calm returned, and so did a memory from the previous week at a nearby beach. Wading chest deep in the Pacific Ocean's crashing surf, a mammoth heron rode the tubing crest of an immense wave that spanned the horizon, occasionally dipping its wingtip into the wave to adjust its flight balance, and, I hoped, to celebrate the day. When I turned my back on the surf, a mother and a colt jogged playfully along the shoreline. Animals play too.

Later that same day on the Costa Rican beach, I enjoyed a sunset. The local wildlife pundit sitting next to me identified osprey and bare-throated tiger herons as they fished in the surf. Breezy sundown rituals as ceremonial turning points rarely disappoint. Then, at twilight, low-flying brown pelicans swooped across the reddening sky. Above the faint thunder of crashing waves, the birdman pointed toward the winged flock, affirming, "There goes the Costa Rican Air Force." (Costa Rica has no military.) I wish he could have shared that news with a flock of NATO Generals.

DIRECTION

GET HIGH (Gulf of St. Lawrence)

We all need higher power.

Until boarding this big old wooden boat, my prior example of an earthling jiving with technology was a noisy city street backhoe operator manipulating two-ton metal plates with the ease of a thumb flipping a nickel. Now, I'm watching a Dutch ship captain choreograph dozens of ropes to tune 27 sails—each catching different notes in the wind. The German-built Europa, a 110-year-old, 265-foot-long masted tall ship, is circling the coast of Newfoundland, and affirming that newer isn't always better.

"It's instinct," says the grey-bearded, sandal-wearing skipper who has navigated from pole to pole. I couldn't think of anything else marine-like to discuss with this Norsemen, so my eyes wandered up the 100-foot mast. Sensing awe, he explained, "The masthead tops the mast for the bird's-eye view. Back in the day, that's where sailors served punishments, similar to a solitary confinement." We pondered oceangoing bylaws before lawyers and workmen's comp.

An hour later, a crab cake salts my blood and stirs me into summiting that mast. Accompanied by crewmember Heidi, we negotiate three successive, narrowing rope ladders. "Just don't look down," she said in her calming Dutch accent. But, peering up becomes the concern. Ascending further requires molting around two cumbersome platforms by disengaging from one flimsy ladder to regrip another. The ladder switches mean dangling while a foot searches for outcrops of steel and wire. Heidi, barefoot and lithe, makes it look easy, "Grab dis, den dis, den dare." I noted her naturally curly blonde hair and absence of makeup, then refocused. A mistake means plummeting to death and disturbing the crew's lunch.

Once settled upon the platform pinnacle, I was left alone, 10 stories high, to reflect. Motoring in windless calm, the ascent recalls the tree-climbing epoch—that arboreal era boys (and some girls) enjoy before adolescent puppy love dislodges after-school bonding high in a tree. With the sails down, my outlook is all North Atlantic Ocean, open sky, and this Canadian island's soaring cliff faces. In a daydream, I'm back atop a sappy pine tree, alone, and free.

We round a peninsula. Suddenly, the wind switches on, and the engine clicks off. A frenzy of sail-raising ensues with pulleys squeaking, ropes whizzing, the smell of something burning, and crewmembers simulating a frantic modern dance. The captain's muffled commands sound like nervous opera. I really am a landlubber. The now bulging sails make the highest crossbeam on my mast pivot 25 degrees, which cancels the view and my preferred route option to descend. I'm encased by enough thrashing sail to wrap a house. The wind redoubles and roars, sails quake, and my lofty lair tilts far enough to spill the pen from my pocket.

I'm on an hour-long ride most weekend warriors would bypass at the carnival. I contemplate descending on the seemingly inverted maze of twine that had recently served as a ladder. A grinning Heidi returns to my perch in the rigging to right the corkscrewed

Dutch flag flapping in my face, and note that "Dee lunch is over. Dare having drinks on deck." Observing my angst, she added, "You okay?" To invite calm, she presented a semi-relevant factoid: "Swimming in dee ocean, the horizon you see is a mile away. From here, dee horizon extends forever, yes?" Tongue-tied in this morass of rattling rigging, a foreboding Viking saying also blows in: "Never walk away from home ahead of your axe and sword." Adrenalized and craving sea level, I spin my head quickly and bang it into a taut rope, presumably a head-rope. Heidi snickers.

Wearing shorts on this wind-whipped perch, it becomes obvious that my veins lack Scandinavian anti-freeze. Quivering, I finally descend through the wild confusion of cordage that's flailing to and fro. Safely back on deck and high-stepping like a royal alpaca, I join the others for a frosty ale. When you change the way you look at things, the things you look at change. Heidi, a Latter-day Viking, walks by and winks—hinting that I'd be back for more—in a code that's for people having little use for land, and no fear of the high life.

DIRECTION

DON'T BE LIMP SEAWEED WHERE THE CURRENT IS STRONG (Palau)

This strange but familiar crossroads, a collection of tiny Micronesian islands in the Pacific Ocean, is tropical Americana on Southeast Asia's doorstep. This multinational intersection offers a taste of Asian diversity, American comfort, and the islands' homegrown friendliness. Rayvon, a grinning local from Palau's largest town, Koror, put it like this, "The Chinese build, the Japanese dive, the Filipinos work, and the well-behaved Taiwanese tourists are like locusts who *never* separate, even when floating in lifejackets." He also noted that Americans ask lots of questions.

Palauan president Johnson Toribiong, wearing a tropical-weight shirt with a floral pattern, told me that "The islands' biggest imports from the U.S. are democracy and Budweiser." But Palau's internationalism runs deeper than liberty and Bud. Locals use chopsticks to eat fries. Another jolly local named Badoi mused on past and present occupiers, saying, "The 1800's German takeover left fat hot dogs in our breakfast buffets, whereas the Japanese occupation can be traced to our prisoners carving fable-sharing wood storyboards. And, now as U.S. allies, we speak English, use the dollar, dig the NBA, and have drinkable tap water." Although Palau is partially Americanized, the locals consider fruit-bat soup to be a delicacy, and you'll likely be woken up by roosters—even at a swank resort.

Palau, however, didn't need any outside counsel regarding its concept of environmental sustainability, which is thousands of years old on the islands. Caretakers of the sea, Palauans maintain their hundreds of species of coral and other sea life via a *bul*, longstanding conservation rulings by the Council of Chiefs that are spread by word-of-mouth and signs posted on the beaches. For example, one biodiversity warning reads: "Go easy on the rabbit fish." Here, an offender's entire family is fined for disregarding the bul. Some of the rules governing Palau's original matriarchal society also prevail. Women are prominent in every aspect of society, which may be why Palauan dudes favor chilling under baseball caps, behind their shades.

As opposed to the moderately effective and rarely enforced U.S. buls, including no littering, spitting, or being an ass, I imagined a conservation sign that Uncle Sam might post upon his soil…

Warning for Women: Guys Who Want Sex The Most Usually Want Kids The Least.

∞ ∞ ∞ ∞ ∞

Just before flying back to my home, I was enlightened about how some Palauans obtain theirs. I met a sunglass-wearing guy whose father named him Corleone after the *Godfather* movies. Santa-like but tan, Corleone told me about the tradition of money-doubling house parties. When you make a down-payment on a house, you invite friends over, and they each give you, say $100. Then, when your pals buy theirs, you have to give them $200.

This reciprocal favor pays it forward—and who wouldn't want to repay a guy named Corleone?

∞ ∞ ∞ ∞ ∞

Hard rain calms rough waters. —Palauan fisherman

DIRECTION

PREPARE TO FAIL WHEN YOU BAIL
(Zimbabwe)

*When a country is politically ripped apart, the seeds
of hope survive.*

S urvey the media on any given day and horrible news about
the country formerly known as Rhodesia is inevitable.
Zimbabwe, as it's now known, continuously made headlines for
the starvation of its people, a 75-percent unemployment rate,
cholera epidemics, an abandoned currency, and the silencing of
dissidents and journalists. That avalanche of bad news cloaks
a reality—Africa's Adrenalineville, the Victoria Falls region,
is still open for business. Rafting on class-five rapids, giving a
full-grown lion a massage, and beholding the epic Victoria Falls
is only a taste. When the Zambezi River—Africa's umbilical
cord—tumbles over the Victoria Falls shelf into an infinite
gorge, it creates a steamy spray that can be seen from space.

When visiting places with bad raps, you have to keep your guard
up but not close yourself off. That goes beyond asking why that
band of submerged hippos, eyes peering from the waterline, are
staring at you.

The theme of never giving up had legs, literally, as I did have to deal with a pesky criminal. While staying in a hotel with a thatched grass-straw roof, a persistent Ververt monkey religiously stormed my balcony to see if my back doors remained locked. A burglar extraordinaire, every two hours, she jumped onto the balcony, marched over to the base of the hinged wooden doors and punched at them to see if I'd forgotten to lock up. I named this unashamed looter Mugsy. Each time Mugsy bounded away defeated, my gaze stretched out over the verdant Zambezi River jungle basin, reminding me that this was her world. As payback for my locked door, she jumped up and down upon my roof twice a day like a rebellious teenager, or more like a warped prison guard reminding the caged man below who's in charge.

I later found out that Mugsy bounded from hotel room balcony to balcony, 72 in all, on a predictable schedule. At least once a day, she scored and scoured a room in 10 seconds. Prized snack targets included coffee and sugar packets, toothpaste, and medications. As I was packing to leave the hotel I noticed that my vitamins were missing and nowhere to be found. Perplexed and hoping I hadn't been outwitted by a monkey, I asked a maid about the vitamins. She explained that Mugsy had recently figured out how to send one of her babies through windows that were slightly ajar to fetch and then deliver the loot to Mugsy waiting on the other side of the window.

Ingenuity.

DIRECTION

PRESERVE THE ICE OR ROLL THE DICE
(High Arctic)

We know more about outer space than our polar oceans.

E ncounters on Arctic islands reveal a region bracing for battle. Our Russian icebreaker downshifts as a fogged-in island comes into view. We anchor near Holman, a treeless seaside village of 400, known by locals as *Ulukhaktok*. A string of modest cabins rim the shore. I climb a rise leading past a graveyard rimmed by a picket fence meet Dave Kuptana, a retired wildlife guide and stone carver. He's working in the yard that doubles as his shop, sitting at his carving table and wearing oversized overalls. All of his 400 pounds seem focused on sculpting, until I get him talking about ice. With squinting eyes, he emphasizes, "Last winter, we only got two polar bears." This fringe above the Northwest Territories mandates that Holman can only hunt 20 polar bears per year; 10 for local consumption and 10 for visiting sport hunters paying as much as $35,000, which supports the community. The meat of hunted animals is stored in underground permafrost freezer huts and also shared communally. Permafrost freezes the ground more than 1,000 feet deep in these parts. The center of their map is the North Pole.

Mellow but judicious Kuptana is a middle-aged Holman native. He remembers decades past when local waters were completely frozen through July, making the area optimum polar bear territory for most of the year. Looking towards the bay, Kuptana explains that now there's no ice in May, only open water, so they're in boats having to go more than 100 miles for bears. He chisels a bit more on his stone polar bear, then adds a merry-eyed muse on the choicest bear parts: "The meat with the fat on it." His grin lingers. Shifting the conversation to the local youth, he explains that the key to winning over kids was insisting that they "follow our tradition" by "listening to the teachers." Then, in a deeper tone he urges, "We can't lose our dialect."

None of Canada's 26 High Arctic communities are accessible by road or rail. The native Inuit—formerly called Eskimos—learned many of their hunting techniques from the bears. But, hunting modes are shifting from dogsleds to snowmobiles, skin kayaks to motor boats, and harpoons to rifles. In High Arctic communities, Christmas comes in the form of one yearly delivery via barge.

Getting to the High Arctic is not easy. Sea carnivalites (soft ice-cream cruisers) seek tropical breezes while cruise extremists deliberately voyage into polar fog—before the top of the world forever tips off its icy hat. My 2,000 nautical-mile voyage through the Arctic's Northwest Passage, a seasonal Atlantic to Pacific Ocean link, navigated the same bays and narrow ice-choked channels that immobilized or killed explorers for 400 years until a crafty Norwegian conquered the maze in 1905.

Unlike Antarctica, a continent shielded by an ocean, the High Arctic is a floating ice-cap encircled by continents. It also differs from Antarctica, which is forever environmentally guarded by the globally signed 1959 Antarctic Treaty, in that the five countries bordering and laying claim to the Arctic region—Canada, Russia, Norway, Denmark and the U.S.—have yet to agree on anything. Mining, oil, and gas claims aside, the accelerating meltdown means the Northwest Passage could soon be a cheaper and quicker freighter ship transit option than the costly Panama Canal. A wave goodbye to one of our last pristine holdouts. Someday we're all going to realize we're in this together. Until then, the geopolitical cash sabers rattle as the disappearance of ice destroys polar bear, seal, and Arctic peoples' habitats.

Another day at sea, the ship battles more ice, the floating chunks resembling an inverted cloudy sky. We eventually land on the island of Gjoa-Haven, another dirt-road survival hamlet where most elders speak only Inuit. A dozen boxy homes upon stilts have porches with banisters that are draped with the skins of caribou, musk ox, brown bear, and polar bear—as a suburban neighbor might dry a sheet. The patchwork of hides slung about made me think of how some metropolitan dwellers share their recent exploits in the form of a mud-splattered SUV in the driveway.

Throughout this region, children seem to be interchangeable among family and friends. There are no rules for the kids as Inuits don't like saying no. Adoption, regardless of fertility, is an integral part of society. They're also not big on small talk; silence is accepted and normal and hellos and goodbyes are unnecessary. Hospitality requires no thanks, and handshakes are pointless. Known for their Herculean stamina and contemplative personalities, Inuits share everything, in fact it's an unspoken cultural mandate. The traditional Inuit, who honed a culture for centuries, on and in ice, had among the fewest natural resources of any people on Earth, making them the epitome of cultural success.

Walking along a beach in this wild north, I'm clutching a pencil because pens freeze. I imagine passing a local 50 years ago as he carries a wet seal over his shoulder. It's one of my Arctic daydreams. When you're cut off from life as you know it, your mind wanders like it was designed to. I pondered my sixteenth story igloo-sized domain back in New York City. Weeks later, riding the elevator up to that cement bungalow, I keep in mind that if you do what you've always done, you'll get what you've always gotten. And then realize the Inuit don't have either option. There's no more dice to roll. No ice, no dice.

As the Northwest Passage opens for business, Arctic political diplomacy will be strained, further straining this way of life. Hopefully, the Inuits' knowing glimpses won't turn into the blank stare of climate refugees. What happens next is largely up to us. Just as winds are designated by the direction from which they blow, a polar visit reminds us that the Earth's warm-up is coming, not going. How we treat our poles, where mere footprints can last a thousand years, is our last chance to do things right. Where the law is silent, ethics should speak.

With the icebreaker anchored off Victoria Island, I strolled into the village namesaked Resolute. An all-terrain vehicle buzzes along a rutted road. Pointing at the teenager's ATV, I inquire "That ATV must be fun on the beach?" "We don't have a TV," he replied, and motored on.

∞ ∞ ∞ ∞ ∞

During British Prime Minister Gordon Brown's first visit to President Obama's White House, he gifted Obama with a framed commissioning paper for the HMS Resolute, a three-masted Royal Navy ship that came to symbolize British-American goodwill. After being trapped by Arctic icebergs, it was then rescued by an American whaler and returned to Queen Victoria in 1856. More telling, the White House's Oval Office desk, the Resolute Desk, was constructed from that ship's timbers and has been used by many presidents since 1880. Until I'd landed on the Inuit island named after that ship, I could only partially define resolute. As it became apparent, some of the *coolest* people in the world live along the world's most dangerous shortcut.

DIRECTION

BE BAD AT SAD (Cosmos)

Take note.

S miling is involuntary, not learned. Even children blind from birth smile. So, you've definitely got it in you. Weathervanes usually complement the type of building upon which they're placed. In that vein, we tend to wear our inner climate on our faces. Smiles, a universal symbol of happiness, can inspire contagious winds of change. Whether forcing a grin through collagen-injected lips that have swelled into a trout pout, proudly showing off missing teeth, or bringing rations into a smile famine, a grin is a gift. So give one up, or inspire one. Let your teeth see the light.

If you're in a rut and struggling, observe and contemplate how other people process ups and downs. You're not the only one sometimes wondering when things are going to improve. But this is easy to forget if you don't commit the communal nature of life's rollercoaster to memory. Archiving is a timeless delight. Pen and paper never lose battery power, and they're discreet. You'd be surprised by the lesson-sharing moments you've witnessed and forgotten because you didn't jot them down. So, throughout life, be a good date for yourself and don't succumb to idea bankruptcy. These road scribbles are testaments to the lightness of the heaviness. There is stand-up comedy everywhere…

"Millionaires leave their tees behind, but billionaires bend over and pick them up—because they know the value of a nickel." —Telling caddy testimonial about Nantucket's rich-and-famous golf set

"I haven't been held like that in a long time."—Elderly British woman after I helped her, practically in bear-hug mode, step down to exit a horse-drawn carriage

"I was really focused, I mean like D.D.A. focused (as in, the opposite of A.D.D.)" —Divorced Trinidadian man on pursuing flight attendant

"If that's true, then waterfalls are rivers giving up and leaping off cliffs." —Albanian optimist negating a pessimist

"Potted trees are not the athletes of trees." —Belgian man's reaction to hearing about the pine trees growing in buckets on my apartment's fire escape

"Trees only look green because that's the name we gave that color." —Same Belgian man, now wearing tiny spectacles

"Your smile is great, but I'm not hanging around to see if your dog smiles." —Sri Lankan woman with dog phobia

"Smile, it won't mess up yo' hairstyle." —New York F-train crooner

"When you all thinks the same, you know, none of you thinks. — Border patrolman regarding my unlawful entrance into Tanzania

"Not all pioneers roamed in the same direction." —Neighbor defending my runaway dog, Ben, a thoroughbred beagle with some listening issues

"I only shoot a camera." —Anti-gun El Salvadorian shutterbug

"Are you an emergency Catholic?" —Woman in Dubai mall commenting on my mention of God while under duress

"I just saw a white guy with Chinese tattoos that were loaded with typos." —Chinatown, N.Y. dumpling shop patron

"I'm right-handed, whereas the guy I see in my mirror brushes his teeth lefty. See, everybody's different." —Bryan Northam

"Here, we all pay our share. Speeding tickets are issued according to salary. A rich Nokia executive was fined $200,000 for his racing." —Overheard in Finnish *Sauna* (the one Finnish word we all know)

"Please try not to be evolution's dead end." —Maltese museum curator, after spying an American tourist stroking a 12th century suit of armor

"Ladies and gentleman, this is your dining car attendant. I had the baked chicken, and it changed my life." —Amtrak employee's train announcement

"What grows together goes together." —Gracious and proudly dressed Zimbabwean speaking eloquently and sharing a wide, white smile. There's a reason for that illuminating grin. Many seemingly poor locals I met, raised in non-electrified villages, ate only organic foods and had never ingested processed foods in their lifetime

"Why *weight*?" —Tahitian beach bartender's play on words to dismiss customer's concern about fancy drink's calorie count

"No way to dull the polish on 'dis diamond!" —beaming outdoor weightlifter in Karachi, Pakistan, who lived outside beneath a tarp draped over his weight set

"Spendonomics...the study of what people buy to make themselves happy...or me." —backpacking panhandler in Luxembourg

"You live to leave!" —New Caledonian bus driver.

∞ ∞ ∞ ∞ ∞

Another on-the-road pastime, and part of a long-standing bet, is observing the number of times that people—conversing in parks, on street corners, and over restaurant meals around the world—physically touch each other within 10 minutes. Here's the tally:

São Paulo, Brazil: 28

Paris, France: 13

Betong, Thailand: 4

Budapest, Hungary: 2

Geneva, Florida: 2

Reykavik, Iceland: 1

London, England: 0

Montevideo, Uruguay: -1

Note: A fleeting cheek kiss may not qualify as touching if it doesn't at least include a mini hug.

DIRECTION

IF YOU WISH TO BE A DIFFERENT FISH, JUMP INTO A NEW SCHOOL (Montenegro)

Do fish living in ponds contemplate other ponds?

O n a mission to dissect what makes traveling such an amazing undertaking, I kept bumping into a singular gist. At the core of travel is asking strangers questions. Randomly doing this, or not, very much dictates your experience. Information-sharing strangers can become temporary acquaintances, or better. This epiphany also revealed how I cope in New York and other mega-cities. You can turn any day into an adventure by striking up conversations with would-be strangers on any street or wherever else you might encounter anonymity.

Way less popular is accosting strangers on public transportation. Not only do I frequently kickstart conversations on mundane trains and buses but I also introduce strangers. These suddenly fashioned focus groups turn heads, and the fun multiplies. Further, decades down the line I still enjoy lasting friendships with several people I've met on subways in my hurried hometown metropolis.

∞ ∞ ∞ ∞ ∞

Life makes some stay and some go. My childhood pals probably wouldn't recognize the kind of travel companion I've become—someone once married to the road and loyal to making that relationship thrive. Friends who join me automatically acquire the travel wand. They decide everything while I suggest tweaks in the path, by spotting otherwise unidentified Most Valuable Players; trusty locals able to help us hone a state-of-the-art jaunt.

While traveling through the former Yugoslavian country known as Montenegro, I was joined by a Boston-bred pal I'd met in Thailand in the 1990s. We hit the capital city, Podgorica, blind and off the rattletrap bus without a plan. There, my friend insisted we first find a hotel near the bus station, then figure out food and leisure, but I swayed him to be open to a goodwill mosey. Letting chance decide led us into a well-staffed but empty supermarket where we parked our packs, shopped for snacks and beer, and chatted with the cashiers about our afternoon options. Acting on a suggestion, we were two mid-life dudes toting backpacks and walking down a broad sidewalk. We stopped easygoing, 30-something Vladimir, who was heading in the opposite direction. We invited him to join us at the riverside place he recommended, and the three of us took off into the summer heat.

We landed at a sprawling open-air restaurant overlooking the cooling Morača River. An ethno folk band with the accordion and harmonica taking center stage served as the backdrop. Talking about Vladimir's life, work, play, and the seismic governmental shifts that upended his homeland was a Balkan highlight. Time evaporated as we got the real scoop about emerging from a dictatorship into a democracy. Nothing comes easy. We enjoyed buying him drinks he wouldn't otherwise be able to afford, while he gifted us with Montenegrin insight. Meanwhile, locals fished and bathed in the nearby river.

As our bond deepened, he insisted we call him Vlad. He then guided us to two more party spots. The first was a trendy Hindugroove-themed mist-spraying hive with overhanging plants and a fancy drink menu where duos chatted. The other was a chain-smoker disco teeming with wannabe lingerie models. The makeup-encrusted dolls were nearly doing backbends to balance themselves above their forearm-length spiked heels. They said nothing as their lipsticked pouts stayed cemented around glowing cigarettes. One of them stared curiously at Vlad. He nodded her way but spoke to us, "An ostrich's eye is bigger than its brain." Vlad's multihued tour shared the abundance found in the pond of a man less traveled.

Years later, I continue trading emails with Vlad, keeping the reason for roving alive. He can't afford to visit the States, possibly ever in his lifetime. Often, life isn't fair on many levels, and fortunate Americans, including me, need to travel internationally to grasp that. Montenegro's landlocked capital is chock-full of uniform, sober buildings echoing the dismal Soviet concrete era, but mannerly Vlad made it shine. He's one of those otherwise elusive people who boosts a visit into a venture—or even better, a special occasion.

It doesn't take much to stop someone on the street and sway the day.

DIRECTION

LET CHOICE AND CHANCE DANCE
(Greece)

What are words worth?

Mulling café options at the base of the Athens Acropolis, I'm hailed by an elderly man wearing a patch over one eye. He's selling sun-bleached postcards that dangle from clothespins clipped on a string suspended by ancient stone blocks. The most crinkled and faded postcard features a smiley face with a Greek caption. Pointing, I ask him about the caption. His buy-sell English vocabulary has expired, so I buy it anyway and tip the tan merchant for a pleasant exchange.

Later, back in an agreeable one-star hotel, the night receptionist translates the postcard, calmly explaining that Aristotle's word for happiness, εὐδαιμονία, decodes as eudemonia, which means human flourishing. "It is," the student continues, "any philosophy that makes happiness central." Folding sheets, she adds, "But, Aristotle's happiness isn't about wealth or power... it's about excellent behavior." You can be enlightened anywhere.

I mail the postcard to myself, and then head for home. Inflight, it occurs to me that the Bible, Koran, and Torah were written by people who believed the world was flat. Unwavering lifestyle advisory clubs overflow with yings and yangs on how to live righteously. What kind of price has humanity paid for surrendering to shrines of identity? Emerson's and Thoreau's philosophy of self-reliance, learning raw lessons from nature, seems timely. In their natural state, plants and trees receive nutrients by recycling their own fallen leaves. Once that cycle of nature is disturbed, non-native species take hold and the strangling vines take over.

Adjust your happiness to fit reality, instead of cramming your reality into someone else's version of it. Perhaps happiness comes not from doing what we like to do, but from liking what we must do. Struggling for most of the comforts and luxuries we consider essential might cost us more than these things are worth. Truth and originality are stronger than deadbolts and chains. Mail that postcard to yourself.

∞ ∞ ∞ ∞ ∞

"No one tears a piece from a new garment and sews it on an old garment; otherwise the new will be torn, and the piece from the new will not match the old." —Jesus parable (Luke 6.5/33), read by Naso tribesman in a rustic Panamanian church

"Nature abhors a vacuum." —Maltese gent, trying to lure customers into empty disco

DIRECTION

REMEMBER, BEAUTY CAN BE IN
THE EYE OF THE BE-OLDER
(North Africa ~ New Caledonia ~ Manila)

Your originality is your greatest legacy.

As a teenager, I had the privilege of living across the hall from my grandmother, Edith, until she passed away at 101 years of age. We attribute her radiant longevity to three factors: cottage cheese with pears, a daily Bufferin aspirin, and a shot of bargain Scotch before bedtime.

A loyal ally, she didn't report my playing hooky from school, or the high school parties I threw while my parents were away at our cabin in the Adirondacks. At such parties—my living room transformed into a classic rock-blaring suburban hippie den— my British-raised grandmother would make 11pm bathrobed appearances in our den-adjoined kitchen to fetch and sip that medicinal shot of Scotch. We'd then give her a rousing ovation, as if she were on stage. She then shuffle back to her bedroom, giggling all the way.

∞ ∞ ∞ ∞ ∞

North Africa

Palm strike to forehead: when in Rome, dress on your own. Real style shouldn't give a damn. While creating North African episodes of *American Detour*, I featured athletic sandals in a video. Soon after, the sandal theme ran away with itself—becoming a time to ponder masculinity and the art of footwear.

The world over, men and women have their respective roles, as do married and single men. Like most bachelors, I have nearly full control of my wardrobe. When I'm in a country boasting ruins from the Roman Empire (and there are dozens), they seem a fit locale to highlight the crucial wardrobe component of footwear. Slaves to fashion perceive the donning of utilitarian Velcro-strapped sandals as a catastrophic style no-no. Yet, in virtually all surviving outposts of the Empire, every male statue features a Herculean God wearing simple sandals—*sandalias*, flat-footed Roman shoes tied around the ankle with thin leather strips that omit gender distinction. Why aren't they cool anymore?

Footwear, like zip codes, now influences with whom you mingle. High-heeled ladies, who won't give a double-take to any fellow sporting open-toed shoes, tend to flirt with slick shiny-shoed guys. When did contemporary men and women lose sight of the shoes that made and shaped history? Fierce Romans conquered the world in sandals, maybe even with black socks.

What do modern Roman guys think about this? Wait, all they want to do is flirt with flashily dressed American chicks. We've got to get back to basics—or create sandalias with laces that go boot-high. Versatile footwear should also be sexy in a world where people in flip-flops can still rock it. Perhaps I've taken the footwear metaphor too far in search of a means of helping people blindly crisscross the fashion finish line. If only those sandal-wearing Roman big-shot statues could speak…

"It never troubles the wolf how many the sheep may be." —

Virgil, 70-19 B.C.

∞ ∞ ∞ ∞ ∞

"Don't age. Mature." —A New Caledonian antique buff's advice...after picking me up hitching, but actually swindling me into an hour of yard work.

∞ ∞ ∞ ∞ ∞

Manila, Philippines

A photographer sets up a tripod on a roadside in a dingy, untouristed neighborhood outside Manila, the Philippine city of 17 million. He aims to freeze-frame the charm of an old rusting bicycle that's leaning against a blue stucco wall flocked by birds-of-paradise. Dozens of elementary students on recess crowd around to watch him vary compositions shot with different lenses from different angles. Halfway through the shoot, one wholly engrossed little boy couldn't resist asking why he was taking so many photographs of the weathered bike, "when there are so many new ones around the corner?"

DIRECTION

DISCOVER WHAT'S COOKING IN THE KITCHEN (Morocco)

The world over, the kitchen is often the most fun place in a house—even if it's portable.

Deep in the heart of Morocco's Riff Mountains, I hiked a rocky hillside shadowed by olive trees and befriended a 30-year-old shepherd wearing a ski cap crowned by a pom-pom. He was the commander of 50 goats and 20 sheep. After a lesson on flock-control fundamentals—tree-branch coaxing, pebble throwing, grunting, and hissing—we exchanged impromptu gifts, butter rum Lifesavers and cashews. I helped bring the herd home to his home, lost somewhere in the narrow, winding byways of Chefchaouen's blue-rinsed houses.

We settled in the dirt-floor kitchen, drank some Moroccan whiskey (sweet mint tea), and smoked *kif* (pipe-tobacco-smelling stuff) from a sixty-inch *sebsi* pipe. The peace-pipe celebration gained momentum when his mother, brother, and sister made their presence known, and we all got chatty playing the name-that-kitchen-utensil game in both Arabic and English. Pot-holder won the most laughs. Meanwhile, in the next room, their livestock baaad, grunted, and mooo'd. Inside three walls but still sort of outside, this was not the Morocco portrayed in brochures. Home isn't a place, it's a mood—where habits have a habitat.

The shepherd explained, "Your home is everything you can walk to," and removed his sandals.

Kitchens are the spiritual hearth of any home and offer the most authentic cultural experience. While living rooms are peoples' deliberate offering (framed pictures, keepsakes, possibly a television), their more confidential kitchen speaks volumes about who they are and how they endure.

Sometimes, a kitchen delivers itself to you, and I don't mean by way of a hot-dog cart. Throughout the developing world, especially in Asia, bicycles and motorbikes are equipped with portable sidecar kitchens, intact with propane or twig-burning grills. These drifting chefs can whip up masterpieces that overhaul the concept of delivery.

While in distant lands—where most travelers' illnesses are foodborne—it is sometimes necessary to chaperone the chef you wouldn't otherwise see. A way to discover what's happening to your food is crafting an invitation into the kitchen while your meal is being prepared. When language barriers are insurmountable, point to the items you want, and see for yourself that meat or other portions are fully cooked. Bring home the recipes. Kitchens shouldn't be confidential.

∞ ∞ ∞ ∞ ∞

"What's a soup kitchen?" —Paris Hilton

"Too much dunking the trunk." —Mumbai elephant pilot's symbolic analysis of what makes people chubby

DIRECTION

DON'T PREDICT WHAT YOUR HEART MIGHT DECIDE (Brunei)

Realize great riches don't mean no hitches.

S outheast Asia is a 10-nation amalgam of wildly diverse cultures. Countries include the democratic Philippines (largely Christian), culturally disparate Indonesia (world's largest Muslim population), wealthy Singapore, agrarian Cambodia, and for decades, a military-ruled Burma. The regional diversity is further spiced by its Sultan-reigned neighbor.

Brunei, a kingdom smaller than Delaware, is ruled by an unbroken line of Sultans dating back 600 years. Asia's version of high-end Islam, the last Malay monarchy is where people play golf and polo, and recline poolside in swank resorts. It's also a decadent place to suspend certain indulgences. Think doable rehab, as alcohol is prohibited.

This version of royalty assures that the country's population has a much higher standard of living than most in Southeast Asia. It's the Asian Muslim world's Vegas, minus the hookers, gambling, and pretty much everything else that might be considered naughty. That said, Muslim men in Brunei are allowed to have up to four wives. The Sultan head of state showed restraint by only having two. Balancing that self-discipline, he has accumulated 5,000 uniquely modified cars worth $4 billion. The ruling Sultan controls religious affairs and is the self-titled prime minister, defense minister, and finance minister. I think that's illegal in Switzerland. Boys and girls holding hands is banned there, which is strange, considering grown men holding hands platonically is common in many other Muslim countries. But not everyone can be controlled. The Sultan's wayward brother's bad-boy antics reassign Charlie Sheen to the choir. There's one in every family.

"If you open the window you get sunshine—but also let in bees." —Brunei tourism official's press conference response to a question about Brunei's strict visa policy for the Chinese

I stayed in the most over-the-top, posh joint imaginable. But, somehow lacked charm. I've never been a fan of marble floors and walls, and mirrors everywhere unsettle me. I'm bored, but hopeful. Luckily, His Majesty's tiny quarter is surrounded by millions of acres of Malaysian jungle. Before heading out into those wilds, I dined with a sage American CEO. He supplied the earthiest moment to be had there. I asked him if he noticed one human personality trait that was a sure ticket to financial success. He apologized for not having more time to go in depth about his observation, but he left me with this concept: When advice boils down to either here's what you should do versus here's what I would do if I were you, the latter is usually wiser guidance.

Here's what I would do if I were *you* in Southeast Asia: postpone Brunei until you crave law and order.

DIRECTION

SOLVE THE MARRIAGE PUZZLE
(Malaysia)

Beat the odds, before cohabiting does.

Knee-wobbling charisma doesn't go very far in Jakun culture, where a bit of tribal technology imposes a buffer between men and women. Here, tenacity outweighs yearning. The Jakun tribe call a wild jungle near Malaysia's Endau Rompin National Park home. Known as animists, they believe that animals, plants, and mountains possess a spiritual essence. They also prefer to be barefoot.

The Jakun have irrepressible smiles and an interesting tradition for determining romantic connections. Complex codes don't govern courtship here. Instead, the people have adopted a Darwinist Rubik's Cube of sorts. Their marriage puzzle is a pencil-sized section of bamboo containing an interior string creating two intertwined loops. From each loop hangs a bamboo ring. In order to marry within the tribe, both men and women must first figure out how to manipulate both rings to one loop.

With coaching from a villager, it took me 10 minutes to figure out the puzzle. Another Western bachelor was still twisting fruitless knots when I departed hours later. Based on his whining and the twisted look on his face, it's probably best he remain single.

∞ ∞ ∞ ∞ ∞

The mountainous spine in this part of Malaysia continues northward along Southeast Asia's narrow landmass and eventually joins the Himalayas. I wondered if this marriage puzzle migrated from—or to—that part of the world. It seems that online matchmaking sites are doing a good job at pre-sorting deal-breaking issues like religion, income, politics, and other possibly polarizing issues. But, sometimes you can say it all with four words: My heart, her sleeve.

∞ ∞ ∞ ∞ ∞

"Do not choose your wife at a dance, but in the field among the harvesters." —Prague tavern scholar citing a Czech proverb

"Wildebeests have been known to run themselves to death while attempting to elude mosquitoes." —Robert Drake Martin III, comparing divorce in human culture to the realm of wild game

DIRECTION

MAKE A BID FOR LOVE (Tunisia)

*Bachelors dine together because they don't choose
to take home the fish.*

S urprisingly, an Arab fish auction can foretell marital status.
When I visited Tunisia in 2008, it was still enjoying an
easygoing vibe. Although that feeling was tested by the 2011
people's revolution, guys and gals continue to court in sync with
their ancestors.

Tunisia, Africa's northernmost country, is an idiosyncratic
melting pot of Arab, French, and progressive Muslim influences.
As a result of various multicultural influences, it's not uncommon
to see Tunisians walking around in football jerseys, carrying
loaves of French bread, and singing in English.

On Jerba, Tunisia's largest Mediterranean island, a fish market
bustles in the corner of a buzzing marketplace. Under the shelter
of a hot tin roof, three auctioneers stood on a stage before 50
shoppers, all male. The hawkers each clutched two to 10 fish
raised above their heads while chanting prices to the bidders. The
guys buying fish, like men everywhere, fell into two categories:
single or married. I was told that the married men bring the fish

home to their wives who then cook a family meal. The bachelors, however, tote their fish to local restaurants where, for a small fee, it's cooked for them.

This reminded me that we sometimes need to change to make relationships work. In our "if it bleeds, it leads" media bubble, it's often difficult to see the softer side of Islam. Many have difficulty even differentiating among people who are Arab, Muslim, or Islamic. It's important to note that not all Muslims are Arabs. Ninety-five percent of the people born in Turkey are Muslim but consider themselves Turks, not Arabs. Sixty percent of the world's Muslims live in South and Southeast Asia, with over 1 billion adherents. Muslims can honor their religion with varying degrees of loyalty, just as Christians' devotion can range from daily prayer to church-going only on Christmas Eve.

One of the challenges creating the culture clash between Western religions and Islam is how the Bible and the Koran are interpreted. The different ways people construe love can also instigate misunderstandings. One evening riding the New York City subway—often a crammed dungeon where strangers seldom chat—I realized that my personal interpretation of relationship bliss had degenerated considerably. Female F-train commuters seem to out-read subway-riding men by two to one. The woman sitting beside me was reading a yellowed paperback with a chapter titled, *Treatment for Divine Love*. I automatically assumed that treatment indicated a cure for love. I inquired about her interpretation of that chapter, and she testified that the treatment specified a recipe for love, as in a movie script that ultimately delivered romance. Whoops.

Finding romance in Tunisia is no less challenging. As I peered about the Tunisian nightlife scene one last time, I wondered which guys were heading home to the Mrs. and which were heading to a public barbeque. In an Arab nation where boys' night is often defined as sitting around wonky plastic tables in a café with 26 other guys—all slugging orange sodas while charbroiling their lungs with cigarettes and arguing about football—marriage seems like the way to go. It's enough to make some consider heading back into that market and bringing that fish home.

∞ ∞ ∞ ∞ ∞

Money can buy things...but it doesn't *make* things. —Tunisian saying, shared by father incensed by his sons' craving of flat-screen televisions more than wives.

DIRECTION

FIND SOMEONE WHO IS WRONG FOR
YOU IN JUST THE RIGHT WAY (Croatia)

"You can have the rock, I need to roll." —*London bachelorette*
fleeing wedlock

E lectricity pioneer Nikola Tesla lived in Croatia. Interestingly
enough, across from Tesla's outdoor commemorative plaque
is one of the city's 250 charming and functional streetlight gas
lamps, an example of history winking at innovation.

A few blocks from Tesla's plaque, old and new mingle again.
The Stone Gate is the last remaining of the five gates that once
guarded the old city, now bustling Zagreb. I huddled beneath
this hulking thirteenth-century arched entrance with other
tourists where there's a much studied and admired painting of
the Virgin Mary that's surrounded by dozens of tribute tablets.
A particular sentiment on the tribute wall praising Mary was
getting considerable attention. It was a remnant of a bygone era
that shared a timeless message: "Thank you Mother for your
help throughout 50 years of marriage."

Everlasting vows are not lost on this former Yugoslavian country.
Croatia was the first Balkan nation to use its own language

for services inside the Catholic Church, and the evolution of language is still being heard outside of it. I was among others silently admiring Mary's homage when a young couple standing next to me broke the silence. The man asked the woman, "Why is it easier to ask for forgiveness than permission?"

We all know a couple who want a peace prize for surviving 50 *weeks* of marriage…

∞ ∞ ∞ ∞ ∞

"Don't judge against the almighty, judge against the alternative."
—Woman adapting her ultimatum for man in bar

"If you do that, many forests of newsprint will die." — Connecticut wife threatening to sell many papers by making news in response to her husband's resolution (an all dude vacation) to ending an argument

DIRECTION

LET YOUR TEARS SOAK THE SEEDS OF BLISS (Mexico)

Communal living tempts misgiving.

Bus rides offer a magnifying glass on humanity. Upstate New York's Woodstock 1994 was a three-day music festival that was challenged by monsoonal rains that created knee-deep mud and a breakdown of all facilities. The bus ride home was especially revealing. Some people grumbled non-stop about the event's misery while others delighted in its chaotic magic. It was as if they'd visited different planets.

Years later, a much longer bus ride presented more irony. Buses as societal microcosms are split between riders and bystanders. Veteran gallivanters wince as tinted-window bus tours pass— and justifiably, such tours usually suck. Heralded by second-generation hippies, Green Tortoise, a long-distance group transport novelty supposedly melded the Partridge Family's tour bus with Ken Kesey's legendary Electric Kool-Aid *Furthur* coach. Dreaming of tales of svelte gypsies rollicking in a rolling hostel, I had to try it.

At the turn of the last Millennium, the Green Tortoise fleet was a nostalgic collection of modified 1970's commuter buses. Excluding the driver's seat, all others were removed and replaced by foam mats. Two card-tables in the forward section folded away at night, making everything camp space. Six kiss-the-ceiling bunks replaced the overhead luggage racks. With no on-board toilet, everyone takes it outside. Peace, brother.

Though most passengers communed, there were some cliques, mostly age-related. Rumor has it that these trips can be intimacy festivals. Thirty-five of us included two drivers. One driver noted that the erogenous temperature of a trip is determined by how many passengers disrobe at the first swimming hole. At the first one we encountered, the hairy-backed driver and a 75-year-old woman were the only ones who stripped to their birthday suits.

Our two-week 2,000-mile loop departed San Francisco, barreled down to the southern tip of Baja, ferried across the Sea of Cortez to Mexico's mainland, and then churned back to California. As the landscapes outside shifted, inside, the atrophy of hairstyles began, except for the guy with the shaved head who was channeling a card shark cooler than himself. By day five, a collage of body odor had taken hold—stinky feet can trip the groovy beat.

The roster was three-quarters male, which meant that after some pecking-order bristling and attempts to wow the two single Canadian women with tall tales, it was about male bonding, longer hikes, and escalated *cerveza* intake. Aussies, Brits, Canadians, and Germans commanded the docket.

Sleeping bodies interchanged like interlocking fingers where the height of the people on either side of you determined the distance between feet and noses. The bus had one entrance up front, so whenever anyone in the back wanted to exit they clambered over the 35 people strewn before them. In the dark, this meant foot-to-groin wake-up calls.

The route favored random driver whimsy, which meant the bus clamored over big rocks, crossed streams, and blazed through forests as tree branches whipped into the windows. Assembly-line meals were cooked communally upon fold-out tables next to the bus, usually in the midst of stunning scenery. The dining routine evolved as the group became familiar with the provisions stored atop the bus, and it became easier with each passing day to figure out who did nothing to help in the open-air kitchen but still ate first. Eventually, the same people cooked each night while others observed in amazement.

After spending a previous decade backpacking on Gandhi's budget, I'd since spliced fancy digs (room service, hot showers) into my itineraries. Though opportunities to swim were frequent, by day 10 it smelled like a few of the bus riders had soiled themselves. All bioethics crashed when one trooper also began reeking of spoiled fish tacos. Pastime shifted from hunting for things misplaced in the swamp of sleeping bags to using windowsills to prop heads outside, making the bus resemble a mobile nest of overheated puppies.

The perils multiplied. One of drivers slept in a coffer located in the rear of the bus while the other one drove. Our beloved in-house therapist, Susan, pleaded for a bathroom stop. The bus pulled over, and she roamed to the rear of the bus to squat. Simultaneously, the driver slumbering in the rear emptied his two-liter pee-storage jug out of the window. We heard Susan yelp, the communal luck-of-the-draw winner of a golden shower.

The frequent pit stops became occasions to breathe, discuss who should be mutinized, compare emerging beards, and ad-lib new terms for beastly stenches. Jumping back on the bus always meant having to reclaim the seat that the same person kept stealing; one pest attempted to claim varying spots like a wild boar rutting its snout in the sand. But, you had to *let go* as the tour proceeded. More personal items vanished into the growing laundry piles, and food items stored atop the bus moldered. But, despite the hygiene dilemma, by the time we crossed the U.S. border again, our rickety ensemble had rebranded itself into a cult of paroled dropouts all on decadent auto-pilot and unsure about adapting to life on the outside.

Over time (well, years), the stench recollections faded. I've stayed in touch with several people I met on this expedition. One, an Australian guy, managed to kidnap one of the Canadian foxes back to Australia, got married, and started a family. Fifteen years on, they're still communing.

∞ ∞ ∞ ∞ ∞

"Dude, the problem with being a Hindu is figuring out which God to please." —Green Tortoise hipster

DIRECTION

BEWARE OF UNEMPLOYED HORMONAL WISHES (Swaziland ~ Spain ~ Mergui Archipelago)

"The man is the head, but the woman moves his neck."
—*Swaziland maxim*

T hroughout the ages, men have endured inner battles about whether to listen to their big head *or* their little one. Guys, without women, there'd be no one to remind us to stop playing hot potato with commitment. Yes, accept evolution and come as you are—but also attempt to defy millions of evolving years by not thinking about sex...for an hour.

Swaziland is an independent African kingdom. Here, people seem to recognize that rain does not fall on one roof alone. Proverbial relationship diplomacy suggests that it's acceptable for men to run the show as long as the woman selects it. During my swerve through this small country, I also learned that its people embrace an adapted universal truth: behind every good man stands a great woman, or rather, great women. Interestingly, the man making this claim had three wives—polygamy is legal here. The bearer of this wisdom fancied himself righteous, as many Swazi men have seven or more wives. One condition of this arrangement is that senior wives must interview and approve any new candidates.

After quietly listening to our conversation, one of his wives chimed in: "Mr. Right usually means a few men."

In parts of our world claiming to be civilized, pornography might be the new polygamy. Bliss is like a kiss, in order to savor either you must give it to someone else.

∞ ∞ ∞ ∞ ∞

Spain

"When a diplomatic man says *yes*, he means *perhaps*. When he says *perhaps*, he means *no*—the diplomat never says *no*. When a lady says *no*, she means *perhaps*. When she says *perhaps*, she means *yes*. A lady never says *yes*." —Madrid street performer mocking high society

∞ ∞ ∞ ∞ ∞

Mergui Archipelago

The fissure segregating fleeting passion and enduring love exists pretty much everywhere. I pondered this divide in Burma, where Buddha manages to trump far and wide. I've been visiting Buddhist countries for decades, not because I'm Buddhist, but because I love the scenery, food, climate, and people—their warm, mellow, and extremely tolerant nature is simply divine. The core philosophy of this 2,500-year-old way of life pretty much eluded me until an insightful Burmese monk from the Mergui Archipelago put it like this: "To love someone is to suffer; to hate someone is to suffer." I think we can all relate to that.

∞ ∞ ∞ ∞ ∞

"My wild oats done turned to shredded wheat." —Lum York, Hank William's bassist/former Drifting Cowboy, beholding a photo of my girlfriend

"Know why it's ladies first? Cuz there's a *booby* trap." —Brook, six year-old American male, on chivalry

DIRECTION

TRAVEL NOT TO ESCAPE REALITY BUT TO PREVENT REALITY FROM ESCAPING (Syria)

Slash stereotypes like wheat before the sickle.

M inds only work when they are open for business. Before turning into another version of Hell—the chapter beginning in 2011—the main dilemma for a visitor to Syria was deciding which type of lemon-infused hummus to sample while peering at mesmerizing Crusader ruins. Smiles and greetings abounded in the midst of Bible-aged buildings, not warfare. Jeans and t-shirt clad women outnumbered those cloaked in traditional hijabs. When I wandered into a hardware store to discuss China's tool manufacturing takeover, the owner kindly put me on the phone with a university professor to get another perspective. On several occasions while mingling on sidewalks, shopkeepers crossed streets carrying plastic chairs and set them out for my comfort.

Maybe soon, the birthplace of the alphabet will reinvite us to reconsider extremist Middle East stereotypes. Every country has wounds that don't represent its entire reality. In the U.S., headlines about murder always trump the work of good people volunteering in disaster areas.

The highlight of Syria's ruin hall of fame is The Krak of the Knights. The prevailing French translation, Le Krac des Chevaliers, has a feminine ring that emasculates the ballsiest of crusader castles. From the fort's wholly preserved towering gothic ramparts, hot oil was poured over would-be attackers to help them rethink their battle plan. In peacetime, the castle housed more than 2,500 people. It was later inhabited until the 1930s by onsite shanties. These are resilient people.

Syria is at the heart of the Silk Road and a cradle of Christianity. Aleppo's majestic 200-foot high Citadel gets all the local applause, probably because unlike the Christian nerve center, the Krak, it was an enduring Muslim stronghold. An arbiter of a coming age of non-violence, the imposing Citadel is adorned with stone-relief snake sculptures. Staring at a snake above one of the Citadel's entrances, an Aleppo local explained to me that while Christianity portrays snakes as devils, Islam instead celebrates their cunning genius.

The Arab world is as mystified by the West as we are by it. It's all about perception, and perhaps, kicking back with a clever snake.

∞ ∞ ∞ ∞ ∞

"To really see, sometime you gotta cut your own bangs." — Metaphorical barber at New York's Astor Place Haircutters

DIRECTION

GET IT DONE (Newfoundland)

...Or at least feel as if you did.

I f you don't script your own story, someone or something else will try. Even though my affection for Major League Baseball has waned—some of us can only endure so much televised spitting and crotch adjusting—I sometimes view life as a series of chances at the plate. My first three books were hits that paved the way for me to develop into a keynote speaker. My print magazine résumé included *National Geographic Traveler* and *Details*.

Despite that momentum, I struck out—even fell to my knees— in 2004 when *National Geographic* sent me to Newfoundland to chronicle a week-long excursion on the *Europa*, a 1911 German-built barque-rigged ship. This floating antique circumnavigated Canada's outlying and storied island using five miles of rope to manipulate 27 sails. The plum assignment resulted from a tavern meeting with an editor who was swayed by my claim that I'd been to every Canadian Province except Newfoundland.

Of course we're all familiar with the old adage: Be careful what you wish for. The assignment led to a scenic but sedate vacation with 10 affluent retired couples energized mostly by wine, cheese, and chat. As a solo act, the romance of it all was lost on me. And as for Newfoundland, the sea route turned it into an evolving but inaccessible painting. Once home, I agonized over my manuscript for days, trying to breathe some life into it, but ultimately failed. *Geographic* killed the story, and I ended up running a rebellious version of it elsewhere. Although the following Newfie epiphany had nothing to do with that publishing strike out, it did give me another swing at the plate...

∞ ∞ ∞ ∞ ∞

Some working folks enjoy the most basic equipment—themselves. Interacting with locals in their trusted establishments is a dependable conduit into the heart of a destination. Emerging onto pavement after a 10-day trek across western Newfoundland's wild, sub-arctic Gros Morne National Park, I followed a picturesque, hilly shoreline road that wound to a Riff's department store. The Atlantic Canadian variety chain "since 1939" was an aluminum-sided mini warehouse with one door and two small musty windows—one posting a Scratch and Save Today coupon sign.

Brimming with necessities and what some would deem as luxury items, the 1960's shopping environment showcased the latest fashions, as indicated by signs atop racks of dated attire, including Adidas cheerleader t-shirts. I mused between knee rubbers (tall boots), glass fruit baubles, cardboard penny holders, glow-in-the-dark Halloween costumes, porcelain cats in sorted poses, and daring ladies wear.

The clerks, middle-age women regarding every patron as kin, caved in to curiosity...

"Hello, come from away?" they inquired in their local vernacular.

I explained my draw to classic retail variety lairs, then, surveying this workplace on a Canadian island with allegedly limited employment opportunity, asked, "How come there's not much work in Newfoundland?"

"Cause we got it all done," a previously silent clerk swore.

DIRECTION

LIFE IS SHORT. GO LONG (Pronto)

"Time passes...will you?" —Garden City, N.Y., teacher

T here are no guarantees in life except that dogs rule, and babies make people smile. People who live outside America tend to think that we're enslaved by jobs and wholly miss the concept of long wine-infused lunches, afternoon naps, and time off each year to go on extended pilgrimages. But, one aspect of the American nine-to-five job thing isn't so limiting, even with the initial two-weeks-off-per-year dilemma. Relax and ask yourself: What are you going to do with your more than four months of vacation this year?

Entry level nine-to-five job days off per year breakdown:

Vacation	10
Saturdays	52
Sundays	52
Holidays	10
Fictional Ailments	5
Days off per year	131

This revelation is not the result of an excursion outside the U.S. but a celebration of simple math. Long ago, I abandoned any worry about my country-folk being viewed as globally ignorant or too loud and chatty by foreigners, because Americans are, statistically, the most compassionate and charitable people in the world.

Whatever your plan, you need money to see the world, regardless of where you tumble onto the job pyramid. Imagine a career hierarchy capped by aspiring movie stars. As you amble down, the pyramid widens, but still narrowly employs yearning musicians, sculptors, painters, dancers, and soon, writers. The impractical career choices near the pyramid's shaky crown beg for unpaid toil, rejection, and an absence of security. But itinerant artists endure, as passion leads to its own riches.

As artists mature, it becomes apparent that people choosing less popular or less glamorous careers—the more bounteous jobs creating the pyramid's wide base—at an early age earn valuable payoffs. People selecting career tracks in waste management, civic duty, medical supplies, or say, metal detectors, buy houses and contemplate early retirement while the creatively bent maestros could still be trying to close in on the big break. Ouch.

Nonetheless, sometimes there shouldn't be a backup plan. Devising backup schemes can diminish the commitment of your primary intent. You don't want to be a watered-down plan-B, especially concerning occupations and vacations. Golden handcuffs are still handcuffs. As they say near the end of up-for-grabs football games, Hail Mary.

DIRECTION

WALKABOUT TO TALKABOUT (Ethiopia)

Wandering is not a chosen option, but a desire written into the human heart.

To mosey is part of our heritage. Ethiopia is the birthplace of the long-distance foot traveler, and perhaps coincidentally, coffee. Africa's oldest royal dynasty is the turf from where humans first began wandering to other continents—primitive pioneers. Historians boil it down to something like this. Africans, from what is now Ethiopia, started tracking toward the Middle East. Once there, the nomads who hung a right evolved into Asians, while the drifters swerving left developed white skin. A rainbow of complexions was born in that midst. Ethiopians certainly still like to roam, as walking is a way of life. The weary catch rides on donkey carts while children as young as four-years-old herd cattle, camels, and sheep. Not surprisingly, the country that invented wandering epitomizes religious coexistence. Muslims and Christians marry and are often seen holding hands while strolling.

Did Ethiopia's eternal status of producing highly mobile people fan rumors of it being the origin of the energy drink? Yielding humanity's oldest traces provided ample time to concoct a few fads, including one that won't quit. Sometime after the sacking of Rome and before Europe slipped into its Dark Ages, coffee was discovered here. A wise herder named Kaldi noted that his goats became hyped up after chewing a plant's leaves and berries, so he munched on some and caught a buzz.

After sharing this discovery with Monks at a nearby monastery, Kaldi was scolded 'for partaking in the fruit of the devil.' That is, until the monks whiffed the splendid aroma emanating from the fire from where they'd pitched the devil's brew. Monks then began drying coffee beans and shipping them to other Ethiopian monasteries, where they discovered it helped them stay chipper for nocturnal prayers. Soonafter, Arabs began importing beans, and the coffee business launched. Fifteenth century Turks invented the modern style of brewing and stamped an adaptation of Kaldi's name on it: kahve.

Ethiopia's coffee houses are about socializing. That's where I met good-natured Addis. He invited me into his home, where like in all abodes, coffee is honored with its own ritual. The coffee ceremony showcases Ethiopia's welcoming nature. The ceremony began with freshly cut grass scattered on the floor to share nature's bouquet, while an incense burner smoked with an aromatic gum. Addis sat on a low stool before a mini charcoal stove. As coffee beans roasted in a pan, he invited me to draw the smoke my way and inhale. Then he ground the roasted beans with a pestle and mortar, brewed it, and served it in petite china cups. Traditionally, three cups are served. The third bestows a blessing, which I happily anticipated.

One of Addis's friends, an accidental model, stopped by and joined us for that third cup of coffee. It's typical to see beautiful women strolling along every bend in these roads. It's also common to see them walking barefoot up and down mountain trails carrying immense loads atop their heads with no men in sight. However, earlier in the week, I saw 10 guys doing laundry together while standing waist-deep in a lake, so I assumed they helped out around the house. I asked Addis about this...

Before he could answer, his friend interrupted with a play on the age-old argument over who does the household chores—"Don't ask the barber if you need a haircut."—her way of saying that no man would admit to *not* pitching in at home.

We all sipped our coffee, then Addis added, "I make my bed."

Foreign but familiar, Ethiopians taught me something about patience—theirs, mostly. I'm rarely star-struck, but every day patches of Ethiopia resemble an epic Jesus-era movie set. Assigned a hue all its own, the country that still embodies the walkabout remains ground zero for pilgrims. This is humanity's starting line for a primitive instinct: manifest destiny. And the country that started it all keeps on trekking.

DIRECTION

SALUTE THE UNDERCOVER NUNS
(County Mayo)

Acing humanity boot camp.

The first gift I gave my mom was a dandelion bouquet. When she turned 80, I brought her to Ireland. It was a gift with a hidden agenda. Born Johanna O'Sullivan, she was one of seven raised by Irish-born immigrants in New York City and later Long Island. There, she was groomed for the convent. With her bags packed for the holy life, she balked and chose a career that eventually led her to Manhattan and to date Hollywood rogue Steve McQueen. Mom didn't know it, but part of our second Irish quest was discovering what might have been if she had taken the oath.

Our search for Ireland's convent lifestyle took an unconventional turn at County Mayo's lakeside Ashford Castle, whose cornerstone was laid in 1228. An intimidating bastion with soaring turrets, this palace featured a celebrity photo hall of fame that's a who's who of former guests. Ronald Reagan's picture triggered mom's buried annoyance because, as she pointed out, "He removed the solar panels installed on the White House roof by Jimmy Carter." It was a far cry from the Spartan life mom would have led as a nun. We quickly fell into a routine that involved long walks on her new knee and reminders to tuck in my shirt. Mom attempting medieval humor, teased, "Where did thee go in eighth grade when you hijacked that golf cart in the middle of the night?"

Paying penance for being a risk-crazed teen, I entertained mom by introducing her to the on-campus falcons and horses. But we still had to find a nun. Rolling across County Galway, our nerves were tested as we sliced between oncoming trucks and roadside stone walls on narrow two-lane roads. Although gorgeous stone churches are at the heart of most villages, Irish convents are rapidly closing, foretelling a fading way of life. It's hard to find a nun in Ireland these days, but we were on a mission.

Our wish was granted by an unscheduled stop at Kylemore Abby, a legendary convent and boarding school. There, we encountered our only nun in seven days as she was stealthily driving along the abbey's utility road in a beat-up minivan. Before she could get away, I knocked on her window, and she emerged wearing a habit and knee-high Wellington boots. She and mom chatted about Catholic school teachers, uniforms, and now forbidden discipline tactics. Fast friends—so close yet so far—they clutched hands for a moment before saying goodbye. Right then it hit me, if mom had donned the habit, my dad would never have been able to use his line, "You have great legs," when they first met on Long Beach, New York in 1949.

Mom's journey from a convent runaway to Manhattan fashionista ultimately led her to my dad, an avid birdwatcher who fashioned a simple honeymoon atop Jayne's Hill, Walt Whitman's favorite spot and Long Island's highest point. It wasn't long before they started a family. Mom relied on a few supposedly Irish traditions to keep her sons in line, including washing our mouths out with soap for swearing and attempting to use a wooden spoon on our behinds—a course of punishment rendered fruitless by a fugitive dance around the dining room table. But it certainly wasn't all tough love. An Irish relative, Sister Eileen, visited us for months when I was barely four feet tall. She pinch-hit for mom as a bodyguard, deflecting attacks from my older brothers that would usually segue into torture experiments. She also never minded when I waltzed into her room unannounced when she was *sans* habit. And, she didn't notice my English-descended, Thoreau-loyal father peering curiously at her when she prayed before every meal.

Nuns the world over are still doing work that most don't consider, such as running orphanages and caring for the homeless. Though my mom never became a nun, her charitable nature was a given. My earliest memories of her include righting environmental wrongs, driving disabled seniors to their medical appointments, and never giving up on integrating black and white students in the divisive late 60s and early 70s. Before moving to the neighboring town, we lived in Hempstead, NY, predominantly African-American and defining the Black Power Movement. She shared her heart, as well as clothes, lunches, and time for tutoring. Nobody ever had to define this undercover nun's "mission."

Ireland is proof that pride can be inherited and magic cons reality. As life is a slowly evolving painting, Irish brushstrokes render lasting memories. I continued the dandelion bouquet ceremonies until I was seven and literally picked up where I left off while strolling by one of Ashford Castle's gardens. We held hands along the bumpy trail for safety like I did with my daughter before "third-grade cool" set in. Hand holding, throughout our lives, says everything without words. There, we chanced upon another patch of pretty weeds. I picked a bouquet of bluebells— dainty purple wildflowers flopping off green stems—presented them, and thanked her for letting me roam out of bounds. In a magnificent ancient setting, but now only partially beholden to an ancient text, this nun on the run is blessed by that underlying wild streak that inspired her journey and mine.

∞ ∞ ∞ ∞ ∞

BASIL LOVES JOHANNA —Cement slab, made by my then courting father, using embedded nails as letters to create an eternal declaration of love to my mom. I later discovered it in a lost corner of our basement, and it will forever soothe my soul.

DIRECTION

ROAM, DRINK, SCREW

*Travel writers need to routinely remind readers that
Halloween-night-style caution is always necessary.*

Streetwise means keen eyes. I nearly wrote a book entitled *Roam Drink Screw*, the male answer to *Eat Pray Love*. That rancorous book title may not resemble one that my father, who suggested my middle name be Thoreau, would appreciate. Although, like Thoreau, I did become a drifting writer, no student of prose can imagine him drinking or screwing—even though he was America's first homegrown activist-style hippie. His masterpiece about living off the grid, *Walden*, is an undying scripture of self-reliance, thriving amid thrift, and how to tell a bullying government to shove it.

I'm the only guy I know who read *Eat Pray Love*, Liz Gilbert's wildly successful travelogue that became a movie starring Julia Roberts portraying the soul-searching editor who met her second husband in Bali. I proposed the male version via an agent, unsuccessfully. A year later an Irish comedian scored with his self-discovery lampoon of Gilbert's dewy bible for solo women travelers entitled *Drink, Play, F@#k*.

Eat Pray Love, on occasion enlightening, is about a visit to three countries by a lovesick and frazzled New York City commuter. Gilbert's travelogue made her the new Queen of travel writing. I forgot about the *Eat Pray Love* phenomenon until I heard about then 23-year-old Aubrey Sacco (a close friend of my cousin), who has been missing since 2010 when she didn't return from a solo trek in Nepal's Himalayas. Sacco's disappearance struck me like a bullet and renewed my urge to warn women about some of the realities of eating, praying, and loving in distant lands.

On behalf of my other travel-celebrating books that mingle the joy of traveling while forewarning about the dangers, I've lectured about world travel on the campus circuit. Discussing travel topics like malaria, inoculations, robbery, rape, and kidnapping is serious business. Writing and professing about travel is a huge responsibility because, although we live in a world full of mostly decent people, the evil ones have a knack for targeting unaccompanied women.

While in advice mode, I always tip my cap to deep-rooted female travel writers—like Lisa Alpine and Carla King—the variety who have either motorcycled, hitched, or hiked around the world by themselves, more than once. These are the sort of empowered solo travel experts I'd want advising my mother or daughter about the realities of globetrotting.

When Gilbert's cinema-ready narrative hit the big screen, my hunch was that it was going to inspire some women to pitch their troubles over the back fence and venture out to distant lands to reinvent their souls, and I'm all for that. However, women and men, unfortunately, still need to endure different rules while traipsing. That said, the same warnings attached to kids on their debut unaccompanied strolls to the candy store should follow us throughout our lives.

Eat Pray Love on the big screen probably didn't motivate an army of women into unsafe situations. But Aubrey Sacco is still missing long after her father, brother, the FBI, and Nepalese authorities scoured a remote region of northern Nepal. Our hearts go out to her family.

Eat, pray, love…and watch your tail!

DIRECTION

CATCH UP WITH FLEETING MOMENTS
(Bulgarian-Serbian border)

There is a bizarre, ghostly border crossing that links Bulgaria's northwest corner to Serbia. Almost exclusively used by foot traffic, the no-man's-land kilometer between immigration guardposts had the appeal of a concentration camp. After a guard rummaged through my passport, I walked quickly past the first lookout towers and barbwire. Midway through the void, a horde of Roma gypsies were delayed indefinitely in their attempt to enter Serbia—and likewise kept from easily reentering Bulgaria.

At first, their quietude signaled another encounter with the refugees of failed communism. One of the men stood up and summoned me, his teeth looking like a picket fence in disrepair. Attempting to enter a country recently bombed by NATO, I was a bit on edge.

"Come from England?" he asked.

I stopped in my tracks and told him and his group that I was American, and they all took a second look at me. The frontman looked back at the crowd, had two conversations, and turned back to me.

"Why you go fast?"

I jokingly looked at my wrist (where people usually wear watches), tapped it repeatedly, and mimed that I was in a rush. He stepped into the crowd and re-emerged carrying a beat-up pogo stick. Setting it before me, he invited me to jump on it. I snapped out of my traveler's trance and sprang into action to discover that this was exactly what I needed to do that day. I bounced around for a while, once springing into the hooting crowd, who were now clapping to the beat of my landings. Repurposed, I handed the pogo stick back to this group's mayor. All around were grins—the timeless symbols of content—uncomplicated by drawn borderlines.

"No connections and only ourselves to recommend us. —Roma interpretation of their immigration dilemma.

Destinies meet from time to time. Good fortune can find those who drift. The rabbit which has only one hole soon is caught.

∞ ∞ ∞ ∞ ∞

Hitchhiking onward from the unshackled side of that Serbian border checkpoint, I got a lift from the owner of a family-run paint store in Negotin, Serbia. He graciously took me in for the night and prepared a time-honored Serbian dinner with his daughter. One appetizer resembled oversized chicken nuggets. The interior of the crisped nuggets were an off-white paste, a shiny, gungy tofu. "What's this?" I asked, ingesting my second sample. "*Pohovani mozak*," came the answer.

The origin of this fatty-tasting, pungent mush was still not clear to me.

"Fried brain… cow," the daughter smiled. My dry heave detonated into a sneeze, and the snack exploded out of my nose.

She corrected herself, "Cow and pig brain mix!"

I remembered that more people die in my home country of too much food than of too little, and I took another bite.

DIRECTION

IF YOUR METHOD OF ESCAPE BECOMES ITS OWN FORM OF PRISON, FIND ANOTHER WAY OUT (Honduras)

Pirate Chic in Central America's Centerpiece.

One definition of a true scholar is someone who knows how to portray an intellectual, but doesn't. Somewhat relevant, my classification of a fashionista is one living by what they wear, but isn't suffering as a result of it. Avoid shoes that look fab, but make toes bleed, or berets worn in hot summer sun that spawn forehead acne. Consider outfits that are road-trip functional, full of pockets, and weather worthy. Aware that my wardrobe doesn't quite leap between fads, I notice those who let their body language do the talking, not the garments upon them.

It's relatively tranquil on the Caribbean island of Roatán, Honduras's bootlegger promised land. Here, accidental innovators entrust pirate chic, clashing outfits—and lifestyles— patched together from different parts of the world. It's as if many of the local ensembles had washed ashore with mixed driftwood, was looted from uncovered chests, or was discovered after a glacier melted. Duds you can dance, drink, and then nap in.

The backdrop to Roatán's idyllic beaches are craggy mountains covered in jungle. Everything smells fertile, and the friendly people talk like pirates. Somewhere between that jungle and beach, locals dress up—but down. European colonizers delivered an array of self-styled characters to Central America, whose flair still paints the region. Settlers-at-large, waterway outlaws, castaways, traders, and militarists stimulated an economy making Roatán a popular hangout for sea voyagers. Britain—always keen on setting biscuits, tea, and bizarre humor upon the global menu—strategically set up shop here in 1550. Today, a few wayward captain types still lurk about.

Slyly commenting on style, a contrary seadog told me, "If you have to ask what's hip—you're not."

Honduran's swashbuckling suave combines gypsy design, expat grunge, gut-level rasta, and the cruise ship day-tripper's silly. Will eye patches and handcrafted leather belts worn high round the waist make a comeback? Locals needn't hijack somebody else's idea of groovy. Welcome to the set of Treasure Island. 1960's San Francisco would be proud.

Stay blind to trivial flashes. Pirate chic's bootleg styling isn't about fabrics married to labels, it's what you do with them. Unleash your buccaneer bravado and ignore the starved-model ads. People (cue the elevating background music), wear clothes that don't wear you!

∞ ∞ ∞ ∞ ∞

"It is, it is a glorious thing. To be a Pirate King." —Roatan 'nonstate actor' and dive instructor, emulating W.S. Gilbert, 1879

DIRECTION

TEST-DRIVE ALTERNATIVE MEDICINE
(South Africa)

South Africa has townships, planned ghettos really, some of which are now flourishing as tourist attractions where locals take pride in their neighborhoods by planting flowers, opening restaurants and bars, and tidying up schoolyards. I've always thought the best hangouts in neighborhoods like these are where people recline on house furniture set out on front porches or lawns and within reach of a cooler. If you poke around these townships, you'll also likely find a traditional African herbalist laboratory.

It wasn't until I visited Langa Township, outside Capetown, that the realities of apartheid truly struck me. Racism was at its worst here. Historically, differentiating between black, colored (mulatto), and white was an evil science, and often a bigger problem between blacks and colored people. With countrywide healing well underway, homeopathic genius survived the racial tension. On the fringe of Langa, I entered a herbalist's laboratory that looked and smelt like the interior of a barnacled ark. Showcasing random roots, feathers, and tonics bottled in recycled containers of every dimension, it smelt like mulched tree leaves mingled with menthol. Cures for all ailments were mixed by a middle-aged man wearing a hawk-feather suit.

"What's that for?" I asked, pointing to a reused Smirnoff Vodka bottle containing a murky, rusting liquid that sparkled with floating pizza-parlor-style red pepper flakes. "South African Viagra," he said, explaining that the tea combo included bangalala roots and African potato juice. I left with a bottle, never asking about the floating red pepper flakes. Back at home, this concoction proved enticing and potent—just like the country that inspired it. I gave it to a married couple, who had their first baby nine months later.

Alternative medicine that's been proven to work is called medicine.

∞ ∞ ∞ ∞ ∞

"It put the *ass* back in cl*ass*ic." —New dad, on South African aphrodisiac potion

DIRECTION

FIND FUN WHERE THE PAVEMENT ENDS
(Fiji)

On the other side of fear is freedom.

I'm on a classic Fijian bamboo *bilibili* raft after a fat rain riding a raging river. Imagine balancing on racing water while surfing a long, tippy, bamboo toboggan through a whitewater maze flanked by unforgiving vertical stone canyon walls. The five fat bamboo trunks lashed together by twine are crackling while the 10-foot guiding pole in my hand seems to be bothering only the fish. The sun stands at high noon between the walls. There is no turning back.

The three local guys on their own rafts—this is how they got around—scratched their heads when we encountered a massive palm tree that had fallen across the canyon creating an impassable dam. Their emergency portage solution would impress a knife juggler. Fretless, they separated to opposite banks. One took a machete swipe at the base of a 40-foot rubber tree, the high end falling next to the guy on the opposing bank. Upriver, I'm holding the rafts close to a vine as I watch them share the machete—to cut long strips of bark—by hurling the

280

hulky knife back and forth to each other across the raging 30-foot wide river. They casually huck the glistening machete back and forth like playground pals underhandedly tossing a tennis ball, systematically cutting enough peels of bark to bind one long piece of forest twine that's used to guide the rafts over the fallen tree.

∞ ∞ ∞ ∞ ∞

Sometimes we must slap ourselves off the tourist treadmill. One-hundred or so of Fiji's 325 islands are "inhabited," and visitors rarely get to know more than a few after landing on Viti Levu. Everyone sees this large island's intimidating peaks; languid, strolling locals; and sugar cane or coconut plantations that dominate the landscape, but they move on. Most options lead offshore where visitors stay on smaller islands embodying the classic South Pacific tropical scenery and predictable resorts.

I understand. Rambler instinct usually necessitates fleeing the busy island in search of adventure. Neglecting that impulse, I dig into the mother island, ascending into Viti Levu's craggy mountain interior and traverse its entire length via the spine of its peaks. The untamed, cloud-misted highlands are an epoch detached from the sea-level resorts.

A steady ascent on Viti Levu, using a medley of buses, taxis, injured pickups, and footwork, leaves the sunblock flock behind. Obtainable though not guaranteed, an invitation from village chiefs is required to enter most native Fijian villages. It's perhaps akin to asking to swim in an unknown person's pool and receiving a wholehearted yes.

After climbing Fiji's imposing zenith, Mount Tomanivi, I pull off my mud-caked boots—now twice their original weight. The settlement of Navai naps at the base of Tomanivi, which the British named Mount Victoria, though it is doubtful any queen scaled the peak. Here, 250 residents live in 75 homes. People still cook over wood fires and the electric bill for the lone fluorescent bulb and listening to rugby on one radio runs about two bucks a month. I'm greeted on the matted floor of Navai's meeting hall by the chief and his entourage for a customary *sevusevu* greeting. This warm welcome ceremony defines Fijian collective pride.

Cool dusk sets in. It is time to gather 'round the kava bowl and drink the elixir used for centuries to mend conflicts between warring tribes; a peaceful happy hour. Kava means to Fiji what football means to Green Bay, WI—a marvelous trance. The rite commenced with a prayer-like communiqué and interpretation of my journalistic curiosity that segued into a kava drinking session; a chief's council breaking bread. Kava is the opiate of a substantial sector of Fiji's one million inhabitants (well, most of the guys anyway). The kava bowl, the *tanoa*, is given an honored place. The tanoa is a block of wood with legs and a bowl carved into its midst. Some bowls sport intricate carvings; others merely serve the purpose of holding the beloved extract. I later celebrated with a bunch of guys in the airport, swigging from a big blue bucket.

Villagers sit cross-legged, shoes off, facing the chief. Primo kava is made from the long, dried root of a pepper plant. After grinding the root into a white, flaky powder, they hand-squeeze the granules in a large teabag-like pouch that's submerged in a gallon of rainwater. The pouch is wrung and redunked until the concoction fogs to brown.

The murky grog is methodically distributed in a dried coconut shell around the semicircle of six seated men. The group ceremoniously claps once—loudly, with hands cupped—to summon a person's six-ounce gulp, then acknowledges the quaff by clapping again three times. The grog tastes like bitter muddy river water but soon nurtures a euphoric grin. This tranquilizer first numbs your lips and tongue, then everything else. The buzz recalls a sort of earthy codeine canapé or a Native American mushroom blessing. The grin widens as the relaxation ritual continues.

My city tempo accepts recess. English-speaking, often literate, low-key Fijians speak in soft tones, switching between English and their native language, which reminds me of serene Italian. They remain calm even when exalting a subject of worship, like rugby.

The seating arrangement of the ceremony is predetermined by tribal seniority and rank, and the imbibing order heeds unspoken pecking orders. The guest (me) sat before the kava mixologist who was centered behind the bowl. The elderly chief sat to my left. Each of us consumed a six-ounce bowl every 10 minutes, happy hour endured four hours. These ageless storytime gatherings combine calling card, telegraph, telephone, television, newspaper, internet, and gossip column—typifying community before electricity.

These are people who have preserved themselves secretly like members of a lodge who are not allowed to give away the untold handshake—a kava ritual unveils the secret.

It is time to talk.

"You live in New York City?" the chief inquiries.

"I do."

"Many people," he nods.

"Too many," I agree, confessing that I often encounter a thousand people in a day, speaking to no one but myself.

That's when I think they prayed for me.

I go for a stroll between kava sessions and revel in the cool fog and full moon rising while two grinning children hide behind a colorful home, encouraging a game of hide-and-seek. To the south, an isolated storm cloud steams over a mountain, a communion of grey-white clouds flaring the high jungle sky with lightning and trailing drapes of rain.

Kava talo (again). Thought: Do they really need tourism here? Travel writing schizophrenia. The kava session waxes pensive, then sleepy. The women and children, who later blend in, sit on the sidelines beaming. I'm asked to dance by one of the women on the sideline, and my glee is transfixed.

I abandon any further oratory attempts, deciding it might result in a spatter akin to implanting a banana into a fan. After a very sound sleep, I wake on a matted floor, without a hint of a hangover, to the smell of breakfast being cooked by a mom.

Contentedness, what all the ages have struggled to achieve.

Leaving Navai the next day to complete my high-ground traverse, I ricochet across a stretch of Viti Levu's aerial backbone in a paint-shaker pickup to another highland settlement, Naitauvoli. En route, wild horses and pigs mosey about the wet, dark-green mulch cloud forest of billowing bamboo tree clumps, rain trees, all amid craggy mountains. Severo, the Fijian cowboy driver, uses both of his wide-splay bare feet on the pedals to navigate the savage Monasavu Dam road. I use the term "road" loosely. Banging down cliff-edged hairpin turns, I inquire, "Ever have a wheel fall off?" then, "Trucks ever tumble off cliffs?" After a skidding pivot, Severo nods, leaving room for imagination.

That night, Naitauvoli's formal sevusevu welcome ceremony prompts another seated tribal ring. I am now on a full-blown kava binge. Several members of the Waiqa River band are in attendance, men who periodically float to the lowlands to play festivals. The band enhances the sevusevu anthem, Fiji's reflective, tradition-steeped chant, with plenty of banter about rain, fruit, and family.

I sit before the patient, nonjudgmental panel of men on a big mat, another human half-circle with the kava bowl at the center. Occasionally, during the thoughtful pauses between dialogue, youngsters peer in. There is a don't-speak-unless-spoken-to respect for elders. Experiencing the respect, politeness, and esteem for elders—in what would be considered a clapboard shanty by the evening news—is a lesson in itself.

This go-round of kava hypnosis approximated a tequila delirium, my heads welling with the "what-me-worry?" vibe. The kava blender is another serious cat, a man-for-all-seasons who's younger than the rest. Outside the hut, I stare at the moon lingering beside a pine tree. As my coordination comes into question, I lean on the tree. Back in the hut, a few men have nodded out. I thank them for making a stranger feel so at home. A senior slowly assures me, "You are no stranger here, Bruce."

As I make my way along Viti Levu's meandering highland vertebrae, several of the doorways I peek into reveal groups of men seemingly drinking grog all day and night. The only side effect of long-term grogging appears to be dry skin—perhaps Grogger's Anonymous waits in the wings. The FDA has banned kava as a mood elevator or antidepressant in the U.S.—the drug companies can't profit from natural remedies easily extracted. The FDA can't play catch with a machete, either.

∞ ∞ ∞ ∞ ∞

My kava-connection walkabout concludes on another island, Taveuni, where the implausible hospitality endured. Rejoining a trail back to my final campsite, fatigue was setting in when I encountered a 60ish man standing in the middle of the path, clutching a machete. At first, I thought he glanced at me in a fairly conspiratorial way, asking if I needed anything from the market back in town. Realizing that I never consulted with the chief before entering this village, I reasoned that I didn't need any supplies. Silence. Though famished, I was simply too exhausted to backtrack.

Eroni Tabua, eldest son of Navakawau's chief, asked if I'd like to have lunch. Again, I explained that if I was to make it back to camp by dusk, I needed to move on. He then insisted that I take a five-minute detour off the trail. I followed the machete man into the thicket, slightly paranoid.

Eroni stopped and shook a few trees and plants, caught a few falling items with one hand and began craftily knife-hacking up a very timely fresh coconut, copra, and papaya variety plate. He tossed each fruit into the air a few times, whacking it rapidly with the knife in mid-air, catching the slices, and handing them to me. I had lunch in the heart of a plantation. Eroni's soft-spoken voice carried a kindness torch for the world, as pleasant and intelligent as any thoughtful professor of the humanities.

I opened my Fijian phrase book to derive another word for thanks. Instead, the knowing farmer took the book, opened it and randomly found *pikiniki*. Definition: Picnic!

Having a sea-level character machete-hack a fruit plate while you stand in the midst of his plantation discussing tarot farming explains some things, like peace. Eroni then contemplated my inevitable return to Fiji and said, "Next time, come home straight away."

Often, the trip begins where the road ends.

DIRECTION

BRING YOUR WEATHER WITH YOU
(Cambodia)

Don't be hot and cold.

To keep things real while visiting developing countries, I prefer to stay in family-run establishments because some of the best aspects of any destination are usually those that pertain to family. Occasionally, I'll spring for air conditioning. Before setting out into northern Cambodia's humid jungles on a motorbike, I spent five nights in a Phnom Penh guesthouse either huddling beneath a mountain of blankets battling teeth-chattering chills, or waking up repeatedly to kick off those blankets and lie drenched and shivering in my own sweat.

The horrors of dengue fever, malaria, and other tropical plagues overtook my mind. Getting into a pattern, I'd fling off the covers and gradually cool down until, an hour later, an Arctic frost would send me back under the blankets to restart the ritual. I became practiced at drenching one side of the bed, then shifting to the other side while the wet side dried. On day three, I got a short 50-cent haircut—via a sidewalk barber using hand-powered shears—so my oft-soddened hairdo would dry faster and not soak the pillow. Anyone who has backpacked extensively doesn't go to doctors unless someone else carries them to one.

Perspiring like a freshly emerged swimmer, on the fourth night, I stormed over to unplug the non-adjustable air-conditioner and discovered instead that sauna-hot air was billowing into the room. As I stood there, relief gushed into my veins. This woeful AC dinosaur had been blowing air ranging from 55 to 95 degrees in two-hour cycles. Just when I'd resigned myself to a hospital visit, I realized that my viral rollercoaster had been instigated by recurring rounds of polar misery upstaged by a humid inferno delirium.

Enjoying a mini triumph, I attached a "broken" note onto the demonic appliance, checked out, met my brother, rented a motorbike, and throttled north.

∞ ∞ ∞ ∞ ∞

"The heart doesn't have to be clever." —Cambodian motorbike shop owner's reply to question about neighboring Thailand and Vietnam being more clever at business.

"Hey man, don't sweat the big stuff." —Humboldt County, California farmer

DIRECTION

AVOID STRANGLING BY THE FOOD CHAIN (New Zealand ~ Switzerland ~ Goa)

"Wine appeals to the nose with aroma, the eye with color, and the tongue with taste. But, the ear was always without sensation. So, a fine crystal glass gives pleasure to that vital sense. Here in New Zealand, to provide a fifth sensation we also spill the wine on our body." —Heavily tattooed New Zealander, freshly self-drenched in red wine, toasting everyone in a Christchurch biker bar.

∞ ∞ ∞ ∞ ∞

Swiss Alps

Shopping for affordable rations in a Swiss ski resort market, I asked a thickly bespectacled employee—crooked over a carton of tomatoes—if the store stocked canned chili. Standing up with shoulders thrown back and without removing his gaze from an unseen ally in the fish section, he steadily replied, "Yes, but much further down the food chain."

∞ ∞ ∞ ∞ ∞

India

In many parts of the world, flushing the toilet and personal cleansing are done with the left hand using a few splashes of rainwater held in a nearby basin. Never offer your left hand to someone in such places.

In 1991, I squatted low within a Goa restroom—an outhouse accommodating a porcelain floor-level crater—when I was frightened by a sudden slosh and clatter. Odd, since traditional Indian toilets don't "flush" Western style unless you manually add water. I checked out the commotion below by looking between my legs. Down below, I saw a spasmodic pink doohickey flapping about wildly. I exited, darted to the rear of the structure, and barreled into the humongous pig who was voraciously groveling its snout deep into the exit conduit of the outhouse.

These "pig toilets" are clever spinoffs of traditional Asian toilets, wherein you hunker down hovering above an opening in the floor. What distinguishes a pig toilet from traditional undeveloped-country latrines is the ravenous, waiting pig that consumes your crap without delay. There's definitely a sensation of a closed-loop ecosystem when your waste is recycled back into the food chain before you've even pulled up your pants. (It grants an updated perspective on pork too.)

Later, realizing that this territorial pig kept a keen eye on his pantry, I waited around until a shocked Swedish sightseer screamed, and then left.

∞ ∞ ∞ ∞ ∞

Martha Stewart-land

Sometimes happiness is about defending your version of it. Is Martha Stewart judging? Pink versus brown can be a meaty issue—why is requesting and consuming well-done red meat considered to be a felony by people who prefer it rare? No stranger to fine dining worldwide via travel journalism, I'm routinely alarmed by rare beef aficionados who never hesitate to glare contemptuously at well-done meat eaters as executable heathens. It seems as rude as someone approaching a stranger wearing pink and stating, without cause, "That color makes you look disgusting." I've never met a browned beefeater who felt compelled to belittle fans of pink cow on a plate. Until now. Why is this transfer of cuisine contempt a one-way street? Is preferring beef that tiptoes toward bacon—instead of raw—a culinary crime? I've ingested underdone parasitic meat before and never want to gamble with that version of poisoning again. And oh yeah, some of us think it *tastes better* cooked.

I decided to do something about this recurring meat preference snootiness at a media lunch in New York City. As it was banquet service, and thus impossible to specify preference beforehand, I cordially sent back the filet of prime beef poached in olive oil that was served for a tad of browning. Someone at my table, a Martha Stewart Living radio personality, leered scornfully at me and announced, "Why ruin a perfect piece of meat? Anyone who wants well-done beef at my house is on their own." Nice to meet you, too?

This heat challenger was the winner of my bottled rant. My first instinct was to approach her later and point to her shirt and inquire, "Seems like *someone* likes to buy tacky clothes on sale?" I'd hit my breaking point and wanted to enlighten this self-elected foodie lord about how it feels to be on the other end of an unprovoked judgment. Instead, when a microphone was passed around to the media to ask the celebrity chef questions, now amplified, I started, "That was a dazzling cut of meat." Then, after a peripheral glint at the carnivore umpire, I continued, "When I sent mine back to the kitchen for a slight browning, someone at my table sneered at me as if I should be beheaded. Is that proper behavior in a humane society?" Message sent, I got a laugh, and the chef mused about options for caramelizing filets.

Then, I explained to this woman that I'm not cuisine illiterate, and not just because I'd eaten pretty much every day of my life. I told her that I've gone without it for three days, adding that I've savored sautéed char while icebreaking near the North Pole in sight of polar bears…and also sipped malbecs infused with glacial ice in Antarctica while watching whales breach. I did not expect to win her over.

When I ask most self-proclaimed foodies—the types most prone to insult brunette beef—if they've ever worked in a restaurant, the answer is almost always no. Starting at age 16, I spent 10 years working in restaurants. That didn't verse me in the truffle shuffle, but it taught me to discuss food with the pros, namely chefs. Since then, I've reviewed restaurants—not posing as a foodie, instead describing restaurants as destinations. By the way, there are entire nations, including Argentina and Uruguay, pinnacles of fine beef, where fully cooked meat is often preferred.

So, beware rare meat connoisseurs, next time you emote an *ew* in the direction of someone who likes their meat cooked through, think about that pink shirt, and your manners. Rant over.

∞ ∞ ∞ ∞ ∞

Ps, Never ask a local where to eat, but rather, where *they* eat.

Note: Rice is great when you're hungry and want 3,000 of something.

"Try the intellectual waffle." —Suggestion made by Norwegian maître d'

DIRECTION

UNCOVER YOUR INDIGENOUS NICKNAME (Guatemala)

Don't fear the darkness.

Ditching hectic Guatemala City for greener pastures, I ascended into a cloud forest and the lush, sleepy hamlets surrounding the pastoral village of Coban. Then, stumbling into a dank cavern, I was led into the darkness. The main attraction—Lanquin Caves National Park—is illuminated by a wire dangling widely spaced lightbulbs powered by a diesel generator found sputtering outside the cave. The origin of the cool Lanquin River, this vast cave burrows deep into the earth and your mind.

After a spooky hour foraging into the slippery, dimly lit bat grotto otherworld, the lights suddenly went out and stayed out for five endless minutes. We're talking pitch black, when the heartbeat in your ears becomes your only functioning sense. Members in my newly formed party all uttered a variety of involuntary gasps. Some of their exclamations were simply vocalized shock, while others sounded like primal babble: Hono. Oshit. Whatdah? And so on.

Ambling half a mile inside this bat-shit-slick, boulder-clogged tunnel teeming with hanging stalactites and underfoot stalagmites is, I found out later, a secret entrance into Mayan mysticism. Caves were sacred to the Mayans, and Guatemala remains as the heart of their mysticism. Mountains and caves served as their first temples. Tikal National Park, Guatemala's crown-jewel, is an above-ground reenactment of these portals to their underworld.

The underground trek became increasingly challenging as people slipped on slimy bat crap. Then, when the lights went out *again* and more guttural wheezing erupted, I wondered if pre-wheel barbarians might have been nicknamed based on sounds they commonly made, especially in perilous moments. (I swear, I only had a sensory deprivation buzz.) If the unintentional noises and grunts we make when surprised, falling down, or suddenly plunged into new environments were, in earlier times, our indigenous calling cards, I'll bet there were many Aboriginal folks nicknamed Whoops. And today, we'd be overrun with Focks.

For the next week, I privately turned Guatemala into a nickname lab. So what's your indigenous name? Jeez? You can try this on friends at home, but not with anyone at risk of heart failure. When they least expect it—and not driving, eating, or petting something—sneak up on a pal, mildly frighten them, and listen to the first sound they utter. Whoa?

Guatemala remains a living legend. On my final day in cobblestone-paved Antigua, I mingled with locals and learn that Maya cosmology considered the Earth to be a clump on the back of a giant turtle swimming in an eternal sea. I passed an elderly vendor in the charming colonial town square. Sitting, she was retailing a pod of wood-carved turtles that were set out on a blanket. When I glanced at the turtles, she calmly inquired, "You-buy?" We can only wonder how far back in time that alias landed in the nickname archive.

DIRECTION

DISCOVER CONTENTMENT IN THE PAUSE BETWEEN TOO LITTLE AND TOO MUCH (Vietnam ~ Scotland)

In the 1990s, as Vietnam emerged from decades of isolation, the headline was "Good Morning, Vietnam." With the country's infrastructure now accommodating Western expectations, a more apt front-page is "Good Evening, Vietnam."

I was leaning my elbow on a plastic outdoor table on a busy Saigon side street when a striking Vietnamese woman with gravity-defying cheekbones came into view. She was pushing an unfamiliar bulky machine on a two-wheeled cart down the street. She was trying to engage passing pedestrians, but I couldn't figure out what she was peddling. I stood up and intersected her path to discover what was on the cart. She motioned with her hands toward my stomach and the top of my head while speaking Vietnamese. A minute later, with the woman still gesturing and offering a faster explanation that I was even less able to decipher, passing locals also began pointing toward my stomach and patting the tops of their heads.

What had I gotten myself into, I thought. When I finally pointed at her stomach and head, she spread out parts of the contraption, stood on it, and shared with me her weight and height. I'd already been impressed that some pharmacies in the U.S. offer blood-pressure testing.

The mobile body-stats lady weighed and measured me for a nominal fee while I pondered her operation. All around us the buzzing motorbike vs. car circus continued—frenzied order without rules. Competing with the endless stampede of sign-and-signal ignoring drivers makes crossing the street here a task not unlike avoiding injury at the running of the bulls. Motorbikes double as cabs and delivery vehicles. It's not uncommon to see someone on a two-wheeler toting cargo more suited to a van. A skinny guy on a sputtering motorbike weighed down by four full-sized old televisions passed and waved hello to the portable height-and-weight beauty.

She bowed slightly and rolled away into the night. I returned to my roadside table and contemplated her resolve, as she resumed shooting the rapids of natural selection. Time didn't just stand still…it laid down and took a break.

∞ ∞ ∞ ∞ ∞

"Live, girls.... Live!" —an empowered woman misinterpreting an exotic dance lounge sign in Cyprus

∞ ∞ ∞ ∞ ∞

I saw a man pursuing the horizon;

Round and round they sped.

I was disturbed at this;

I accosted the man.

"It is futile," I said,

"You can never—"

"You lie," he cried,

And ran on.

—Stephen Crane

∞ ∞ ∞ ∞ ∞

Scotland

Back-to-back assignments—a survival school bout with starvation in the parched Utah desert segueing into a VIP splurge at Scotland's legendary Glenlivet founder's home—set the stage for my graduation from depravity into no gravity...

The airtime linking Salt Lake City and Aberdeen, Scotland, initiated a voracious two-day food binge of triple servings with extra salt. As opposed to being homeless in the desert, I'm now bunking in a royal countryside castle where, outside finding the fitting wordiness to illuminate the ultimate whisky swill, adjusting my kilt is my sole worry.

I'm still frail, feeling rather like Walt Whitman emerging from a hunger strike, and certainly an alcohol lightweight—an easy target for the amber spirit. Inside the stone-built Minmore House, former residence of Glenlivet's forefather and neighbor to the world's first licensed distillery, I fall prey to Scotch-enhanced babbling. Midway through our long-table dinner in an oaky dining hall full of Celtic art and 40-foot-high vaulted ceilings, I begin to concern the staff when I borrow a bit of glee from an involuntary childhood flashback...

"This is as much fun as being a kid when two crowded school buses pull alongside each other at a red light!"

What tumbles out as starved caveman-speak is lost on this venue for worshipping the juice from these heath-covered mountains of Scotia. I try again: "Did you know that it says 'Study now pay later' on the 500-peso bill in the Philippines?"

"Yes…?" the master of ceremony inquires. I should just cut and run, but I stay.

Single malts are only five percent of the Scotch market, and this corner of Scottish royalty is only comprehending five percent of my musings. Perhaps because the "cigar and scotch" craze of the 90s escaped me, or because I'm still in-flight.

Credibly, I surmise, "The Native American Navajo language has more than 200 words for auto parts, but there's not one curse word."

Stillness. A raindrop crawls down the window.

My headlong into highland fermentation annuls my sober-in-the-desert piety. The statuesque butler, the maid who polishes my mammoth bathtub twice a day, the tuxedoed staffer who only seems to dust things in the library, the haggis chef, three adorable waitresses, and the teenaged violin and bagpipe performers all avert their eyes.

The butler raises his glass of Scotch and chimes in: "The fusil oils and impurities inspire the taste."

Attempting to resonate that narrow slice of DNA that separates us (here, just mine) from chimps, I sip again, and then make a toast: "Adventure before dementia."

They all peer at each other and change the subject back to the log fire in the corner. My brain starts smoking. I am not surviving this Celtic State Dinner. I did learn that *livet* means valley, and, as the glow of one more "wee dram" burns my gullet, I silently recall an Eskimo saying—every taboo is holy—and remain seduced by my own spin.

∞ ∞ ∞ ∞ ∞

"You are what you lean on." —Firefighter, City Fire Brigade Social Club, Gibraltar Fire Department

DIRECTION

LET THE GOOD OLD DAYS BE NOW
(Azores)

In some places, religion is no bull.

Although I've sailed on icebreakers to both poles, I'm largely a landlubber whose footwork is spliced by frequent flying. Yes, cramped planes percolate claustrophobia, but for me, more than a week on a boat crosses that line. Boaters are usually hardy, welcoming folks, but on long sails it's nearly impossible to dodge anyone you don't like, and knock-kneed boat toilets are reliable like four-year-olds on sugar buzzes. I do envy international mariners, like my boat-building cousin Brendan, a wood purist who cringes at the sight of fiberglass yachts and is blind to airport security shakedowns and immigration toil. Maine-based Brendan has always raved about the mid-Atlantic Ocean's Azores Islands, and assumed a dreamy, farsighted gaze while describing them. So I had to go. Sorry cuz, I flew there.

The only islands between the U.S. and southern Europe are claimed by Portugal. If measured from their ocean bottom base, they rival the tallest mountains on the planet. These pinnacle-cap islands are rolling checkerboards of farms and pastures partitioned by mossy stone walls. The villages are dappled with homes and windblown churches borrowing color from the surrounding sea and sky as inspiration. The craggy shoreline melds rock wall bluffs and jagged black volcanic outbursts, both battered by dark-blue waves. Volcanic activity gurgles from these tides, and up in the interior mountain forests, volcanic chimneys sputter.

The Azores were once the only stopover for voyagers sailing between Europe and North America. Happily stranded, these sealocked islanders seem to be immune to continental conflict and fast food. I explored Terceira, an island that produces naturally preserved, non-refrigeration-worthy seagoing food, including organic goat cheese, hot peppers, and overcooked corn. "Food that's for sail," a shopkeeper joked. Much of this island feels like the 1700s, uninterrupted.

Religion has found its way onto nearly every earthly acre—it surely landed on the Azores. But, here in the midst of breathtaking nowhere, it's not all holiness. The isolation seems to have hatched at least one obsession. Terceira's version of the running of the bulls happens 270 times a year on various neighborhood streets. Tromping wildly, an out-of-sorts bull romps the length of these odd block parties. On the entertainment agenda since the 12th century, this *largada* is interpreted as "bulls run free," or "get loose." This demolition derby mentality is similar to lining up alongside a hazardous highway hoping to witness a gory accident. Inviting a deadly, unpredictable *bull-dozer* to ravage your otherwise calm street seems harebrained, but it trumps indoor video gaming.

Amateur daredevils taunt the darting animal with umbrellas, towels, or frantic gestures—each volunteer vying for idol status. Kids and grandmothers wave red shirts from partially barricaded windows while bands of friendly, drunk men mingle alongside bar carts on wheels. As locals calmly hang along the roadside awaiting a 2,000-pound typhoon of mad burger, every door and alleyway is temporarily boarded up as if a major hurricane looms. After the run, the town is quickly unfastened. Typically, the bull isn't harmed. When a bull injures a person, the bull's stock value soars—rare animal justice, a flicker of natural law. Here's to being sealocked but free in the Azores.

We may have isolated ourselves from nature, but we still rely completely on the *services* it provides.

DIRECTION

IF THE ONLY FAMILIAR THING YOU CAN SEE IS THE MOON, PINCH YOURSELF (China)

Culture shock is sometimes best enjoyed in a rear-view mirror.

I zigzagged across China in the mid-80s when it first opened up to freestyling backpackers. Before then, independent travelers weren't allowed in the country. The only tourist options were quarantined group bus tours that visited a few fixed sites, and only those the government permitted.

Back then, bicycles reigned supreme over the cars that rule today. Now, thick smog and franchise branding dominate their cities. The dizzying changes there are disturbing—incomprehensible traffic displacing cyclists, neon insanity, and fast food empires that have all but bulldozed local outdoor food stalls.

Traveling in pre-globalized China was not easy, especially in the countryside. In three months, I dropped 20 pounds off an already slim frame. The only soup I could find was hot water with limp vegetation steaming over random animal parts, such as snouts, claws, and intestines (what many Westerners happily ingest as hot dogs). It was nearly impossible to find an inviting place to eat. I winced when I caught my first glimpse of skinned and glazed beheaded dog torsos sitting in the corner of restaurants. Many of my gypsy budget meals in China were botched when shallow buckets of dog and cat heads returned my gaze. You soon realized that anything moving in most of the mainland is edible. There were entire streets and neighborhoods dedicated to slaughtering and selling anything alive that wasn't human. Refrigeration was nonexistent. A bit of an aroma neurotic, I regularly found myself sprinting to the end of one of those streets of carnage, deep in the throes of nausea.

Before China "opened up" revealing what seemed to be a medieval existence, a translation dictionary was vital here. Because I lacked one, my sanity fuse was tested on a three-day third-class train ride while my appeals to a man in uniform to enter the empty sleeper car were met with an unrelenting "no." It was my third sleepless night. There were scores of snoozing Chinese families on the floor and in the spaces between cars and nowhere to stretch out. Flocks of chickens ran up and down the aisle, a caged piglet moaned beneath my seat, and lumbering sides of butchered meat covered in flies swung from the overhead luggage hooks. Mothers periodically hovered their babies outside the windows of the moving train so they could poop. Black diesel engine smoke blew into the car, which never exceeded 40 miles an hour. All the while, vendors paced back and forth, endlessly peddling odd dried crustacean snacks.

One group snacking on a greasy chicken carcass drooled profusely and orally expelled undesirable foodstuffs about the car. I searched my empty pockets for napkins. Coughing up and spitting phlegm onto the floor was also part of the drill. If I'd had a phrasebook, I could have asked the right question sooner. I finally comprehended that an 80-cent payoff was required when the conductor held up a banknote and made the "shhh" gesture. He then led me into a totally empty sleeper car where I immediately passed out and dreamt about life on another planet.

When traveling is like oil and water, make cerebral salad.

DIRECTION

DON'T RUN OUT OF IDEAS—RUN OUT
FOR IDEAS (Adirondacks)

"A little rebellion, now and then, is a good thing."
—*Thomas Jefferson*

N ow that childhood seems to be officially over, only occasionally do I dare people to do things. Not the case with my eldest brother, Basil, who routinely challenges me to perform illegal tricks for his amusement. I routinely caved into his cons until I turned, well, about 35.

Our family summered in New York's Adirondack mountains annually starting in 1967 after my father bought 16 acres of remote hillside land there for $800 from a farmer who needed that amount to buy an oil burner. That was back when achieving the American Dream was doable, even affordable.

As seasonal Adirondackians, July Fourth is my father's favorite holiday. Although he's still mad about being persecuted as a Walden-carrying Communist during the 1950's McCarthy era, he remains a loyal transcendentalist. His favorite Americans, after Henry David Thoreau and John Muir, include Abraham Lincoln, Benjamin Franklin, and Thomas Jefferson. Our family beheld the annual fireworks show on a hillside overlooking touristy Lake George, N.Y. Throughout the crackling airborne display, my otherwise publicly measured dad would loudly thank our founding fathers for all to hear. It embarrassed his three boys, but his glowing pride let us know this was important.

After my father's 1972 patriotic public declaration, "Thank you, Thomas Jefferson!" my brother Basil challenged me, a fourth-grader, and brother Bryan to summit the lakeside A-frame roof of a nearby fast food restaurant. With Basil and hundreds of people watching from the fort's hillside, Bryan and I galloped up one side and over the other side of a roof that we soon realized was made from soda-can-thin aluminum-bubble shingles that crushed audibly under the weight of our steps. For everyone crammed on the hillside, we became the show.

The audience lounging on the hillside applauded our crunchy roof summit. The ovation surged when, once back on the ground, we sprinted into the crowd hoping to disappear. Feeling safe, we then strolled calmly away from the scene of the crime until the restaurant owner grabbed me from behind, spun me on my heel, and screamed "You're coming with me." As he dragged me back toward his damaged snack shack, the still attentive crowd booed my capture. Basil yelled out at the top of his lungs, "Boo... Run!" (Family, old friends, and a few cousins occasionally still call me Boo.) I twisted out of the man's grip and bolted. The onlookers, thankfully not including my parents, gave me a howling standing ovation as I sprinted toward freedom. And so the lessons on eluding authority continued. Once I caught my breath, far in the distance I heard *someone* yell, "Thank you, Benjamin Franklin!"

DIRECTION

**UNFOLD YOUR DAYS—AND LIFE—LIKE
A MAP, UNDERSTANDING WE CAN'T
ALWAYS REFOLD THEM THE SAME WAY
(Wales)**

*The roaming gene should not become out-selected over time.
Motion creates emotion. Walking never disappoints; it's a
whimsical celebration of right now.*

M y father and I walked together a lot. We undertook a
200-mile trek across Wales, coast-to-coast along Offa's
Dyke—the great dirt wall conceived in the eighth century by
King Offa of Mercia to separate England from Wales. The
immense earthen barrier, intended to keep the Welsh out of
England, eventually became the border between England and
Wales. Old grudges die hard; some English and Welsh folks still
eye each other warily.

Our walk along this border was a celebration of sorts. A year
earlier my father was seriously ill, having undergone open-heart
bypass and back surgery.

Now we were walking together atop the long, curving ridge of
Brecon Beacons National Park. The valleys below, pardoned by

the Industrial Revolution, are where heaven and earth appear to have been reversed. En route we befriended Holly, a Welsh woman who was seemed oblivious to the beck and call of stress. On a bluff overlooking opposing valleys, the three of us encountered an elderly woman and her beagle hiking toward us. Teetering along on a walking stick, she wore a motoring cap and held a bunch of wildflowers. After offering up a greeting, I asked her where she was going. She replied in Welsh, "Rydw i yna yn barod." We looked to Holly for a translation.

"She said, 'I'm already there.'"

They continued their quiet conversation in Welsh until the old woman and her dog resumed their walk. As she faded into the distance, I declared my envy for her simple outlook.

"Let's catch up with her. There's something else I'd like to ask."

We spun around, caught up with her, and bade for more time. She walked a few more steps along the trail, traded her flowers to the other hand, and raised an eyebrow. We traded glances; beings from different eras and opposing sides of an ocean.

Holly asked my question, "What's the secret to a long and happy life?"

She directed her answer to Holly, but now in English.

"Moments."

Then the old woman smiled, squinted at my father, and spoke slowly, "Moments…moments are all we get. A true walker understands this."

After a silent, timeless minute, we all clutched hands and waved goodbye. Just before she faded into the horizon, I looked back at her, plodding on with eternal poise and bearing. As we turned to continue on our way, my father and I exchanged shrugs.

She's right—that is all we get.

DIRECTION

DODGE FOOD FIGHTS (Antarctica)

Multiculturalism gets a workout.

T he last thing I expected to discover on my second excursion
to Antarctica was a reminder about how rapidly tourism
demographics are shifting, even at the bottom of the earth. In
total, we were 18 nationalities; a Chinaman painted the character
for water, a seaworthy Dutchman told seagoing tales, a British
chairman reflected on the horrors of doing business in Nigeria,
an Italian woman cried over the glacial beauty overload.

While sampling Chilean Malbec in the most inhospitable, yet
intoxicating, place on earth, I marveled at the two nimble wave-
challenged Chilean waiters serving the meals. Daily desserts
were presented as a buffet of opportunities, literally. That's when
the international *ship* hit the fan.

I'm no stranger to China. My three-month stay in 1987 introduced
me to the Chinese tendency to cut lines, hack up and spit publicly,
and sidestep other common courtesies that were ingrained in
us by our parents. In 2005, Chinese tourism accounted for one
percent of Antarctica tourism. That figure in 2011 rose to 30
percent, and our ship reflected this trend. Millions of Chinese,

now flush with money, can vacation anywhere.

When dessert was presented the first day on the ship, a huddle of Chinese passengers rushed the buffet table and wiped out the daily offering of cut fruit that was displayed on a turkey-sized serving tray. As they walked away with heaps of fruit on their plates, other passengers mourned the site of the empty tray, which was not replenished. The evolving daily assaults on the post lunch and dinner fruit tray became a sociology circus. The next day, other country-folk nonchalantly raced toward the just-arrived fruit plate. Game on. Similar to poolside resort loungers who claim lounge-chair real estate by putting towels upon them the night before, the Chinese posse then began sending out scouts before each meal to claim the table beside the coveted produce. A Canadian couple then parked their empty shoes at the front of the imaginary starting line. The fruit war at sea had begun.

The Polar Front needed an intervention. By day six, a quick elbows-out jog was required to get in the lineup and still have any shot at produce. Sympathizers, including an Australian woman (please pass the Pickwick Sterrenmunt Tea), reasoned that the Chinese didn't fancy the Western food served, making fruit their sustenance. Critics, such as the salty Dutch seaman, personally scolded them for hoarding. Of course, a Swiss woman blamed the ship for not being able to present enough daily fruit. A previously "barking mad" Brit softened up when, after ample whiskey, he decided the Chinese painter had the kindest face on earth, and they became pals.

The final solution required the chef to park himself at the crime scene and ration fruit individually via tongs. Sightseeing demographics are changing fast—no matter how you slice them.

In a fitting finale, at the last dinner, the Chinese assembly sat back and waited to receive their tonged fruit last. But, with everyone distracted by the resolution of the ongoing tussle, I noticed that a tactical German couple had finagled table-delivered plates of fruit. As the war of fruition was resolved, peace returned to the remotest curve of the earth.

DIRECTION

DON'T BE AFRAID TO SCARE YOURSELF
(Utah ~ Zambezi River ~ Puerto Rico)

M y wilderness survival course in the southern Utah desert included three days completely alone in a red canyon so beautiful it made other parts of the earth seem lonely. Mother Nature's sandbox dyed me red-orange. My senses felt alive. I smelled the sage breeze, heard the wisp of darting vultures, saw the dry earth crackling under my feet, and felt the precious seconds ticking.

This desert, like most, can experience 60-degree temperature swings in a day. One chilly night in sandstone-cactus backcountry, I tried lulling myself to sleep with thoughts of an all-you-can-eat buffet. Simulating sleep, I burrowed deep inside my burrito-fashioned poncho, pulled my hat down over my face, and listened to my breath. Then, a large-footed animal, possibly a human linebacker, encroached. The sound of legs brushing against dry shrubs started and stopped abruptly. My adrenaline flooded as it drew close. When it stood above me, I lay stone-still. The steps became more erratic, and my heart raced. I froze, waiting for the intruder to decide my fate. It just stood there. I blinked. It stepped. Blink. Step. The sound of my heart thudding against my eardrums overtook the clamor. I held my breath, then realized that the nerve-racking commotion was really just the sound of my eyelashes brushing against the inside of my hat.

∞ ∞ ∞ ∞ ∞

Zambezi River, Africa

If you do frighten yourself, it's important to bounce back. A touristy bungee jump wouldn't be in these pages unless my premonition came true. Before leaping off Victoria Falls Bridge, the world's third highest bungee bridge, located above Africa's raging Zambezi River, I stood atop the 365-foot-high span connecting Zimbabwe and Zambia. As I was about to freefall toward chugging whitewater, the number one thought banging around in my skull—what if the equipment fails—must occur to every jumper.

Other musings about this suicide practice were of the rumors that this high-velocity leap causes people to have strokes, wet their pants, or suffer detached retinas. Finally, I realize the triviality of stressing over an optional recreational danger in a region boiling over with inevitable danger every day.

Needless to say, I survived the jump. However, not long after my leap, the same bungee cord snapped, sending an Australian woman, ankles still bound, plummeting into the alligator-infested river below. Cuts and bruises aside, she amazingly survived. Talk about nearing the end of your rope.

Testing your limits is a joy to reflect upon, and leaps of faith are often worthwhile…many moons later.

∞ ∞ ∞ ∞ ∞

Puerto Rico

And then there are those times you don't intend on scaring yourself, but stupidly do. New York City's Puerto Rican Day Parade had been my reigning image of this Caribbean island until a 10-hour layover from Aruba in the 90s became a few nighttime hours of partying. When the bar closed, I hoped to bypass paying for a fancy San Juan hotel by napping outside for a few hours. Sand flies convinced me that heading inland to get a bit of shuteye behind a hedge near an inviting villa was a better idea. Shortly after dozing off, a loud, angry voice yelled "*Policia*," so I jumped to my feet and emerged from the hedge to behold a man crouched in a position with a gun pointing at my chest. Likely a private security guard, he was 10 feet away, shaking and serious. Fearing for my life, I summoned some high school Spanish. Somehow "*Sueno, no criminale, sueno!*" tumbled out of my mouth. No bang, yet. As I continued begging for forgiveness, I had to go back into the hedge and fetch my backpack, which didn't amuse the gunman. Fortunately, I managed to skulk away and escape the grounds alive. Although my first book was called *The Frugal Globetrotter*, this *el cheapo blunder* changed my travel tact forever. Stingy nurtured by stupid can be deadly. I resolved to never again risk my life for frugality's sake.

DIRECTION

DESIGN YOUR *OWN* COAT-OF-ARMS
(Indonesia)

Some people wear their heritage on their sleeves, literally. You might want to give it a try. A traditional coat-of-arms, the brainchild of London's College of Arms, is a family crest of accumulated values. It's typically an image of shield-wielding ancient warriors with nifty logos. Want your own badge of honor? Overlook the College of Arms, which, until now, was required for development and registration—even if you don't have ancestors who kicked ass in a medieval war. Royalty Schmoyalty.

Start by amassing your personal collection of the significant symbols in your life: wars (firing your boss), faces (kids, mate, pets), symbols (favorite band's logo, alma maters, brand of chocolate, charity), weapon (pen, intellect, tennis racket, mouth) and a Latin motto of choice—heck, stitch one in English so it can be read. Still not picturing your ultimate logo? Regardless of your take on tattoos, ponder the one's you'd get if you could instead sew them into your design.

The components of a coat-of-arms are the 'arms,' the decorated shield, the 'crest,' a three-dimensional object, and decorative paraphernalia known as the 'coronet.' Most important, your 'motto scroll,' is a life-affirming maxim. 'Just do it' is taken. Cut and paste your favorite symbols and personal maxim as you like, because, starting now, your 'helm' needn't be an armored warriors helmet...a bicycle, fencing, kick-boxing, or welding headdress may do.

I'm gradually pulling together my coat-of-arms, which includes connections to my family (we love white pine trees), a scroll (best job I was ever fired from), my daughter's eyes, my life partner, and a beagle. Also circling in my head are hiking boots, a guitar, my dad's forest-green 1972 Ford Torino station wagon, a "No Littering" sign, and a pen. The coat-of-arms tradition probably started as identification insignias on Crusade soldiers' shields. If I had to waltz around with a shield today, it would declare: *Violence is a problem to be solved—not a contest to be won.*

What would be embossed upon your shield? Think epitaph with legs, while you're still standing.

∞ ∞ ∞ ∞ ∞

Indonesia

Jakarta, Indonesia, was a grim city in the late 1980s. This made arriving in lush Bali even more magical. The Balinese have no word for future. Not hung up on linear thinking, the here remains the now. While there, this dawned on me: when lured by temptation, if you have to pause to decide yay or nay, it usually mean yes—because the thought process concluding a no pops right up.

My decision to ride a motorbike along Bali's north rim was a good one, until a rainstorm created a flash flood that made a raging river overtake the road. A throng of onlookers watched as more and more vehicles showed up at the impasse and realized their fate. Turn back, or wait a day.

I revved my engine and prepared to attempt an emergency crossing. Two men came up behind me and grabbed my torso, not the motorbike, and advised me to not test fate. This coat-of-arms saved the motorbike, and possibly my life.

∞ ∞ ∞ ∞ ∞

"That coat has no arms?" —my daughter (age 4), pointing at man wearing a down vest

DIRECTION

PACK YOURSELF FIRST
(Chile ~ Hong Kong ~ Portugal ~ Macau)

Risk Flight.

For any journey, the first thing you pack should be yourself. Our computers and gadgets have memories, but no remembrances. During my early decades of hardcore vagabonding, there was no internet or cell phones, so a traveler's umbilical cord to home was completely severed. You had no choice but to be where you were, and it forced people to connect. Now, I see hunched-over "travelers" spending hours in internet cafes or constantly peering into phones and remaining shackled to their homebound circumstances, missing the life happening around them. This bums me out. People have forgotten how to truly leave home home.

Irrelevant studies may claim that being constantly wired means remaining informed, but people offline—the ones talking and bonding—don't need such studies. The wired generations needs to gaze away from its devices to notice the wind-rustled trees, tail-wagging dogs, skipping kids, and people near them.

Here's something to ponder. Pre-genocide Native American

groups traded with one another. They had no horses, so their trade goods were hand-delivered or floated by canoe, often for great distances. Natives along the coastal areas valued stone, while natives living inland prized shells. Likewise today, it seems that we still want what we can't have. But you can have the free, anonymous therapy gifted by travel on any and every corner of the globe. Traveling makes people feel better not just because of the escapades to be had in new horizons, but also because we're re-triggered to share our life story—and hear someone else's. That typically only happens in our hometown orbits when we meet new friends or lovers, which for some, can be an uncommon occurrence.

Find the edge in the ordinary. Pack your best intentions, and don't be homesick for yourself—even while driving across town. Forge on. Blurry plans provoke adventure; blind plans crash into it. Pass it on. Not planting the seeds of adventure in children is a national security threat! We're heading for a plague of nature-deficit disorders. Get some forest therapy.

Ps, It doesn't get better without you.

∞ ∞ ∞ ∞ ∞

"A fly doesn't mind drowning in Coca Cola." —overheard outtake of a conversation in Chile about alcohol dependence… and, I forecast, a metaphor for computer gadget addiction

REMEMBER YOUR LEVEL —Hong Kong parking garage sign

"Following other people's advice usually leads to making other people's mistakes." —Portuguese taxi driver speeding wrong way down a one-way Lisbon street

"Every road doesn't lead to Rome." —losing gambler in Macau

DIRECTION

DON'T FEAR FOUL BALLS, THEY STILL
FLY OVER THE FENCE
(High Line ~ Turkey ~ Palestine)

Roaming is how discovery sounds.

I f you hit a foul ball instead of that hoped for home run, remember it may have still cleared the fence. When people hit a foul ball in life, give them a break.

∞ ∞ ∞ ∞ ∞

Akin to a Roman ruin rebirth, one of New York City's elevated railways made a comeback as the High Line. Originally built in the 1930s to lift freight trains 30 feet above Manhattan's then industrial West Side, it was abandoned, and decades later, revived into a public park. In the mid-80s, the High Line was still a desolate, elongated slab of crumbling concrete sprouting spindly trees and wildflowers. Mixed in were homeless people's campsites, pigeon roosts, and rodent hideouts. It was a secret society hovering above the buzzing city.

Back then, the ominous railbed still extended north of 50th street above the West Side Highway—a block from my Hell's Kitchen apartment. Skyscraper rooftops aside, this corroded section of tracks was my favorite urban escape. Getting up there meant scaling vertical steel support columns to locate entry points in the barbwire that barricaded this otherworld. The holes in the barbwire were constantly relocating, as it was cyclically slashed by itinerant squatters and then repaired by city workers.

I've always sought out railroad track environments. Before girls dismantled my pre-adolescent bicycle gang, we wandered for miles along the Long Island Railroad, day and night. A highlight was parking coins on the rails to be pulverized by commuter trains. There was other mischief, but I won't admit any of it until I'm 70.

Some habits are hard to kick. In my early 20s, on a midnight ramble with my brother Basil along the pre-restored, then apocalyptic High Line, I tripped on a rope that was supporting a drifter's plywood and tarp gazebo. Tugging the rope caused the plywood to shift, which alarmed the dweller and made rats scatter. My misstep actually expanded the size of his shelter. Like an earthquake instantly freeing a prisoner, my actions caused him to bolt from his hovel. Nearly naked in the August sizzle, he resembled a tortoise without a shell. I apologized for tripping over his home, but he was still visibly angry, and not yet fully awake. As he fidgeted with reasons to battle, the logic of his own argument led him towards a conclusion he tried to avoid. A grin overtook his face. Because his lean-to had morphed into a larger safari tent, he extended a hand and praised me for the upgrade.

My brother resecured the structure while I asked the man about the vagaries of living upon the lowly High Line. One more nomad at home, his head spun away from his modified fortress and smiled at me without front teeth to say, "VIP baby. Vagabonds In Power!"

You never know when you'll encounter a radical utopian. Wild turkeys in the woods are hard to find, no less catch.

∞ ∞ ∞ ∞ ∞

Turkey

Sometimes you wander, and the pictures stare at you. The remarkably preserved and photogenic Roman coliseum in the ancient metropolis of Ephesus made me wonder what it was like to be a gladiator waiting in an underground tunnel before surfacing to fight for your life. Sometimes, it ain't easy being human.

Seating hundreds, this coliseum is still in use today—for mellower spectacles. The restored coliseum hosted full-on rock acts until the mid-80s when, apparently, a vibrating Sting show damaged the stone structures. Throughout the Greco-Roman world, once-abandoned relics that weren't looted for new construction materials or foreign museums (or rocked by Sting) have been given new lives.

I met a charismatic carpet-vending Turkish elder near Ephesus' spa ruins. He had probably slept in the oversized, dusty sweater he wore like a robe. When his lively carpet pitch—a hurried medley of outdoor furlings and unfurlings—failed, he told me that he lived in one of the tunnels where "the gladiators prayed before battling the lions." When I asked him what it was like to live among lions, he stood up straighter and announced, "If lions could talk, the gladiators would not."

∞ ∞ ∞ ∞ ∞

"A foul ball is still a home run to the person who recovers it." — Guy in Jericho, Palestine, wryly commenting on his neighborhood

DIRECTION

DON'T LET AN ENEMY BURY YOUR SPIRIT (Slovakia)

"When soldiers come, grass never grows again."
—*Slovak Dobro player*

S lovakia inherited some of the best aspects of its five neighbors. It enjoys Czech-inspired brewing, Polish diligence, Austrian architecture, Ukrainian good looks, and Hungarian stews. The one thing Slovakia can claim outright—imagination—was revealed to me by a local woman's Slovak-to-English musing: "You have to use your fantasia." Her Slavic accent recalls the Soviet Union while this evolving part of Europe salutes her free will.

While some Americans deem a 1950's Los Angeles diner a historic landmark, Slovakians won't soon forget the 1500s, as castles from that period crown many hilltops. Often confused with the former Yugoslavian country Slovenia, Slovakia seamlessly blends the best of romantic Europe: Renaissance churches, a picturesque countryside, ghostly bastions, and some timeless insight. Modern artist Andy Warhol's parents, Byzantine Catholics, emigrated to the U.S. from Slovakia. But, tourism still doesn't flow freely between these two countries, as your chance of meeting an American here is similar to a Middle American's chance of meeting a Slovakian. It's a lucky strike either way.

Leaving the captivating capital city of Bratislava, I discover that much of Slovakia is made up of mountains that attract cloudy halos, like the Smoky Mountains. It seems as if every tenth pinnacle has a regal fourteenth-century castle upon it, or at least the crumbling ruins of one. My ears led me to a bellowing, mustachioed mountain-living man who was playing a Dobro guitar on a restaurant patio. In 1925, a Slovakian invented the now globally famous Dobro, which uses an eye-catching bowl-shaped reverberater to enhance the sound of an acoustic guitar played with a slide. After plucking a folksy tune, he explained that Dobro is also a word meaning "goodness" in his native Slovak. A few songs later he told me that the last man to visit the moon had Slovak heritage. He continued picking tunes while I weighed his messages. Across the valley, another set of eerie medieval ruins kept me on the lookout for a reincarnated knight passing on horseback. I've probably seen too many beer commercials.

I made my way back to the flatlands, which are salted with 500-year-old manor houses now doubling as swank hotels. During the 50-year Soviet Regime, most of these country houses were converted into orphanages, schools, hospitals, and retirement homes, or left to fall into ruin. The transition from noble family mansions to communist facilities took its toll. Because it was a Soviet pawn, a few otherwise quaint, rural, medieval-flavored valley towns were overshadowed by huge, hastily constructed factories near ugly off-color communist-bloc-style apartment buildings that don't exactly blend with the preexistent antiquity.

A little nation with a big spirit, the atmosphere of reinvention energizes Slovakia as the resurrected geographic center of Europe. This sentiment was endorsed by the parting words of the Dobro-playing troubadour, which I later found out, is an off-the-record Slovak maxim linked to its succession of foreign oppressors: If you dig a grave for someone you oppress, you'll eventually fall into it yourself.

Something else, Soviet domination, ultimately tumbled into that pit—it surely wasn't the unbroken Slovakian will. Cheers. The old chapel bells toll yet again.

DIRECTION

BECOME YOUR WONDER (Earth)

This old, spinning ball we live upon.

Get dressed to the benigns (As opposed to "dressed to the nines," meaning flamboyantly. By the way, nine makes a showing in other sayings of uncertain parentage, including "cloud nine" and "whole nine yards.")

A true-blue nomadic man named Satch lived in consumer exile for decades before transforming into a popular spiritual leader. While evolving into a visionary, he chose a wandering, impoverished lifestyle to comprehend suffering and desire. In his travels, the still unacknowledged Satch, wearing tired clothing and sporting wild hair, applied for a clerical job but was not hired by the shortsighted CEO because of his appearance.

Forty moons later, Satch, now a sought-after motivator of the masses, returned to the CEO's town. Arriving in a fancy limousine, Satch was met with great fanfare. The CEO contacted Satch at his hotel to offer high-salaried employment at his company. Satch then instructed his driver to go to the company's office. When the CEO rushed outside to greet Satch, he found an empty limousine. He called Satch to ask, "Why did you send over an empty limo?"

Satch replied, "I sent you what you really wanted. Some years ago I came to your office, and you wouldn't fathom hiring me. Now you wish to have me. I'm the same man I was then—what has changed today? What do I have now that I then lacked? A fancy car. Apparently, that's what you really wanted."

DIRECTION

ASK THAT QUESTION, NOW (England)

"We make the road by walking it." —Rosa Parks

What if you only had one more opportunity to take a long walk with your dad and ask him those ultimate questions, the ones you wish you had asked before it was no longer possible?

Where a son takes his father for a precious ramble depends on his dad's favored backdrop. Mine treasures sweeping fields and birdsong, and no haven for wide-open strolls matches England's countryside. But I knew that our trekking savvy would be put to the test this time around, our fourth in Britain, because dad was more fragile than during our earlier rambles. After initially declining my suggestion for one more trek—at 79, dad didn't want to slow me down—he thought better of it. We used this trek to discover England's Midlands, and our shared history.

Our 10-day walk navigated the 147-mile Viking Way, a trail across Lincolnshire, which borders England's central east coast and the North Sea. Named at the suggestion of the Ramblers Association to reflect the influence of Danish law in Britain's eastern counties, The Viking Way met dad's demands for mild hills, woodlands, livestock encounters, and villages of stone houses with gracious inhabitants.

Our previous experiences in the U.K. had impressed upon us the respect Britain pays to its walkers. Foot travelers rule in Britain, on ancient rights of way. Once, Madonna (locally known as "Madge") purchased a mansion adjacent to a public footpath and then spent millions trying to block its public access to no avail. A testament to ramblers' solidarity, the right to roam endures.

Our wanderings led us to villages forgotten by modern highways and high-speed trains. In Lincolnshire's rolling forested wolds, the most timeless scenery on our itinerary, each village offered a weathered stone church from the 13th century, usually positioned on the settlement's highest point and left unlocked. We stayed in homey bed and breakfasts (you must adore dogs and horses) and archetypal English inns that make New England's historic buildings seem like new. Viking helmet signage marked the trail, and when it escaped us, the British national habit of tending gardens made getting directions easy. Birds and sheep galore provided the soundtrack.

Most English homeowners post the nicknames of their houses on a placard out front or along the driveway. Handles like Willow Croft and Lilac Cottage prompted me to ask my father, "What should we have named our house?" Dad first suggested a memoriam to our dog and cat, "Ben and Chelsea's Pee Palace?" Then he corrected himself with a moniker honoring his three sons' reign of mild suburban delinquency: "Wild Antelope Range."

My father imparted my middle name, Thoreau, hoping that I'd sympathize with the philosophical naturalist. Today my standing as a professional wanderer pleases him. In high school, I had difficulty distinguishing the family station wagon from a daring off-road all-terrain vehicle. Dad frequently discovered muddy grass clumped in the wagon's wheel wells and forbade me from borrowing it. No measure of lawn mowing, firewood chopping and stacking, or kitchen Nerf-basketball tournament victories could reverse his decrees. We were the lone residents in suburban Garden City who burned storm-toppled trees for heat and used our backyard as a hedge-to-hedge vegetable garden.

During our trek, Dad enjoyed interviewing unguarded Lincolnshire locals about birds, flowers, and heritage. These included the truck driver who rescued us when we had to hitchhike our way back onto the vanished route. Our feet held out without incident. I'm told that when my English-born great-grandfather and his son walked the south coast of England together, my great-grandfather had some trouble with his feet and poured a bit of whiskey into his boot "to make the leather more supple."

Dad's sporty, self-styled, extreme suburbanite hiking outfit for the ramble was an evolving mélange of trusted sweaters over button-down shirts; khaki or corduroy pants; his hiking boots plodding a confident, sturdy gait; and a game face shadowed by a traditional British flat cap or farmer's cap, as it's called locally. Plus, a nose devoted to smelling blossoms.

Swinging through charming Normanby le Wold, in need of directions, we encountered a woman hosing down her mastiff who demonstrated the Anglo-specific custom of agreeably ending nonquestioning sentences with either "isn't it?" "doesn't it?" or "wouldn't it?"

"Well, it would be that way then, wouldn't it?" she said.

I looked hard at Dad. He looked hard at a bird.

We used the ubiquitous medieval churches—cool and still inside, stained-glass light bleeding in, bird chorus outside—as pit stops. The All Saints Church, its 1226 character intact, sits on a hilltop overlooking Walesby and beyond. Dad decided "The Ramblers

Church," nicknamed that because it holds Sunday services and weddings for rambling enthusiasts, was an apt place to pray for the continued absence of fast-food franchises on Long Island's North Fork, where my parents live.

Lectures on art and Long Island history aside, Dad declared another signpost of his retirement from teaching: The self-appointed status of back yard-reclining, binoculars-raking-the-sky air traffic observer. An elderly couple dining at an adjacent table pretended to not hear the conversation, but then I suggested an attempt to short circuit the often obligatory jests about anyone's Long Island heritage by renaming it Isle de Long. The couple broke down and peered red at us. When Dad steered the chat toward our family's established legacy of "booming," a familial term for inspired but aimless wandering, they left.

After getting our urban fix from an Indian meal, we returned to 360-degree views of the horizon. Trotting past another screaming-yellow crop of rapeseed (harvested as cooking oil and a base for butter alternatives), Dad reminded me that "prostitution is not the world's oldest profession ... farming is." Dad's flora identification computer was heating up again as we crossed into a young green field of wheat. He petitioned the next three people on genus and species. Isaac Newton, a Lincolnshire native, would have been proud.

Whenever I stopped to take pictures, Dad obliged by allowing me to tilt up his farmer's cap stylishly to allow sunshine on his face. After a fence-leaning shoot, I tried talking him into taking up modeling back in Manhattan, such as Mom did in the 1950s. He immediately focused on the dung stuck to his soles.

Walk talk stimulates recollection, anywhere. While ensuring the survival of bottomless memories, my two-week trip abroad with Dad transcended the proverbial pat on the back after watching a game together. We retuned to that global circuit of father and son connections. It was the perfect time to thank him for helping me earn my Walker Laureate.

On the path, I enjoyed the role reversal of being in charge. When we inevitably found ourselves lost in a muddy field of cows— and all of us wondering what we were doing there—I drove the boat, er, station wagon. I intentionally delayed answering his question about what sort of meat was hiding in that Indian food.

The 30 meals we shared along the route afforded me ample time to encourage Dad to recount his life story, the entire odyssey. These discussions made us realize that our greatest fortune was also our supreme bond: my mother. Rural England is a rare zone where humans have improved upon nature. Somewhere in the dream of hunting for Viking Way signposts, I discovered my best friend, the bird and jet watcher.

In the end, after hiking at least 10 miles a day, wiry Dad slept less and ate more than I did and seemed to have more energy. He also noticed every birdsong, flower, shrub, tree, gardener, and cloud. Once again, we'd simplified parent-child recreation, without props. At the Viking Way's lakeside end, Dad unlocked from an expression recalling a medieval frieze we'd seen and raised an eyebrow to declare, "When my mother turned 100 on Long Island, she received a congratulatory telegram from the Queen."

Pause. "But it was routed through Philadelphia?" he added.

At London's Heathrow Airport, my dad, who loves Big Band jazz and once suggested his epitaph read simply "Clown," let his inner actor shine by faking a docile, demented stare to secure me a standby seat to New York.

The eternal revelation surfaced mid-trek, en route to Tealby, while strolling along a green hillside as magpies chattered to each other. I finally asked, "Dad, what gives you hope?"

He paused to reflect, there in the midst of England's secret rambling magic, changed his expression to glad, and declared, "You."

Looks like I've got another shot at borrowing the station wagon.

DIRECTION

CONSIDER A DIFFERENT STATE OF *MINE*
(Yukon)

Courting life's most elusive prize.

After I declined a shot of whiskey, a scruffy saloon man cracked, "You've come a long way to behave yourself." While fond of mischief, I'm still an amateur in Dawson City, a Yukon River-side port in the midst of the Yukon Territory's pure vastness—a flash in the gold pan, defined. In its 1898 heyday, this gold-rush mining settlement, flanked by mountains, was the largest city north of Seattle and west of Winnipeg. At least 100,000 gold seekers set out for its riches, but only 40,000 made it.

Since then, it seems most people drawn to the Yukon Territory are searching for something. I also encountered a long-anticipated plateau here—my inner grown-up. Although getting to Dawson is no longer brutal, settling down certainly was for me.

This checkerboard of dirt roads unites a gritty Canadian West living history museum with boardwalk sidewalks, bush-bearded brew-sippers, sassy female bartenders sporting armpit hair, and First Nation elders mingling in wooden establishments. Dawson also attracts at-ease ski bum types in a region without ski-lifts. They all have a story and share it with Canada's trademark sentence-ending uptone, which makes their declarations resemble inquiries.

One exchange involved self-appointed Klondike Kaye. I happened upon this quintessential mountain woman outside the Snake Pit tavern. She was a vision with muscular arms jolting out of a cutoff plaid shirt and sporting muddy hiking boots. An over-served logger I was chatting with turned and asked her "Are you left-wing or right-wing?" Smoking and illuminated by a golden rush of sun, she stepped off the boardwalk onto the road and mused, "The whole bird." Then she walked away with that Arctic cowgirl strut. She made the women I see every day putting makeup on in the subway seem fragile.

The mellowing me didn't accost Klondike Kaye. Various landmarks inspire men to come of age—finding or losing jobs, becoming a parent, finding grey hairs, caring for aging parents, experiencing a health scare or loss. I had difficulty locating my fun off switch and extended the shenanigans into my 40s. I began accepting adult scheduling when I simply tired of hollow sex, late nights, boozy babbling, and bedbugs. Moreover, having a daughter renders womanizers into girl guards. Sometimes getting away from it all—the Yukon certainly fits that bill— sends everything you're fleeing right back to you.

Everything evolves. With an eclectic mix of restaurants—Greek, French Canadian, gourmet moose burgers joints—it's not hard to imagine this river valley town having the potential to become a tourist trap in 20 years, but still salted with harmless outlaws. Meandering between bars, I watch a strolling cop nod toward a cougar wearing a *CANADA: It's Better on Top* t-shirt and smirk, "This is a drinking town with a sightseeing problem." I peek at his watch, and it's still happy hour. I talk to the cop instead of the cougar.

Canada's three Arctic-hugging territories are only loosely tied to the constitution that governs the rest of the country, and the rules that concern most people. You can still stake land here. The Idaho-shaped Yukon Territory borders Alaska and the Arctic Sea. It's home to 35,000 people and encompasses the same land mass as California, which hordes 38 million souls. Flanneled locals who refer to "outside" as the rest of the world simply call it, "The Yukon." Our northern neighbors, way northern, puzzle over why we live on top of each other. The human population of the Yukon was higher in 1898 than it is now. Even today, moose outnumber Yukoners by two to one.

Dawson City was known as the Paris of the North because the abundant gold afforded all the luxuries that money could buy. But it wasn't the high life for many. The oft delusional hordes that didn't perish en route were fleeced of their riches by conmen or prostitutes, and left broke. And then the town was basically abandoned. Repopulated, this is not the sort of place that identifies with city slickers bumbling blindly down the road ogling their smartphones. Gnarly tavern patrons lowering an eyebrow at anyone speed-thumbing their gadgets buoyed validation for my adaptation of an iPhone—an 8x11-inch piece of paper folded in eighths, etched by a pen. Without screaming I'm ignoring you or I'm not really here, my inconspicuous reporting mode allowed me to blend in, sort of. I'd just shaved and was on beer number two, not eight.

This resuscitated prospector outpost still attracts modern fortune hunters, and I don't mean internet tycoons. Pioneers continue staking land—a version of homesteading—as new gold finds are discovered. It lures people in search of alternatives, whether it be gold, avoiding pop reality, or a different take on conformity.

Next stop northbound: Arctic tundra. Next stop for me: a jog instead of a joint.

Canada's Wild West movie set's wooden footways groan just like they did in the late 1800s. Storming Dawson seems to be a Canadian rite of passage, akin to Americans reaching Key West. On a college spring break, I managed to never stall the flow of beer even while hitchhiking from Virginia to Florida's Keys and back. The next afternoon, immersing myself in this far-flung escape's multiple personalities, I danced to live bluegrass with locals, miners, musicians, and showgirls. Later, I told them about that hitch. My amateur status temporarily gave way to semi-pro. Then, a Yukon roots music maverick invited me to an all-night bash that promised to see the sun rise. The guy—me, who once flew to New Orleans' Mardi Gras and didn't leave for two months—reached down, clicked the on switch off, and went to bed. Jack London's *The Call of the Wild* drew worldwide attention to The Yukon—the same Yukon acknowledging the overdue taming of my wild.

There are some places in this world where humans cooperating with nature means more than pitching nuts to a squirrel. In Canada's version of rapture, it implies leaving wildlife as is—summoning nature head-on without hitting it. This is the place to ponder our nearly extinct roaming nature. The native Yukon culture was based on mobility, which explains why they didn't establish villages with permanent structures. I can relate. From age 18 through 40, I called more than 50 places home—some in Southeast Asian bungalows, others in dank North Carolinian boatyards.

The Yukon is a trout nirvana where ethical fishermen throw back would-be trophy lake trout measuring more than 40 inches—a resurrection of the native understanding that killing the biggest members of any species weakens its gene pool. I testify to a girl-crazed fishing guide that I've retired from that mode of trophy hunting. Wait, truth be told, I might have been forced into retirement. When the last of my childhood wingmen moved away to start family life in the 'burbs, I endured as a lone wolf for another decade until finally growing a conscience—when I reported this news to my older brother Basil, he countered that I'd only caught one, temporarily, like a flu.

Like the first First Nations Aboriginals on the Bering Strait migration route following the animals they hunted, I'm now tracking with my mind instead of my midsection. Here, it also occurs to me that these permafrost-bedded roads need more maintenance than a marriage—I may claim to be more settled, but I didn't pursue that custom. Neither did Klondike Kaye, who I ran into again at an acoustic rock concert inside a church heated by a wood-burning stove. She mentioned the previous night's all-night bash, and I confessed that I'd opted for a pillow, adding, "We're more bull-headed in youth."

Kaye, in a corrective tone, muttered, "Yeah, but a wise bull will still charge a vegan."

Yukoners needn't declare what's mine is yours—there's plenty of everything up here. In Canada, a loonie is slang for their one dollar coin, whose backside depicts a floating loon; the front is a stately portrait of their Queen. This odd flipside pairing reveals royalty's irrelevancy in these parts. Here, in a retreat from predictability, the loons reign supreme.

I found my phone, called my daughter, and headed home to that gold mine.

DIRECTION

DON'T WORRY ABOUT WHO IS
TEACHER AND WHO IS STUDENT

A child is God's take on hope.

Children sense the secrets to enjoying life. Their take on what adults might consider mundane can inspire non-surgical facelifts. Kids are unpaid pros at keeping boredom at bay. While happiness can be the adult fulfillment of childhood dreams, children do not dream of money. Put an ear to the ground to listen for that music only children hear. Day to day, the shrewdest advisers we encounter might not be grownups. My daughter Bella, like most children, routinely recasts reality with her uncanny insights...

THREE YEARS OLD

"*Why* do we have to leave...and what's wrong with him?" — assertion made in playground, pointing at three-year-old boy, flat on his back from dizziness, after Bella made the swing they shared spin into oblivion.

FOUR YEARS OLD

"What are those?" —pointing to lines on dad's forehead

"Cities don't make cricket sounds."

"Who knows more, God or Santa?"

FIVE YEARS OLD

"Are their bodies inside the wall?" —question about mounted animal heads on ski lodge wall

"Why does everyone tell me I'm beautiful?"

SIX YEARS OLD

"When you say 'absolutely' I know it's not true."

"When you die, do you disappear?"

"When people are poor, are they bored?"

"Do they speak English in Virginia?" —after meeting southern U.S. couple in Santa Margherita Ligure

"I can't get this yawn out." (re-opens mouth)

"It's like you're having a staring contest with the TV."

SEVEN YEARS OLD

"Two places I'd never live are China or Florida."

"I'm so sick of this *ladies first* all the time."

Dad to Bella: You just swam in Long Island Sound ... Reply: I didn't hear it.

"It's funny fresh, not real fresh."—on defiance

"Don't I look the same every day?" —response to "You look beautiful today!" (in midst of doing fearless back walkovers)

"I was going to apologize, but I was relaxing."

EIGHT YEARS OLD

"It was just a silly question." —regarding equation on otherwise-aced math test.

"If dogs talked would you get one?"

"Oh, don't worry daddy, I've got a *million* excuses."

"I don't really get perfume. Nobody's ever going to walk up to you and say 'can I smell you'."

"I like sushi, lobster, oysters, crabs, and any kind of seafood—I'm not a cheap date."

NINE YEARS OLD

"Just for the future, I love all things sparkly."

"Did they just start this today?" —watching Hare Krishna's chant in Union Square.

∞ ∞ ∞ ∞ ∞

Because I slighted Socrates in this book's prologue, I'm sharing what seems to be an eternal but fleeting observation...

"Children today are tyrants. They contradict their parents, gobble their food, and tyrannize their teachers." —Socrates (469-399 BC)

EPILOGUE ON COUNTRY COUNTING

WANDER, DON'T TALLY

Roaming the world should be a matter of art, not math.

There is always that one person in the office or at a party who has just returned from a trip and treats it more like a checked box than a profound revelation. Whether they have discovered the soul of that destination or not is of no significance. It's like that overzealous elementary school classmate who earned all the stars on that chart on the wall. In our internet-driven culture, one-upmanship has become all too common. Well, as it turns out, counting countries is like judging cuisine—it all depends on the referee.

Country counting is misleading and no way to measure a world traveler. If today's hardcore globetrotters had been born near European seaports in the 1500s, they'd surely be the ones volunteering to crew on those outbound world exploration ships. And they'd be landing in undeclared territories, unconcerned about ticking off country claims. I cringe to tally up destinations visited, but have done just that to justify the arrangement of this book.

On the other hand, country calculating does arouse contemplation, as many of us do aspire to feel every country. However, the global count depends upon who is doing the math. The U.N.

currently recognizes 193 official countries with Sudan's split adding a digit. It ignores Taiwan and also Martinique, the latter which it lumps it with France. FedEx delivers to more than 220 countries and territories, including North Korea.

Border disputes are as old as time. The U.N. views Puerto Rico only as a U.S. Territory, which it is, but it still feels like its own country. Perhaps the most humane approach toward country counting would be to use the 205 nations that competed in the 2012 Olympics, which includes Samoa and American Samoa, though the latter is actually a territory.

As for those keen on padding their stats, there is the Travelers' Century Club. This club spikes the number to more than 300 by including places that are removed from their parent country by geography, politics, ethnicity, or culture. For example, Papau, recently known as Irian Jaya and before that Dutch New Guinea, is not only a great distance away from its parent country, Indonesia, it's also culturally light years away. This kind of categorization makes sense within the many shifting nations in today's world.

The geographic location, politics, and customs of Alaska and Hawaii are a far cry from what makes Georgia tick. To consider these places as individual countries, however, as the Travelers' Century Club does, is an argument for the ages. Heck, New York City smells different from block to block. You can wander its five boroughs for years and will never experience its every note.

I can testify that Antarctica's Deception Island, which is part of South Shetland and one of the Falkland Islands Dependencies, is a world unto itself. Travelers' Century Club even subdivides the White Continent into seven countries, not including the regions leased for research. Acing their test would be easier said than done.

Whichever destination calculus you choose, you should remain wary of relying on a tally for bragging rights. You can knock off

10 in as many days traveling through Europe, if that is your thing. A manic tour of Southeast Asia can log 10 more countries in less than a month. Africa's 55 countries make it a handy field of dreams for counters. However, you will miss the most precious takeaway of allowing the people from these destinations to saunter over and discover *you*. I've been to a dozen countries a dozen times. That didn't increase an inconsequential nation ticker, but it forever connects me to those places.

One aspect to value is the Travelers' Century Club recognition of how so many countries can have many diverse vibes that are blind to nationalism. The regional enchantment within such massive spaces as Canada, China, India, Indonesia, Russia (nine time zones), and the U.S. should alter how we perceive the world. None of these countries adhere to just one dogma or brand. Geographically and culturally, these sprawling realms have provincial variations that are so distinct from one another that each of these nations could subdivide into a dozen or more provinces. Exploring these bigger countries and all countries, for that matter, at a slower pace will allow you to gain the insight lost in a check-the-box race.

For those looking to merely slap a number on where they've been, do airport stopovers and day-tripper cruise ship dockings really count? One confirmation of a contented soul is to be absorbed by one's surroundings. So don't tally the countries you visit but take your time wandering through them. Be available for the magic and roam out of bounds.

∞ ∞ ∞ ∞ ∞

I celebrate my exploration of Canada's 10 provinces, three territories, and high Arctic—incredible variety for one country. And I do that with far more passion than visiting every country in Western Europe, which is the size of New England. New England represents about two percent of Canada's landmass. Canada is the world's second largest country, geographically diverse, and wondrous.

Few Americans seem to know that Canada has provinces and territories, while (guessing with my eyes open) most Canadians can name the 50 U.S. states. Americans often fail to acknowledge that Canada is also an American country—as in North American. For that matter, if you spice in Central and South America's 19 countries there are actually 20 Americas. So-called "Americans" are actually citizens of the United States of America, and it can be argued that every Caribbean island is also part of the Americas.

Enough math. Go ramble until the moon gets lost in the trees.

∞ ∞ ∞ ∞ ∞

Keen on not ending this contemplation in calculus mode, here's a few alternative takes on whereabouts...

"Who's with me on the whole 'center sun' theory?"—Bewildered Galileo reincarnate campaigning at *party* in Goa, India.

"We are doubly landlocked." —Liechtensteiner clarifying that his country is surrounded only by other landlocked countries, meaning they must cross at least two borders to reach a coastline.

"Whoever has the most fun wins." —Basil F. Northam

EPILOGUE ON TRAVEL WRITING

TRAVEL WRITING IS *NOT* BREAKING NEWS

This final footnote may be a detour from these directions to happiness—but needs to be addressed because the field known as travel journalism, a craft of possibility and one of the engines powering this book, is showing cracks in its finish...

One afternoon in the late 1970s, my big band music-loving dad heard Led Zeppelin booming from my bedroom and opened the door wanting to know why "that man" seemed to be "screaming like he's in pain." This was a preview of how every generation beholds younger generations with a combination of fascination and fear. These days, generation gaps have grown into gorges. People who still favor landlines gawk in amazement at their counterparts nimbly thumbing gadgets while walking across crowded intersections but unaware that they're begging to collide with pedestrians *and* speeding buses.

Two high school jobs, supermarket cashier and busboy, and moreso, college summers as a Manhattan horse-drawn carriage driver, were my humanity boot camps. Later, backpacking and travel writing fanned that fire and helped me step out and shake hands with the world on its vast turf.

Perhaps my biggest lesson of all while compiling this book was realizing that a person living solely in one village for a lifetime can comprehend many of the same discoveries—possibly more—about human nature that may dawn upon far-and-wide travelers. I also discovered that it's not necessary to be rich to experience the best of what our world has to offer. Although there were some years when the combination of freelance writing, book royalties, and keynote speaking was rewarding, others years rode a month-to-month rollercoaster, or suddenly derailed. Nonetheless, I've confirmed that it's possible to flirt with an income deemed as poverty in the U.S.—for decades— and still be able to experience what amounts to a never-ending ramble through new universes. True happiness may be thought, sought, or caught, but never bought. Wealth is relative when you're one of America's poorest millionaires.

Confession. That cited jet-set lifestyle is exclusive to my life outside of New York City. My modest apartment, slingshot distance from bleak housing projects, is where in the midst of nocturnal writing binges, dinner or breakfast meant standing in a flickering light-bulb kitchen, forking cold cans of ravioli…after daily prayers begging a dismal elevator to not faint between floors. This brand of glory is part-time. We all keep secrets. There can be sacrifices to seeing every curve of this planet, including foregoing home ownership, chunky investments, and a gauged retirement plan.

Isn't life sharing the information you gather? A few of the tales gathered here were written while on assignment, but most of them were not—the niftiest tales seem to hide where you're not looking for one. Writing about travel won't win most fame or fortune, but it can send you and your pen to corners of the world that inspire alternative outlooks on life's choices. For me, the evolving and devolving field known as travel writing is simply about encountering accidental gurus, asking can-opener questions, and taking notes.

One test for a story's readability is imagining the writer telling it aloud in a group or one-on-one setting. The explosion of travel content creators, especially on the web, forever changed the game. Some, who never muddy their shoes, are simply rewriting press releases where nobody ever seems to get robbed, conned, injured, or laid. Where are they going? Similar to how we often inherit our parents' political views, travel writers' styles are usually steered by how their family vacationed. When fantasy trumps reality, only a fraction of what's really happening out there is revealed. Travel writing is nothing if not streetwise. Nobody learns how to be a writer, nor a traveler. You make it happen.

The motivation of a writer shouldn't be *look at me*, it should be *see with me*—or through me. Just as you don't see kids climbing trees anymore, as trees were traded for digitized trances, an army of vacation bloggers are shackled to devices, taking selfies, and sending instant updates. Meanwhile, a useful or entertaining travel story is almost always *not* breaking news.

Career-wise, travel writing is a rutted road, but it salvaged my freedom. Thanks world. Beating the system, as they say, I remain faithful that the light at the end of the tunnel isn't an oncoming high-speed train. We only stumble when moving.

Parting thought. Unplug every now and then. Hours-wise, Mozart spent most of his life in horse-drawn carriages crisscrossing Europe to meet the demands of his touring schedule. It's important to make the most of our mobile moments, since, do we really ever arrive? In roughly three million years, when the sun becomes a red giant heating our puny planet to over two-hundred degrees and boiling earthly life as we know it, this proverb from the Kama Sutra will still reign…

"It is better to have a pigeon today than a peacock tomorrow." — read in a Karachi, Pakistan slum, while eating unidentifiable yet tasty slop at a fly-fetching outdoor food stall on Christmas day

ACKNOWLEDGEMENTS

Cover design by Stuart Inglis

Earth, for staging chance meetings, and trying to forgive humanity's blunders. We owe ecology an apology.

Joe Satriani and Jorma Kaukonen for their guitar inspiration.

The marvelous kin and comrades who never give up on simplicity, hope, and chuckling.

Heather Mikesell for her love, thoughtfulness, editorial counsel, and taking the cover photo.

My brothers, Basil and Bryan—*American Originals*—who'll always enjoy the final wink.

My nonconforming parents, Basil and Johanna, for everything. May the road-tripping family hunting campsites at the end of random dirt roads never go extinct.

My daughter Bella, just for being you.

---

* Note: This book visits countries and territories. Not every chapter represents an individual country, as some chapters fuse places or quote citizens from others. My country tally recognized claims made by sources including the U.N., the Olympic Committee, FedEx, and the Travelers' Century Club.

ABOUT THE AUTHOR

B ruce Northam is the award-winning journalist and author of *Globetrotter Dogma, In Search of Adventure*, and *The Frugal Globetrotter*. He is also the creator of "American Detour," a show detailing the travel writer's journey. His keynote speech, *Directions to Your Destination*, reveals many shades of the travel industry, including how to entice travelers. Northam's other live presentation, *Street Anthropology*, is an ode to freestyle wandering. Visit AmericanDetour.com.

Made in the USA
Charleston, SC
23 March 2015